Curriculum for Special Needs

Wilfred K. Brennan

Open University Press
Milton Keynes · Philadelphia

Open University Press
Open University Educational Enterprises
12 Cofferidge Close
Stony Stratford
Milton Keynes MK11 1BY, England.
and
242, Cherry Street
Philadelphia, PA19106, U.S.A.

First published 1985
Reprinted 1985, 1988
Copyright © Wilfred K. Brennan 1985

British Library Cataloguing in Publication Data

Brennan, W. K.
    Curriculum for special needs. – (Children with
    special needs)
    1. Curriculum planning – Great Britain
    I. Title
    371. 9′0941   LC3986.G7

ISBN 0-335-10575-0
ISBN 0-335-10421-5 Pbk

Library of Congress Cataloging in Publication Data

Brennan, W. K. (Wilfred Kayran)
    Curriculum for special needs

    Bibliography: p.
    Includes index.
    1. Handicapped children—Education—Great Britain—
Curricula—Planning.   2. Slow learning children—
Great Britain.   I. Title.
LC4036.G7.B74.   1984   371.9′0941   84-19087

ISBN 0-335-10575-0
ISBN 0-335-10421-5 (pbk.)

Text design by W.A.P.

Typeset by
Gilbert Composing Services, Leighton Buzzard, Beds.
Printed in Great Britain by
M. & A. Thomson Litho Limited,
East Kilbride, Glasgow, Scotland.

Curriculum for Special Needs

Open University Press
Children With Special Needs Series

Editors

PHILLIP WILLIAMS
Emeritus Professor of Education
University College of North Wales, Bangor.

PETER YOUNG
Formerly Tutor in the education of children with
learning difficulties, Cambridge Institute of Education;
educational writer, researcher and consultant.

This is a series of short and authoritative introductions for parents, teachers, professionals and anyone concerned with children with special needs. The series will cover the range of physical, sensory, mental, emotional and behavioural difficulties, and the changing needs from infancy to adult life in the family, at school and in society. The authors have been selected for their wide experience and close professional involvement in their particular fields. All have written penetrating and practical books readily accessible to non-specialists.

TITLES IN THE SERIES

Changing Special Education Now
Wilfred K. Brennan
Curriculum for Special Needs
Wilfred K. Brennan
The Early Years
Maurice Chazan and Alice Laing
Residential Special Education
Ted Cole
Working With Parents
Cliff Cunningham and Hilton Davis
Understanding Learning
Difficulties
Kathleen Devereux
Special Education: The Way
Ahead
John Fish
What is Special Education?
John Fish

Special Parents
Barbara Furneaux
Deaf-Blind Infants and Children
J.M. McInnes and J.A. Treffry
Educating Hearing-Impaired
Children
Michael Reed
Helping the Maladjusted Child
Dennis Stott
The Teacher is the Key
Kenneth Weber
How to Reach the Hard to Teach
Paul Widlake
Special Education in Minority
Communities
Phillip Williams (ed.)
A Glossary of Special Education
Phillip Williams

Dyslexia or Illiteracy?
Peter Young and Colin Tyre

Contents

Editors' introduction

The curriculum used to be described as a secret garden, a garden to which only teachers held the key and from which all others were excluded. But the garden is secret no longer. The curriculum is now more open for all to see and to debate, and while no one doubts the central importance of teachers' roles, others are starting to influence their decisions. 'What shall we teach?' is a question which not only teachers can answer.

If the ordinary curriculum has been a secret garden, then in special education that garden has been not only secret, but neglected, too. The hard-pressed professionals working with children with special needs have had to be more concerned with extending scarce facilities for the children than with the content offered by those facilities. All too often, *where* to place a child had to take priority over *what* was actually taught. The purposes of special education were rarely explored and formulated: the school for children with speech problems was presumed to specialize in teaching communication skills; the unit for maladjusted children was meant to 'adjust' them – but few had thought through what those deceptively simple aims might imply for the curriculum.

Now that the special education service has grown, now that we increasingly appreciate that the education of our children matters at least as much as their medical care, our attention is turning to what is after all the key question in special education, as in all education – what shall we teach?

There are few as well fitted to write on this topic as Wilfred Brennan.

His wide experience, first as a teacher and lecturer, then as an inspector and assistant education officer for special education with the Inner London Education Authority, made him a natural choice to direct the Schools Council project on the curriculum for slow learners. At the time the report of that project was published, special education could almost be described as a collection of tiny independent city states, each specialism attracting its own loyalties and defining its own route to professional membership.

But this description is no longer valid. For one of the many interesting developments of recent years has been a growing awareness of the common ideas and principles shared by the separate specialisms. The increasing emphasis on integration has been one factor in this, for any one school may now have to cope with a wide variety of special needs.

Another factor has been the abolition of legal categories of handicap, for this has meant that educational programmes have to be more clearly specified than hitherto.

Thus there is an urgent need for an authoritative text on the general principles underlying the design and development of the curriculum for children with special needs, whatever those needs may be. And that is precisely the aim of this book.

In his approach Brennan builds on the foundations laid by the Warnock Report. He first deals with general issues, discussing the nature of the curriculum and providing a wide review of the various influences on it. He then reviews the idea of special needs and examines the way in which the range and levels of special need affect the curriculum. After this, he turns to the central issues of the book – problems of the design and implementation of curriculum for special needs. At this point there is some separate discussion of the different demands of children with different handicaps, which serves to illustrate the main theme. Brennan is just as concerned with access to the ordinary curriculum as he is with the design of an individual programme.

Brennan then offers a masterly survey of some of the resources – of people, of the school and of the community – which can be marshalled to enrich and develop the curriculum on offer. The survey is supported by useful appendices. Finally he examines some of the wider issues which interest those concerned with the curriculum – and that means all of us.

As teachers and parents everywhere come face to face with the education of all children with special needs, so the problems of creating and nourishing a sensible and satisfying curriculum become clearer.

To adapt a phrase from Brennan himself, the way we face those problems may prove to be the supreme test of the new system. The garden of the curriculum must be cultivated and made to flourish. Here we have a book which sets out the principles, techniques and resources of good husbandry to help and guide us in that task.

Phillip Williams
Peter Young

CHAPTER 1

Curriculum in education

Curriculum – what is it?

A curriculum may be regarded as a course of study to be followed in the process of acquiring education, a concept which goes back to the earliest use of the word. This fundamental meaning tends to become obscured through the use of other words which may be part of curriculum or take over its function according to the context in which they are used. For example:

Syllabus: the subject contents to be taught by the teacher to the pupils.

Topics: themes which the teacher will develop with the pupils which have a focal point but may involve more than one traditional subject.

Field of study: transactions between pupils and teacher, broader than a topic, with more planned interaction between subjects included in the field.

Centres of interest: focal points chosen to interest pupils and motivate their learning, around which the teacher will organize activities in terms of topics or subjects.

Integrated learning: similar to fields of study though possibly broader, more concerned with conceptual relationships and with more direct involvement of pupils in shaping their learning. Often involves the abandonment of a strictly structured timetable.

Educational experiences: descriptions of situations organized by teachers for presentation to pupils at the appropriate time, from which it is intended pupils will derive experiences which contribute to their educational development.

These approaches are not exclusive of each other. The subject contents of a syllabus may be described in terms of topics or centres of interest, while the description of a topic may include close specification of the subject areas involved and their interrelationships. Educational experiences probably represent the most open of the situations; but even here the specification may involve definition of subject areas to which the experience may contribute. In general, though, this way of organizing curricula is confined to the more personal, aesthetic areas, to the arts, humanities and some aspects of religious and moral education.

In one sense these approaches may be regarded as different ways of describing a school's course of studies or curriculum. This notion of a curriculum as a description of a course of study is of limited value. It is useful only where concern is for the knowledge acquired by the pupils, in particular knowledge in a form which may be tested through written examinations or checklists. Once concern goes beyond what the pupils 'know' and becomes involved in the kind of persons they are, or are becoming, broader aspects of curriculum assume importance. Alternatives to traditional subject organization provide evidence of this. The concepts of topics or centres of interests arise from understanding the need to motivate the learners, while fields of study, integrated learning and educational experience show additional concern that knowledge acquired be interrelated and conceptualized. And insofar as these approaches involve group learning and pupil interactions they indicate awareness of individual personality being fostered and developed through social activities. It is important to examine this broadening of the notion of curriculum in contemporary usage.

A modern concept of curriculum retains the idea of knowledge to be acquired by the learner but sets it in the framework of cognitive development. The premium is not upon the possession of knowledge in itself, but knowledge to be manipulated and applied in the process of thinking and problem solving. The curriculum is concerned with the acquisition of skills, their application, and their synthesis with knowledge in emerging techniques, an important experience in learning. Broader, common experiences are also the concern of curriculum and relate to the attitudes and values pupils should acquire or assimilate in the process of education – attitudes and values shaping personality and social relationships and generating motivation for the learning which the school exists to foster. In the curriculum *process* there must be the flexibility to allow for the development of unique individuals who differ in personality, potential and background; at the same time, common experiences must enable the individuals to relate, both to each other within the shared society of school and to those aspects of development common to all. Thus in a democratic society the curriculum has both individualized and common aims. Tension usually exists between them – sometimes to the point of conflict.

The enormous pressure on the contemporary school curriculum of complex, and sometimes conflicting, needs, aims and developments is usually overlooked. Take as examples the communication explosion of the last two decades, and the rapid development of microelectronic techniques now reaching down into the primary school. Add to these the power of tradition and a reluctance to remove from the curriculum those features which have outlasted their purpose, and the lesson of the 'saber-tooth curriculum'[1] has a modern application. The aims of the curriculum are no longer achievable solely through the formalized teaching of academic knowledge. How the knowledge is communicated and how the pupil learns may be more important in terms of personal and social growth. So teaching method assumes importance in relation to aims and needs to be specified within the curriculum. Less formal activities within the school also relate to the wider aims and claim inclusion and concern as part of curriculum. A school's curriculum may also be said to include the model of human relationships which the teachers and other adults present to pupils, and these may be consciously related to those pupil–staff and inter-pupil relationships considered appropriate to broader curriculum aims. Wide aspects of total school relationships, then, become part of the 'planned curriculum', which extends far beyond the formal or 'taught' curriculum.

The concept of the broader 'planned curriculum', highlighting the importance of methods of communication and quality of human interactions, owes much to insights from social psychology and, to a lesser extent, sociology. From these arise the understanding of the importance of classroom and school culture as well as the effect of outside influences, to be discussed later in this chapter. Barnes,[2] Bennett,[3] Dreeben,[4] Jackson[5] and Keddie[6] have discussed specific aspects of this development. Equally important is the contribution of studies investigating the 'unplanned learning' which issues from the nature of the school as an institution and the way curriculum and learning are handled within it. Dreeben[7] and Hargreaves[8] have provided insights into aspects of this 'hidden curriculum' about which too little is known, though the last decade has seen a growing realization of its importance by teachers.

The points made in this section are perhaps best summarized by extracts from recent publications. The first, from *A View of the Curriculum*,[9] offers a definition.

> The curriculum in its full sense comprises all the opportunities for learning provided by the school. It includes the formal programme of lessons in the timetable: the so-called 'extracurricular' and 'out of school' activities deliberately promoted or supported by the school; and the climate of relationships, attitudes, styles of behaviour and the general quality of life established in the school community as a whole. Whatever formal programme is adopted, account has to be taken of that other less formal and seemingly less structured programme, and of the interactions between the two.

The second extract, from *The School Curriculum*,[10] demonstrates the breadth of modern school curriculum. It is a list of broad educational aims to which local education authorities (LEAs) and schools are invited to refer:

(i)   to help pupils to develop lively, enquiring minds, the ability to question and argue rationally and to apply themselves to tasks, and physical skills;

(ii) to help pupils to acquire knowledge and skills relevant to adult life and employment in a fast-changing world;

(iii) to help pupils to use language and number effectively;

(iv) to instil respect for religious and moral values, and tolerance of other races, religions, and ways of life;

(v)   to help pupils to understand the world in which they live, and the interdependence of individuals, groups and nations;

(vi) to help pupils to appreciate human achievements and aspirations.

The definition and list - appropriately an overview, from the central Department of Education, which shares responsibility for curriculum with local education authorities and the schools - indicate a broad curriculum framework and direct attention to the magnitude of the curriculum task. However, they say nothing about the objectives which must be defined and pursued on the way to achieving the aims of the curriculum. Skilbeck[11] moved closer to establishing broad criteria by which curriculum matter might be judged, presenting his view of what qualities teachers should require of curriculum content:

(1) rational, coherent and fundamental - ordered and organized

according to a framework of rules, principles and basic ideas; capable of being systematically related to other themes, topics and bodies of knowledge; rich in powers of explanation, criticism and problem solving; able to stand up to relevant tests of validity and reliability;

(2) contemporary – true according to current knowledge and theories; relatable to contemporary problems and issues;
(3) socially relevant – having wide and varied applications to society, its needs and issues;
(4) action orientated – so selected and designed as to enable learners to undertake tasks, confront problems and achieve intellectual and practical competencies;
(5) broad and balanced;
(6) learnable and teachable – having a structure and sequence which fit the needs and capabilities of teachers and learners;
(7) intrinsically interesting and meaningful.

A curriculum which measures up to this list will communicate knowledge; it will also be relevant, synthesized and relatable by the learner to the world around him. At this point we leave the curriculum definition, with issues to be taken up later in relation to special needs. First, factors which influence the curriculum are identified and examined.

Influences on the curriculum

The curriculum does not operate in a vacuum. It is itself influenced, often in a subtle and indirect manner, by pressures from the society it seeks to understand. In this section, we consider some sources of pressure and influence.

The organization of education

It is not necessary to delve deeply into the history of education in order to show a relationship between the curriculum and the organization of education. The progressive lengthening of the period of statutory education has been a major factor in the broadening the school curriculum.[12] Tripartite secondary education had a direct effect on curriculum, particularly in the 'modern' and to a lesser extent in the technical school.[13] Flexibility of curriculum arrangements for pupils was enhanced by the move to comprehensive secondary schools while the associated abolition of selection at eleven years of age liberated the curriculum of the primary school.[14] Nursery education, where provided, permits many children to enter infant school better prepared to make the most of the curriculum offered. Provision of advisory and support services with their associated teachers' centres, museums in education and outdoor education centres, and linked courses between schools and colleges of further education are all examples of educational organizations which extend and enhance curriculum possibilities. The influence of these facilities on curriculum often passes unnoticed until, as in recent years, the curtailment of funds available to LEAs leads to the facilities' reduction or elimination. It is then quickly realized that without them curriculum is poorer.

The developmental aspect of curriculum merits close examination in relation to the organization of education. Curriculum in nursery and infant education consists almost entirely of experience-based teaching with little subject differentiation apart from emphasis on language and quantitative aspects of experiences. As progress is made in junior school the curriculum broadens and specific objectives in language, reading and number are added to or shaped from the experienced-based curriculum according to the school's style of teaching. Project work now involves a more distinct element of pupil involvement in selection and planning with more precise recording of outcomes, often including the beginning of objective observation and its recording as 'science'. Secondary curriculum tends to be more subject orientated even where study is organized around grouped or integrated subject fields. Specialist subject teachers are more in evidence, as are the effects of traditional public examinations. At the same time more responsibility for learning passes to the pupil and increases as he or she moves through the school. Most pupils are now expected to handle the interrelations of learning more competently, to conceptualize more readily and to think in abstract terms.

At this stage, the wide range of intellectual ability among the pupils begins to create curriculum problems. Individual needs which at primary level were resolved through *individualized learning* now appear to require in addition *individualized curriculum*, so that in mixed ability groups the teacher must resolve not only the problem of different methods and presentations but also problems of different curriculum priorities. This is a consequence of mixed ability teaching in comprehensive secondary schools – a curriculum problem arising directly from the organization of education. For all pupils the secondary curriculum begins to relate to the outside world in terms of their post-school options and prospects. Yet vocational aspects of curriculum tend to be absent, except perhaps for some work experience or linked courses with colleges of further education. It is in the latter, in the post-school years, that a vocationally based curriculum may be developed.

For further evidence about the relationship between organization and curriculum, consider, first, the curriculum activity generated by the introduction of middle schools; and second, the flurry of activity resulting in the outward looking ROSLA courses following the raising of the school-leaving age from fifteen to sixteen.[15][16]

Examinations

The persistence with which the examination system has influenced curriculum, particularly in secondary schools, justifies separate consideration, though in many respects the system has become part of the organization of education. The examination tradition, arising in the academic grammar school, persisted as the new secondary schools were established following the Education Act 1902 into and beyond the Secondary Schools Examination Council constituted in 1917. Through the examinations, university interests ensured that an academic curriculum was appropriate in content and standard to the requirement of university entrance. That was not an improper objective, but it had unfortunate side effects. First, the majority of selective secondary school leavers did not enter university, so to some extent the curriculum was not appropriate to their post-school experience. Second, the non-selective secondary schools, fearful of being second best, directed much effort into the development of courses leading to GCE examinations, which diverted attention from the task of developing curriculum related to the needs of the majority of their pupils, many of whom were left with 'watered-down' versions of academic syllabus. Third, the curriculum of the primary school was unduly influenced by the type of examination at eleven plus which had the objective of selecting pupils suitable for the academic grammar school.

Some of the tensions between the academic curriculum and the needs of pupils for whom it was considered unsuitable were eased by the introduction of the Certificate of Secondary Education. The CSE organization offered a more flexible approach to curriculum, regionally based and with a high degree of teacher control. Mode III arrangements in particular broadened curriculum options through being school based and related to the pupils for whom it was intended with outside monitoring of standards.[17] In practice Mode III gave impetus to integrated studies.

Nevertheless the dichotomy between the academic and broader

curricula remained, with universities and the Schools Council engaged on both sides – progressive in relation to the emerging initiatives, while traditional in academic demands for those pupils likely to continue in higher education.[18] The CSE examination was not considered appropriate to the lower 40 per cent of the secondary school population, yet in a survey of 118 secondary schools 98 per cent were presenting for examination individuals from that section of the pupils, including 51 per cent of schools expecting CSE passes for all except 10 per cent of their pupils.[19] It may be argued that the practice fosters motivation in the pupils and avoids the distinction between those who are examined and those who are not: equally it could be replied that motivation should be intrinsic with appropriate curriculum, and that far from removing the distinction, the practice merely moves it lower down the range of ability in the school population. Whatever the answer, the examination system continues to influence the curriculum of secondary schools in a manner making it less appropriate than it might be for some of the pupils.

Relationships within the school

In any school, teachers differ in personality, self-concept and their view of their role as professional practitioners. Pupils are equally different and usually represent a variety of social backgrounds. Often the social and educational background of the teachers is different from that of the majority of the pupils they teach, which means that their insight into the circumstances of the pupils may be based upon generalized impressions and concepts rather than upon personal experience. Further, as pupils develop and mature each aspect of curriculum calls for adult–child relationships appropriate to the contemporary situation. These are complex relationships, but their influence on the taught, planned and hidden curriculum of the school cannot be doubted. Yet the individual schools do generalize in reaching a consensus about curriculum content, teaching styles, discipline, order and acceptable attitudes within the school. From authoritarian through democratic to *laissez-faire*; from tough- to tender-mindedness; from conservative to radical; and from the prescriptive to the enquiring – curriculum transactions are influenced as much by people, personalities and relationships as they are by theory.

One important aspect illustrates the influence of relationships. When problems arise which cannot be accommodated within the consensus, serious situations develop within schools: Rising Hill[20] and William Tyndale[21] are extreme but important examples of this. At Rising Hill an attempt by the headteacher to introduce a more liberal and democratic regime was followed by opposition from some staff members and divisions which eventually led to the closing of the school by the LEA. The introduction of child-centred methods at William Tyndale primary school led to similar divisions among staff which eventually involved governors and parents. Some parents withdrew their children; others supported the headteacher and the new methods; publicity was given to opposing staff views; and the headteacher and some members of staff refused to accept instructions from the LEA. Drawn into the dispute, the LEA organized an independent public enquiry and eventually the headteacher and some staff members were dismissed.

Relationships in schools, then, are subject to external pressures not only *on* the school but *in* it.[22] Pupils bring to school attitudes assimilated from homes and neighbourhoods within which tensions may exist as well as a lack of harmony with school values. These are realities to be taken account of in curriculum analysis, with the important consideration that their most subtle influence may be through the hidden curriculum of the school.

Central government

Central government has exercised its influence on curriculum through its specialized department, first the Board of Education, then the Ministry (MOE) and currently the Department of Education and Science (DES). The length of statutory education, the divisions within it and the examination system have been shown to affect curriculum; all are shaped by political decisions incorporated in Acts of Parliament administered by the central department for education. In administrative terms the DES continues to exert powerful influence. The capital programmes allocated for education are controlled by the DES, as are the number of teachers in training at any time and the basic teacher - pupil ratio in the schools. There is strong DES influence on the design of schools, not least in the control of the 'cost per place provided' which defines the constraints on designers and architects. The results set limits to what can be provided by the LEAs and therefore on practical curriculum options in their schools. The DES, moreover, is not a free agent. As a department of government it is engaged with other departments (Health and Social Security, Defence, Environment, etc.) in counter-claims on the available funds controlled by the Treasury. The allocation of the funds among the contending claimants involves wide political decisions about priorities and national interest, the results of which may limit DES options and, indirectly, the quality of curriculum and teaching in the schools.

The DES has influence other than administratively, through Her Majesty's Inspectorate (HMI). In a characteristically British arrangement, HMI is part of the DES but operates with a high degree of freedom from administrative and political control. 'Eyes and ears of the DES' is one shorthand description of HMI – one which is only half true, for the inspectorate is involved in intercommunication between the DES and the Minister, the LEAs and the teachers in the schools, covering all parts of the UK and involving in addition the Schools Council and voluntary associations concerned with education. Curriculum innovations and development are fostered through reports and pamphlets, in-service courses for teachers at national and regional level, and a continuing dialogue with schools and teachers which has an important role in disseminating effective curriculum practice. At a more specific level, in terms of individual schools, the inspectorate provides objective advice and reports on curriculum and teaching to both the LEAs and the DES. In contributing to curriculum, HMI operates entirely in terms of influence, for it has no direct power, though evidence of its independence is exemplified in reports on the adverse effect of central government economies on education at a time when politicians in power were striving to convince the voters otherwise.[23]

Since the Board of Education relinquished control of examinations and curriculum its successors have disclaimed any direct responsibility for the curriculum and have acquiesced in the tradition of local and school responsibility guided by DES circulars and HMI reports. The arrangement has always had its ambiguities, in particular those arising from political pressures already noted. However, teacher control, as it came to be regarded, has been jealously guarded by the profession. A threat emerged in the early 1960s when a MOE initiative resulted in the setting up of a Curriculum Study Group. The unrest and dialogue following the event resulted in the establishment of the Schools Council for the Curriculum and Examinations; this was explicitly for the purpose of fostering curriculum development, with a controlling arrangement which included the DES and LEAs (the funding bodies) but gave teachers the voice on professional committees, and a constitution which emphasized that responsibility for curriculum rested within the individual school.[24] (The work of the council is considered later.) Public concern and political pressure

continued and came to a head with the setting up of the DES
Assessment of Performance Unit in 1975, followed by the Oxford
speech of Prime Minister Callaghan which launched the 'great
debate' in October 1976 and an agenda which included standards
of numeracy, use of English, teaching of science and mathematics,
the need for assessment and the desirability of a common core
curriculum.[25] Though there was great stress on 'consultation' at
the time, there were those who saw a conspiracy by the DES to
gain control of curriculum. The suspicion was not allayed by the
arrival in power of a Conservative government which had made
standards in education part of its election manifesto.

Central government can also influence education at local level
outside the sphere of the DES. Local authorities depend for part of
their income on rate support grants from central government
intended to supplement income raised locally through property
rates. Where local expenditure exceeds a figure set by central
government (often through refusal to reduce education or social
services) it has become the practice of the government to withhold
part of its grant, leaving the deficit to be made up from local rates.
As this has not deterred some local authorities, the government
has taken legal power to set an upper limit to locally incurred
annual expenditure. Such legislation represents interference with
local responsibility and will almost certainly effect educational
expenditure and through that the breadth and quality of
curriculum in the schools.

Another central government initiative is causing concern in
further education (FE). The Manpower Services Commission,
through its training division, has played a leading role in
expanding FE opportunities for unemployed school leavers,
including those with special needs. The courses have been
provided in co-operation with LEAs, FE colleges and voluntary
bodies. Now the commission is acting directly through its
Technical and Vocational Education Initiative, and in the white
paper *Training for Jobs* the government is proposing to allocate
responsibility for some 25 per cent of work-related non-advanced
further education to the commission. The LEAs and teachers in
further education are resisting this development. Though the
commission is independent of the government, it answers to the
Secretary of State for Employment. The LEAs and teachers see the
development as a reduction in the role of the DES and of
educational influence in further education, carrying with it a
danger of increased central government power.

Local government and LEAs

Local government control of education is exercised through the local education authority,[26] within a structure established by Education Acts and the political constraints noted above. Duties of the LEA include the provision of schools, appointment of teachers, and the framing of instruments and rules of management which determine the nature of the school and the relationship between the LEA, the headteacher and the school governors. Governors are usually made responsible for the conduct, curriculum and discipline of the school in consultation with the headteacher and within the parameters established by the LEA. The arrangement usually leaves some doubt about who is ultimately responsible for curriculum; in practice the main responsibility rests with the headteacher, though in large schools he or she may delegate responsibility to heads of departments.[27]

The influence of the LEA on curriculum is generally indirect but broad. The facilities available in the school, the amount of capitation money for books and equipment, the pupil–teacher ratio, the provision of specialized off-site learning centres and the quality of local library resources all affect the curriculum. In addition, most LEAs maintain a local advisory service with general and specialized functions in relation to school curriculum and its development. The resources available to the service and the quality of personnel are likely to affect the quality of work in schools. However, the relationship is indirect, usually achieved through influence on appointment policy, in-service courses for teachers and other staff, judicious use of additional resources, influence on LEA policy, publication of curriculum documents and the development of teachers' centres and curriculum conferences and working parties. All these techniques operate in the medium and long term and it is difficult for the advisory service to achieve short-term results. The service is also responsible for keeping the LEA informed about the quality of curriculum in the schools and for indentifying any deficiencies or weaknesses. This inspectorial role of the advisory services has tended to be neglected in recent years but there are indications of it being accorded more importance as part of the LEA response to criticism and the 'great debate'.

Currently the LEAs are in a difficult situation. On one hand, in response to public concern and debate, they are tending to take a more positive attitude in their responsibility for the quality of curriculum in the schools, in particular in primary education and in those areas of secondary education not dominated by external examinations. On the other hand, they are under increasing financial pressures generated by central government which require reduction in the facilities and services they are able to make available to their schools. Nor does it help that criticism of performance and curriculum often arises from the very source which imposes restrictions and creates difficulties.

The strength of the LEA should reside in intimacy. It is close to the local community, representative itself of the many groupings and interests within it. It should be aware of local needs, of the pattern of industry and commerce, and of the prospects which they present for school leavers. Not that these should dominate the curriculum, but they represent factors to be carefully considered. Aware of these factors and interests, the LEA is in a position to see that they are represented on the governing bodies of schools and are contributing to discussion at that level along with parents and teachers.

The Schools Council

The Schools Council for the Curriculum and Examinations, to use its full title, is the only major body at national level which has the development of curriculum as its main purpose. Through joint funding the DES and the LEAs were involved from the start, but committees other than that concerned with finance had a majority of teacher members. Teachers' unions were strongly represented and have been closely associated with the work of the council, as have professional educators from universities and colleges, the advisory services of LEAs and HMI. In its original form the council represented a balance of the parties most interested in and directly concerned with curriculum, teaching methods and examinations. The constitution of the council emphasized the position of individual schools:

> that each school should have the fullest possible measure of responsibility for its own curriculum and teaching methods based on the needs of its own pupils and evolved by its own staff.

The principle was reflected in the appointment of practising teachers as field officers and on the consultative committees of council curriculum projects.

In its first phase the council conducted over 150 projects at national and regional level, examples of which are listed in Appendix 1. Some major projects were involved in the production of curriculum materials for use by teachers in schools; others examined specific curriculum areas or problems and reported in a series of working papers or curriculum bulletins. There is no doubt that in this phase of its work the council was a powerful influence on the development of curriculum, though attitudes to its work were varied, as might be expected in a system marked by different opinions about curriculum and its control. Supporters saw its balance of powers, emphasis on choice for schools and involvement of teachers as reflecting all that was best in education, the basis of freedom from direct political control and a major strength of the system. Critics from the right alleged a lack of coherent policy towards the curriculum and far too radical a diffusion of effort away from the 'basic' standards, while the left saw the apparent radicalism covering a conservative concern for the status quo. Elements in the DES found it difficult to live easily with the dominant teacher representatives over whose appointment they had no control. Teachers in the schools divided between these attitudes – some seeing council work as too late, too little or both, others as a radical plot or an imposition.[28]

One criticism bears directly on the subject of special educational needs. It focuses on the separate projects for early leavers and non-examination pupils, arguing that the policy prevents a majority of the school population from participating in high-status knowledge which is the key to power and influence in society.[29] In ideological terms it would be difficult to refute this view totally. However, it overlooks the practical situation in the schools. Curriculum for these pupils leaves much to be desired and needs to be improved, in particular the 'watered-down' diet considered suitable for many of them. By working out appropriate curriculum efficiently taught, their education can be improved, they can be offered alternative means of access to high-status knowledge, and the convergence of curricula may bring nearer a working common core.[30]

Eventually the Schools Council became the victim of growing criticism, of economy in educational expenditure and of a government which seemed determined to increase the degree of centralism in education, or at least to strengthen its own influence. The result was the abolition of the council. The Schools Council, as an independent body with a large measure of professional teacher control, disappeared. In its place two separate bodies have been set up: the School Curriculum Development Committee and the Secondary Examinations Council. Membership was by DES appointment following nomination by bodies such as the Association of Metropolitan Authorities, the County Council Association and the Society of Education Officers. At the time of writing the National Union of Teachers has declined to make nominations to the School Curriculum Development Committee, and out of a membership of twenty only six were teachers and all headteachers.[31] Two other members are educational advisers.

The future of the new curriculum body is difficult to forecast, but the separation of curriculum and examinations has not been well received by the teachers' associations, and suggests that there will be more direct DES influence. No machinery or pattern yet exists for co-operation between the two bodies. Financial restriction will undoubtedly curtail work on the curriculum and it may prove difficult for the new curriculum committee to gain the confidence which teachers in general gave to the Schools Council. The new arrangements are considered by many to have lost much that was good, to have weakened the position of the schools in curriculum matters, and to be a source of apprehensions about the future.

National bodies

No other body approaches the original Schools Council in terms of involvement with curriculum, though a number have made contributions. Of the permanent organizations the Nuffield Foundation stands out through its funded work in science, mathematics and modern languages and its co-operation with the Schools Council[32] (see Appendix 1) and, to a lesser extent, some work of the National Foundation for Educational Research has curriculum implications.[33] In Scotland the Consultative Committee on the Curriculum and the Scottish Council for Research in Education have similar curriculum influence, as does the Northern Ireland Council for Educational Research.[34]

Considerable influence on curriculum has arisen from committees of enquiry set up by the Central Advisory Council for Education. These committees investigate specific problems which are put to them, operating nationally in terms of both membership and scale. The reports identify excellence where it is found but also highlight weaknesses or omissions, while their suggestions and recommendations frequently stimulate curriculum change and development. Examples from England are the Plowden Report on primary schools and the Newsom Report on below-average pupils in secondary schools;[35] in Wales, *Primary Education in Wales*[36] and, in Scotland, *Remedial Education in the Primary School*,[37] fulfil a similar purpose. Usually the reports are not without their critics and it is unusual for committees to follow up their recommendations in any organized manner. Their effectiveness arises from the wide involvement of teachers and LEAs through the presentation of written and oral evidence; the incorporation of report material in the initial and in-service education of teachers; and the fact that LEAs are likely to call for reports from their administrators on steps being taken to apply national report recommendations.

The context of the curriculum

The economy

It is doubtful if the national economy has any direct effect on the school curriculum, though indirect effects are easily identified. The total wealth available for investment in the public sector and the priority decisions as to its distribution bear on educational resources and through them on curriculum options in schools. Changes in the pattern of industry feed back into schools, as witness the growth of computer studies in recent years. Relations between nations, such as Britain's entry into the European Common Market, may influence the place of a second language in curriculum. Conflict may arise in the opposition of 'training' versus 'general education' as the purpose of education, though this is frequently over-emphasized. Employers most often demand general education and good grounding in basic subjects in entrants into commerce and industry, relying on 'job training' and further education for the specific learning required. A cynic might say that this is an area where there is general distrust of the schools; what the industrial system requires in its workers is discipline, order and the willingness and ability to concentrate on a task for long periods. This might be stated as 'controlled people', a concept not easily developed in a democracy and consequently rarely stated directly when the school curriculum is criticized. Nevertheless, the discipline aspect of popular education has a long history and is in opposition to curriculum trends which emphasize pupil interest and involvement, exploration and freer relationships between pupils and teachers.

In some respects the opposition between training for a life of work, on one hand, and individual growth, on the other, may already be outmoded. Changing economic conditions and the prospect of accelerating change suggest that what entrants to industry need most is the ability and willingness to acquire new skills in the course of a working life, an attitude more likely to be communicated through co-operative and exploratory learning than through the didactic. The other economic trend is reflected in the reduction and levelling off of economic activity, with associated unemployment, which is unlikely to change dramatically for some time, with the possibly permanent reduction in traditional semi- and unskilled jobs requiring mastery of a simple routine and a modicum of strength. This projection has two major curriculum implications. First, leisure and the knowledge and skills required to use it positively must be accorded increased importance and extended time. Second, the curriculum should *now* engage pupils in an analysis of the work-style changes which will become necessary: shorter working day, week and year; work sharing; the balancing of an economic and social 'wage'; extended education; re-entry to education on the pattern of Danish folk schools; planned job changes to accommodate to changing personal needs with age; and an increase in the number and status of jobs which 'service' the community but are currently rated low in prestige and in wages. The emerging economic conditions may require considerable participation of individuals within the socio-economic complex, and that itself may call for increased interpersonal skills – another challenge for curriculum, taught, planned and hidden.[38]

Ideology

Ideology may be regarded as a system of beliefs shared by a group of people and influencing their view of society, economics, politics and education. The individuals may not have complete identity of views, but what they hold in common is sufficient to maintain cohesion within the group. Ideology may be subject to shifts in relation to particular subjects, but continuing common attitudes across them will maintain it. Some beliefs may rest on verifiable facts, others may be without objective basis; all will be regarded as truth. Ideology provides its holders with a basis for action. Education and politics appear to be fertile fields for ideologically based action, since both create access to power, the one through knowledge and the other through government, which may account for their close association.

The rapid social changes of the postwar years focus attention on the ideological dichotomy between the 'traditional' or 'conservative' and the 'radical' or 'progressive'. Both ideologies have direct implications for curriculum content as well as indirect influence through views on teaching methods and the organization of education. In the traditionalist or conservative ideology, emphasis is placed upon the past, its real or imagined stability, its personal and social values and the sense of individual responsibility and obligation which contributed to national achievements. The main purpose of education is seen as the transmission of the heritage of the past to the young of today. What is transmitted, and how, will differ for individuals, since the ideology involves an hierarchical view of society and curriculum appropriate to the levels. Good curriculum will be formally organized on a subject basis, with stress on standards of basic subjects for the majority and selection of those thought to be appropriate for different curriculum, leading to high status knowledge for an élite. Discipline and obligation permeate the curriculum taught, planned and hidden, and pupils are expected to conform.[39]

In the radical or progressive ideology, the forces of change are accepted as a natural part of human experience, capable of being shaped through intelligent social action. The past is now important in that it assists with understanding the present and shaping the future. What has value from the past is retained, but given expression in contemporary terms likely to secure its acceptance and application to a changing future. In curriculum terms understanding and insight rank above rote knowledge; the learner should be involved, active and seeking; knowledge is organized through associated fields, is problem orientated and seen as subject to continuing revision. Teachers explore learning with pupils; there is a sense of equality and a belief that social and individual aims are not in opposition but complement each other. The views find expression in a belief in the importance of a common curriculum conducted in mixed ability groups.[40]

To many traditionalists the progressive ideology appears as 'socialist', is held to undermine discipline, reduce standards and contribute to deteriorating social behaviour and economic performance. Those less extreme react to the challenge by developing a view which has been called 'revisionist'. The revisionist ideology puts a premium on economic efficiency, making it the justification for the modernization of curriculum seen as necessary to the production of an intelligent work force able to come to terms with industrial change and maintain or improve the nation's competitiveness. The changing curriculum remains teacher controlled, though the teacher becomes more accountable to some (undefined) authority, with terms like 'vocational', 'relevance' and 'evaluation' featuring in discussion. Subjects remain, with a focus on scientific and technological studies related to the efficiency objective and available, if not to all, then to all who have the ability to benefit from them and add to the skilled work force. It is possible that the revisionist ideology attracts both traditionalists who acknowledge the necessity for some change and progressives who are uncomfortable with the more socialist tendencies in that position.[41]

There is a further ideology in the educational system which sees the exclusive purpose of the curriculum as the development of the individual pupil. It finds its strongest expression in the early stages of education, in nursery, infant and junior schools and in many involved in the education of children with special needs. In the extreme of this ideology the very concept of a curriculum is rejected except in terms of an individual curriculum for each child on the basis that each is unique. Childhood is valued for itself, as a process of development neither a hostage to the past nor beholden to the future. In the educative process, learning requires first-hand experience arising from the child's exploration of the environment in 'play' activities to which each child contributes a personal structure and through which he constructs his own reality. To the holders of this ideology the concept of predetermined outcomes is anti-educational, so that goals or objectives are rejected as meaningless. Consequently the other ideologies are unacceptable, for all involve the concept of education as having purpose and predetermined ends. So far as the individualist ideology admits of ends, they must be self-formulated as, in the process of development, the individual becomes his or her own educator.[42] [43]

It would be wrong to think that individual teachers belong exclusively to one or other ideology. In general the individual's view of the curriculum is likely to include a variety of aspects, though overall one ideology may predominate. A similar combination of viewpoints will exist among the teachers forming the staff of any school, with the complication that the staff will change over a period of time with associated changes in the ideological 'mix'. Nor are only teachers influenced by ideology. Headteachers are not immune, nor advisers or HMI, though they may recognize ideology at work in others more readily than in themselves. The view of the curriculum in a LEA may be influenced by the majority party in power and may be altered by a swing of the political pendulum with indirect consequences in the schools – though it would be wrong to associate any political party exclusively with any one educational ideology. The DES itself may be affected by the political ideology of a government expressed in its policy towards the curriculum, often indicated in statements by Prime Ministers.[44]

The most insidious operation of ideology could be through the hidden curriculum of the school. Differentiated adult attitudes to successful or unsuccessful pupils; the adult view of the nature and purpose of school order and discipline; the quality of respect shown to pupils and their families; attitudes to industry, management, workers or trade unions; the measures through which the adults assess success; the teachers' attitude to communal property; the degree of courtesy shown to pupils, visitors and each other by the teaching staff; and the consistency of treatment of boys and girls, indiginous pupils and ethnic minorities: through these the adults influence the hidden curriculum. Perhaps these factors are of sufficient importance to be included as part of the planned curriculum in the school. They are specific to relationships in individual schools; they cannot be centralized or achieved by legislation. Here the autonomy of the teacher exists whether or not approved of by those who would control curriculum from outside.

Democracy

The belief in democracy may itself qualify as an ideology, though it has the distinction of widespread acceptance among people who might belong to any of the more particularized ideologies outlined above. Democracy also has important implications for curriculum. Men and women in a democratic society have equal rights which include the right of access to education and equality of educational opportunity. Further, each individual must have the opportunity to develop fully as a person without limit other than those made necessary by respect for the rights of other individuals.

Part of the concept of a democratic society is that society itself is in a process of free development. While the educational system has the responsibility for turning out individuals able to participate in the developing democratic society, there is no pattern or stereotype of democratic man or woman to guide the process. More than anything, the citizen of a democracy requires a critical attitude towards the society which he or she basically accepts and values in order to make a positive contribution to the refinement of the democratic ideal and practice. To achieve this the individual must, in the process of education, assimilate the essential values of democracy; but he or she must not accommodate inflexibly to the contemporary practices through which the values are expressed, since changing circumstances may require altered forms. In a developing society principle will at times overtake practice, the spirit will transcend the letter of the law. This creates a curriculum dilemma, for the claims of the individual must be balanced with the requirements of society, with neither allowed to permanently dominate the other. It also raises the question of by what right any individual is denied access to any area of curriculum, a question sometimes overlooked when seeking a curriculum appropriate to the real or imagined special needs of individuals. This will be an important consideration in later chapters.

Time and the curriculum

Time as process In the first place, the curriculum is a process in time. It is concerned with learning; and learning, in its complex forms, is rarely instantaneous. The curriculum is concerned with children, who enter it as infants and leave it as adolescents, with all the consequences for developments and appropriate learning which that implies. It follows that the curriculum may be regarded as a sequenced learning plan extending over years, taking account of the development of the pupils for whom it is intended and related to their pace of learning. Revision and application will be allowed for in the plan. This is necessary so that knowledge and skill may be assimilated, related and generalized in achieving quality of learning, something achieved over time. Some critical experiences may be re-presented to pupils in the manner of a spiral curriculum. The re-presentation takes account of the time-development aspect through a realization that an experience presented to the ten-year-old may have different and richer meanings than had the same experience at seven years, as a consequence of the intervening learning and maturation.

Time as limitation In the second place, the curriculum is constrained and limited by time. In general pupils enter the curriculum at five and leave it at sixteen years of age, with intermediate time limits allocated to successive phases in the organization of education. Within the given time limits, it is impossible for the schools to present pupils with every learning experience which would be beneficial to them as adolescents leaving school. What is presented represents a selection from all the possible learning experiences that could have been chosen. It is this inescapable constraint which makes curriculum necessary and it is the presented selection that forms the curriculum. Time limitation is the factor which forces teachers to become involved in the selection of learning experiences, of knowledge and of skills, but the selection cannot be made intelligently without reference to the learning abilities of the pupils, which will determine what may be achieved in the time available.

Future time It follows that curriculum is concerned with the priorities which should shape the decisions about what is to be included and what is to be left out. Now another time aspect presses for consideration. At what point are the priorities to be assessed – is the only concern the pupil as he is, or as he may be by the time he leaves school? Or should there be some consideration of the demands likely to face him as a young adult? Consideration of the latter may change the pattern of inclusion suggested by exclusively contemporary considerations. This question is raised to establish that some aspects of the curriculum may involve consideration of future situations, a less tangible aspect of time than the two discussed above, but one that cannot be ignored.

The social context

The wider society In a free society there are many groupings of citizens with interests in education, in the schools, and in curriculum and teaching. They generate criticism but they rarely influence the curriculum directly. The influence operates through members of parliament who influence legislation; through LEAs and the governing bodies of schools; through parent–teacher associations; and through the staffs of the schools. Mass media are used where possible, pamphlets and statements are circulated, and convinced and committed individuals promulgate their point of view in organizations noted above. This is an essential freedom in a democratic society.

In many respects the views put forward form part of an ideology or belief system and may be mainly directed at aspects of curriculum concerned with moral education, the teaching of religion, human relationships and the study of society in its economic and political aspects. The churches, now much wider than the Christian, form a grouping possibly more influential than their size of membership would justify. Trade unions and employers associations express views locally and nationally. Political parties produce educational policies and seek influence on bodies controlling education, and in some areas ethnic minorities may operate in a similar manner. The Home and School Council and the Confederation for State Education are examples of parent organizations with a close and legitimate interest in curriculum. Many of the pressures thus generated are in conflict and compete for influence in the schools, where they may operate not only in the open but also in the hidden curriculum.[45]

Home and community Consideration of the context of the curriculum should conclude by focusing on the family and the subculture. Curriculum is about pupils and their needs – as they are and as they present themselves in school. They do not enter school as blank sheets upon which the teachers collectively write 'education'. They enter with attitudes and values assimilated from family and neighbourhood; so far as they are able to express them they do so in language derived from the same sources; and from there also they bring expectations of what the school is and how teachers will behave. There is a world of difference between a child who has been told to listen to teacher or he will be in trouble, and his contemporary told he must listen to teacher or he will not learn. One home sees school as a place of discipline; the other as a place of learning. Homes and subcultures should be known and taken account of in the formation of curriculum. Strengths should be utilized and built upon, while the school curriculum should attempt to compensate for any known weakness in the life experience of the pupils. Schools should seek to make more use of

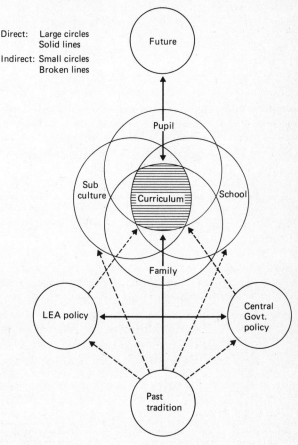

Figure 1 Influences on curriculum: direct influences – large circles, solid lines; indirect – small circles, broken lines

the skills, experience and insights of parents in developing curricula, and in doing this more account should be taken of community views and resources. The Taylor Report[46] gave recognition to this feature in considering the government of schools. Parents and community representatives were to have a defined place on the governing bodies of schools which would be more closely connected with the development and oversight of the school curriculum. It was further suggested that there was a role for senior pupils in the government of secondary schools.

Notes and references

1. BENJAMIN, H. (1969) 'The Saber-tooth Curriculum' in Golby, L. *et al.*, eds. (1975) *Curriculum Design*, London and Milton Keynes, Croom Helm with Open University Press.
2. BARNES, D. (1976) *From Curriculum to Communication*, Harmondsworth, Penguin.
3. BENNET, S.N. *et al.* (1976) *Teaching Styles and Pupil Progress*, London, Open Books.
4. DREEBEN, R. (1968) *On What is Learned in School*, New York, Addison Wesley.
5. JACKSON, P. (1968) *Life in Classrooms*, New York, Holt Rinehart.
6. KEDDIE, N. (1971) 'Classroom Knowledge' in Young, M., ed. *Knowledge and Control*, London, Collier Macmillan.
7. DREEBEN, R. (1976) 'The Unwritten Curriculum and its Relation to Values', *Journal of Curriculum Studies*, 8.
8. HARGREAVES, D. (1978) 'Power and the Paracurriculum' in Richards, C., ed. *Power and the Curriculum*, Driffield, Nafferton Books; Schools Council (1981) *The Practical Curriculum*, London, Methuen.
9. Department of Education and Science (1980) *A View of the Curriculum*, London, HMSO.
10. Department of Education and Science (1981) *The School Curriculum*, London, HMSO.
11. SKILBECK, M. (1976) 'Ideology, Knowledge and the Curriculum' in *Curriculum Design and Development*, Units 3 and 4, Milton Keynes, Open University Press.
12. The school leaving age has been progressively extended as follows: 1880, 10; 1893, 11; 1918, 14; 1947, 15; 1972, 16.
13. The tripartite arrangement followed from the Spens Report (1938). Grammar schools for 'bookish' pupils; technical schools for those with a 'practical' bent; modern schools for the others.
14. Department of Education and Science circular 10/65, London, HMSO. A comprehensive secondary school is designed to eliminate selection for secondary education at 11 plus by providing secondary education for pupils of all levels of ability except those who are thought to require education in special schools because of their

special educational needs. See HARGREAVES, D. (1982) *The Challenge for the Comprehensive School,* London, Routledge & Kegan Paul.

15. The Education Act 1964 permitted the development of 'middle schools' normally providing a four-year course from 8 to 12 or 9 to 13 years of age in place of the existing organization of primary 5 to 11 and secondary 11 to 16 years.

16. ROSLA is shorthand for Raising of the School-leaving Age. The new courses were often referred to as ROSLA courses and their participants as ROSLA pupils. See Education Act 1972, London HMSO; (1963) *Half our Future* (Newsom Report), HMSO; (1965) *Raising the School-leaving Age,* Schools Council working paper No. 2, London HMSO; (1967) *Society and the Young School Leaver,* London HMSO. For criticism of the courses, see LAWTON, D. (1970) 'Preparation for Changes in the Curriculum', in Tibble, (ed.) *The Extra Year,* London, Routledge & Kegan Paul.

17. The Schools Council (1964) *The Certificate of Secondary Examination: an introduction to some techniques of examining,* bulletin No. 3, London, HMSO.

18. SHIPMAN, M. (1971) 'Curriculum for Inequality?' in Hooper, R., ed. (1970). *The Curriculum,* Edinburgh and Milton Keynes, Oliver & Boyd and Open University Press.

19. From the unpublished full report of the Schools Council project (1974) *The Curricular Needs of Slow Learners.*

20. Rising Hill: a London comprehensive school. See BERG, L. (1968) *Rising Hill: The Death of a Comprehensive School,* Harmondsworth, Penguin.

21. William Tyndale: a London primary school. See AULD, R. (1976) *Report of the William Tyndale Junior and Infant School Public Enquiry,* London, ILEA.

22. BRENNAN, W. K. (1979) *The Curricular Needs of Slow Learners,* Ch. 4, London, Evans/Methuen Educational.

23. Department of Education and Science (1982) *Report by HMI on the Effects of Local Authority Expenditure Policies on the Educational Service in England, 1981* London, DES; see also *1982* report.

24. The brief of the Schools Council is wider than the curriculum. Its purpose includes teaching methods, examinations and other ways which help teachers decide what and how to teach.

25. Speech in Oxford reported in *The Times,* 8 October 1976.

26. The local education authorities outside London are the metropolitan district councils or the non-metropolitan county councils. In London they are the councils of the outer London boroughs and a special committee of the Greater London Council known as the Inner London Education Committee.

27. Instruments and rules of management my differ between different LEAs but the general situation is as stated. There is also a complication of voluntary schools and the restriction relating to denominational religious instruction. For the legal position, see TAYLOR, G. and SAUNDERS, J. B. (1976) *The Law of Education,* 8th

edn, pp. 100–109, London, Butterworths.

28. WHITE, J. (1968) 'Instruction in Obedience', *New Society*, 2 May; CASTON, G. (1971) 'The Schools Council in Context', *Journal of Curriculum Studies*, Vol. 3; RICHARDS, C. (1974) 'The Schools Council: A Critical Examination', *Universities Quarterly*, V.28.

29. YOUNG, M. (1972) 'The Politics of Educational Knowledge', *Economy and Society*, V.2.

30. BRENNAN, W. K. (1979) *The Curricular Needs of Slow Learners*, Ch. 7, London, Evans/Methuen Educational.

31. *Report in Education*, 18 Novemeber 1983.

32. Nuffield Foundation, Nuffield Lodge, Regent's Park, London NW1 4RS.

33. National Foundation for Educational Research in England and Wales, The Mere, Upton Park, Slough, Berks SL1 2DQ.

34. Consultative Committee on the Curriculum, Scotland, Education Dept, St Andrew's House, St James Centre, Edinburgh EH1 3SY; Scottish Council for Research in Education, 16 Moray Place, Edinburgh EH3 6DR; Northern Ireland Council for Educational Research, 52 Malone Road, Belfast BT9 5BS.

35. Department of Education and Science (1966) *Children and Their Primary Schools*. V.1, London, HMSO; Ministry of Education (1963) *Half Our Future*, London, HMSO.

36. Department of Education and Science (1967) *Primary Education in Wales*, London, HMSO.

37. Scottish Central Committee on Primary Education (1974) *Remedial Education in the Primary School*, London, HMSO.

38. LAWTON, D. (1974) *Social Change, Educational Theory and Curriculum Planning*, Dunton Green, Hodder & Stoughton Educational; HALSEY, A. H. *et al.* (1961) *Education, Economy and Society*, New York, Free Press; HOLLY, D. (1974) *Beyond Curriculum*, London, Paladin; FREIRE, P. (1970) *Pedagogy of the Oppressed*, Harmondsworth, Penguin; WILLIAMS, R. (1965) *The Long Revolution*, Harmondsworth, Penguin.

39. BANTOCK, G. (1968) *Culture, Industrialization and Education*, London, Routledge & Kegan Paul; COX, C. and DYSON, A. (1969) *Black Paper II: The Crisis in Education*, London, Critical Quarterly Society; COX, C. and BOYSON, R. (1975) *Black Paper 1975*, London, Dent.

40. WHITE, J. P. (1973) *Towards a Compulsory Curriculum*, London, Routledge and Kegan Paul; (1969) 'The Curriculum Mongers: Education in Reverse' in Hooper, R., ed. (1970) *The Curriculum*, Edinburgh and Milton Keynes, Oliver & Boyd and Open University Press; LAWTON, D. (1974) op. cit.; WILLIAMS, R. (1965) op. cit.

41. This movement may have something in common with the political trend which led to the formation of the Social Democratic Party in Britain.

42. DES (1966) *Children and Their Primary Schools* op. cit. reflects something of this ideology. See also COOK, C. (1919) *The Play Way*, London, Heinemann; MARSHALL, S. (1963) *An Experiment in Education*, Cambridge, Cambridge University Press.

43. The traditionalist–progressive dichotomy is becoming difficult to sustain as it does not allow for the middle field. DAVIES, I. proposed a four-category system: democratic, revisionist, romantic and conservative (*New Society*, 8 May 1969). I have used this revisionist category, and his romantic category approximates to the description of the individualist ideology. Davies's model is briefly discussed in TAYLOR, P. H. and RICHARDS, C. (1979). *Introduction to Curriculum Studies*, Ch. 2, Windsor, NFER.

44. Prime Minister Callaghan's Oxford speech op. cit.; also Prime Minister Thatcher's constant references to 'Victorian values': no doubt she means those of the drawing room rather than the gin palace.

45. Details of the organizations are available in *Education Year Book*, published annually by Councils and Educational Press, in particular the sections on denominational education, parents' organizations, Confederation of British Industry and Trades Union Congress.

46. DES (1977) *A New Partnership for our Schools* (Taylor Report), London, HMSO.

CHAPTER 2

Curriculum and special needs

What are special educational needs?

One of the difficulties in discussing special needs is the fact that agreed definitions are difficult to achieve and consequently rare. In specifying special *educational* needs, the field is limited on the assumption that not all special needs affect the curriculum; however, not all teachers agree with this position. All pupils may be regarded as having special educational needs of some kind. One approach is to regard as special educational needs only those which require more than the skill of the classroom teacher for their solution; in other words, needs which call for intervention in support of the teacher or the creation of an alternative learning situation for the pupil.[1] This position is consistent with that of the Warnock Report,[2] where a special educational need is defined as one requiring:

(i)   the provision of special means of access to the curriculum through special equipment, facilities or resources, modification of the physical environment or specialist teaching techniques;
(ii) the provision of special or modified curriculum;
(iii) particular attention to the social structure and emotional climate in which education takes place.

This definition marked an important advance. By concentrating on the facilities required it became possible to assess whether or not the child's needs were being met by comparing the facilities available with those required. It is also an *educational* definition in that it centres on curriculum, allows for those children who may follow the normal school curriculum given appropriate support, includes those for whom the normal curriculum may be inappropriate, and makes the point that curriculum to be effective must be conducted in a situation appropriate to the child's *learning* needs.

But the leap forward became a small step in the Education Act 1981.[3] There a child has a special educational need if he has a 'learning difficulty which calls for special educational provision to be made for him'; a child is defined as having a learning difficulty if:

(a) he has a significantly greater difficulty in learning than the majority of children of his age; or
(b) he has a disability which either prevents or hinders him from making use of educational facilities of a kind generally provided in schools, within the area of the local authority concerned, for children of his age . . .[4]

Gone is the precision of concentration on facilities and curriculum. Learning difficulty is referred to the generality of children of the same age and any difference must be 'significant'; there must be difficulty with facilities 'generally provided' for the age range; and all this must relate to what happens in the local authority. The outcome of this may be that the special education which the pupil requires is determined more by the standards existing in his LEA than by his personal needs. The Educational Act 1981 confirms this conclusion in its definition of special educational provision:

Special educational provision means educational provision which is additional to, or otherwise different from, the educational provision made generally for children of his age in schools maintained by the local education authority concerned.[5]

Comparing this definition with the following, from the Warnock Report, emphasizes the Act's loss of precision and scope:

special education . . . should therefore be understood in terms of one or more of three criteria:

(i) effective access on a full- or part-time basis to teachers with appropriate qualifications or substantial experience or both;
(ii) effective access of a full- or part-time basis to other professionals with appropriate training; and
(iii) an educational and physical environment with the necessary aids, equipment and resources appropriate to the child's special needs.[6]

The Warnock concern with curriculum, facilities and teaching has been lost between the report of 1978 and the Act of 1981.

There are now two definitions of special educational needs: on one hand, the legal definition of the Act which will be attractive to administrators; on the other hand, the educational definition of the report more attractive to educators. While it would be wrong to regard educators and administrators as inevitably divided, tension between the *roles* is a distinct possibility in times of financial stringency and scarce resources. In a discussion of curriculum it is clear that only the Warnock definition is helpful, and this definition will be assumed throughout this book.

On one point the definitions are as one. In the report and in the Act there is acceptance that special educational needs extend over a range from mild to severe, and both establish a critical point in the range as that where the LEA finds it necessary to determine a pupil's special needs in a 'statement' to be maintained by the authority.[7] But even here there is a difference. The Act says nothing about pupils with special needs for whom a statement is not considered necessary; the report defines five stages of assessment of needs, the first three within schools and considered appropriate for pupils who are not candidates for LEA statements.[8] The statement does not alone determine curriculum, for that should relate to the pupil's needs and these will not be changed by placement, which the statement influences. The main purpose of the statement is to ensure the pupil's needs are kept before the LEA and reviewed at regular intervals, though the *content* of the statement should relate to the curriculum appropriate for the pupil and must be taken account of by those responsible for teaching him.

Another important point in the Warnock Report with direct consequence for curriculum is the concept that special educational needs are not necessarily permanent needs. While at any time one in six of pupils is likely to have special needs, one in five may have such needs *at some time during their school career* and at that phase will require special education delivered through all or part of their curriculum.[9]

It is now possible to arrive at a working definition of special educational needs and associated special education:

SPECIAL EDUCATIONAL NEED.   A special educational need exists when any disability (physical, sensory, intellectual, emotional, social, or any combination of these) affects learning to the extent that any or all of special access to curriculum, special or modified curriculum, or specially adapted conditions of learning, are necessary if the pupil is to be appropriately and effectively educated. The need may be at any point on a continuum from mild to severe; it may be permanent or a temporary phase in the pupil's development.

SPECIAL EDUCATION.   Special education is that combination of curriculum, teaching, support and learning conditions necessary in order to meet the pupil's special educational needs in an appropriate and effective manner. It may form all or part of the pupil's curriculum, may be delivered individually or in association with others, and may form all or part of his school career.

These definitions form the basis for subsequent discussion of curriculum. They make no distinction about level of severity of need, nor any assumption about the place in which special education is delivered.

Special needs and curriculum requirements

Aims

The Warnock Report, in examining the education of children with special educational needs, took the view that the aims of education are the same for *all children* and are twofold:

> first, to enlarge a child's knowledge, experience and imaginative understanding, and thus his awareness of moral values and capacity for enjoyment; and second, to enable him to enter the world after formal education is over as an active participant in society and a responsible contributor to it, capable of achieving as much independence as possible.[10]

This statement is fully compatible with the nature of the curriculum described in Chapter 1. The degree to which the aims may be achieved will vary between individuals. Some children with exceptionally severe learning difficulties will achieve the first only through small increments carefully taught and reinforced continually, and what is achieved must be evaluated in terms of the individual child. But the nature of the aim is not changed. For other pupils, those who may be regarded as profoundly mentally and physically handicapped, the second aim may not be achieved in terms of wider society, but progress towards it may come as they interact with those who care for them and constitute their, albeit limited, society. So even at this extreme level special needs are accommodated within the overall aims of the curriculum. In a democratic society it must not be otherwise – one cannot exclude humans from human rights, and the right to education is fundamental. Curricular aims are stated in the Warnock Report in general terms which provide a frame of reference within which individual schools may operate. Any statement from outside a school, whether from central government, DES or LEA, must be subject to that limitation. Each school has a specific responsibility for the formulation of specific aims directly related to the perceived curricular needs of the pupils in the school. The specific aims must be consistent with the general aims of education and this also applies where specific aims are designed to meet special educational needs.

Objectives But the responsibility of the school extends beyond specific aims. If aims are to be achieved then the school must select the activities and experiences which are to form the curriculum and assist pupils to attain the currciulum aims. The selection itself will imply certain knowledge, skills and values and will, in turn, be shaped by what the teachers hold to be valuable for the pupils in the school. The knowledge, skills and values are the *objectives* of the curriculum the attainment of which is necessary if the aims of the curriculum are to be fulfilled. Education for special needs is most clearly reflected in the objectives of the curriculum and associated teaching methods. Both these must be realistically related to the pupils for whom they are intended and must therefore take account of individual potentials and disabilities while remaining as close as possible to those for all pupils of the same age. It is here that the wide variety of special needs generates curriculum problems.

The range of special needs

Problems arise from the wide range of special educational needs and the associated circumstance that within any group of needs there will be equally wide variation in the severity experienced by individual children.

The situation has not changed over the years. The National Bureau for Co-operation in Child Care, dissatisfied with legal categories of handicapped children, looked for more useful groupings of disabilities in 1970. The report produced listed ten groups including sensory disabilities of sight and hearing, physical disabilities, intellectual handicap, severe environmental handicap, severe personality disorder, emotional handicap and severe multi-handicap.[11] Around the same time Gulliford[12] proposed nine groups: emotional difficulty, intellectual handicap, specific learning difficulties, communication difficulties, social and cultural differences, hearing impairment, visual handicap, physical handicap and multiple handicap – all capable of generating special educational needs. A decade of development passed before the Warnock Committee discussed the curriculum for children with different special needs.[13] The Warnock Report first stresses the number of children with multiple special needs, either dual primary needs or needs generated through the stresses accompanying a single primary disability. Then the curriculum is discussed relevant to visual disability, hearing disability, physical handicap, epilepsy, speech and language disorder, specific learning disability, learning difficulty (at mild, moderate and severe levels), and emotional and behaviour disorders. In their discussion the committee had to identify important specific conditions creating special needs within each of the groupings, for example reading and perceptual difficulties within the specific group, and childhood autism within the emotional and behavioural group.

Brennan[14] illustrated the range and levels of disability in a different manner by describing children within his experience of special education. In all he described twelve children, all different and all with their own special needs; they included: John with severe physical handicap, without legs or arms but successful in academic subjects in the comprehensive school; Molly, with education interrupted by violent outburst followed by with-drawal, posing problems in her special school; Kathleen, inert and without sight or hearing, depending on others for any mobility, severely mentally handicapped; David, a boy with a rich intellectual life and exciting hobbies finding it hard to keep up in secondary education because of perceptual and fine motor difficulties; Ann, blind; Donald deaf; Molly, severely withdrawn and losing touch with reality; and Susan, whose education was interrupted by absence due to poor health. In Brennan's discussion the varying school programmes are indicated along with the possible post-school outcomes from each individual.

Mary Wilson has conceptualized the diversity of special needs and has proposed four groupings which relate directly to the curriculum:[15]

1. *Children with defects of hearing, vision or mobility without serious intellectual or emotional problems.* These pupils must acquire special, additional skills to overcome their disability, learn to use special equipment for recording or mobility. They are capable of following the normal school curriculum, though the time required for their necessary additional learning may reduce the number of subjects with which they can be involved at any one time. That problem may be overcome by extending their time in school or arranging follow-on curriculum in further education.

2. *Children who are educationally disadvantaged.* Social or psychological reasons account for the difficulties in this group, with the result that they are not able, or are not prepared, to

accommodate to the learning tasks presented in their schools. Their attitudes are inappropriate and they do not relate to the values of the school. In Wilson's view sensitive handling is called for if these pupils are not to become totally alienated. Many schools do succeed with the pupils, not necessarily because of what they are taught, but through the respect and encouragement which they receive. In terms of this discussion success arises from the planned and hidden curriculum.

3. *Children with significant learning difficulties.* Some of these children need broadly based curricula closely related to their general intellectual and personal immaturity, and they may require it throughout their school life. Others are less immature and may eventually participate fully in main curricula. Yet others are near normal in intellectual capacity and maturity but with educational progress at risk through severe specific learning difficulties. Wilson points out that that where the latter group have specific language difficulties they may be underestimated by their teachers. All this group are at risk emotionally through their experience of failure. To be successful with these pupils, schools need flexibility of approach and curriculum allied to sound assessment techniques; and it is important that the pupils are not denied appropriate access to the main school curriculum.

4. *Pupils with emotional or behavioural difficulties.* These pupils present the most serious problem in school and have usually experienced scholastic failure, frustration and social stress. At present, Wilson suggests, 'they benefit particularly from warm, caring attitudes, consistent though non-punitive discipline and opportunities for talking things over', allied to a 'two pronged attack on their cognitive and social/emotional development'.

The above sources of discussion, though widely separated in time, all direct attention to the fact that some children have multiple handicaps. As such children present complicated problems in the design of appropriate curricula about which little is known at present, some indication of the frequency of occurrence would be useful. Information is not easy to obtain due to the practice of classifying children with special needs in terms of their major, primary disability. Cave and Maddison[16] have produced a broad survey of the incidence of multiple disability, noting illustrative studies in the UK. A DES survey [17] showed that

60 per cent of deaf children had at least one additional handicap after discounting emotional disturbance. In schools for pupils with moderate learning difficulties Williams[18] found half with disturbed behaviour, a third with speech defects and one fifth with visual defects, while a Manchester study[19] of children with severe learning difficulties discovered 20 per cent with epilepsy, 27 per cent physically handicapped, 33 per cent with visual and 9 per cent with hearing disabilities. A well-documented Isle of Wight study[20] was concerned with intellectual retardation, educational retardation, psychiatric disorder and physical handicap. These conditions were found in 16 per cent of the pupils studied. Among the handicapped pupils 90 per cent of the intellectually retarded, 43 per cent of the educationally retarded, 36 per cent of the psychiatrically disordered and 29 per cent of the physically handicapped pupils had one or more additional handicap. Subsequent studies have shown that a similar situation exists in inner-city areas.[21] There is reason to believe that multiple handicap has increased in recent years, though this may be *identified* multiple handicap arising from improvement in the assessment of pupils with special needs. The fact remains that multiply handicapped pupils present a curriculum challenge and will continue to do so.

The level of special need

If the range of special educational needs presents a curriculum problem, so does the wide difference between mild and severe within any one disability. A further complication arises in that there is no simple relationship between the severity of the disability and its effect on learning. Take, for example, two physically handicapped boys:

John

John is severely physically disabled. He has no legs or arms and his mobility is totally dependent on a wheelchair. He requires assistance, not only to move around the comprehensive school, but also to move around the classroom. His school timetable must be carefully organized so that the support he requires is capable of ensuring he is in the right place at the right time. Once there he learns normally in academic subjects though he requires special help with recording. School progress is satisfactory. John has successful GCE 'O' level studies behind him and he is continuing at 'A' level.

Robert

Robert at rest has a perfectly normal appearance. He moves around the school without assistance though there is a lack of co-ordination in his movements; in spite of care, his grasp is haphazard and he is uncertain when he has to lift objects. Robert certainly has a physical disability but why should he require a special school? Consideration of Robert's learning provides an answer. In class he is almost unable to concentrate, through lapses of attention due to distraction caused by almost any external stimuli. He misses some points, misunderstands others and has difficulty in sustaining thought sequences. Reading is hesitant and retarded, handwriting uneven and misaligned, drawing immature, and craft work lacking in accuracy appropriate to Robert's age. Yet it is believed that Robert is within normal limits of intellectual ability, and apart from slight slurring of speech he communicates at an acceptable level.

Both these boys have physical disability. John's is exceptionally severe but he is making educational progress which would be considered satisfactory even in the absence of physical disability. He is working within the normal school curriculum. John's severe special needs require the provision of comprehensive support service necessary to give him access to the normal curriculum. In contrast, no amount of support would give Robert access to the normal school curriculum, though the physical handicap is mild. Robert's main special needs are directly concerned with learning. He requires most carefully organized and structured learning situations with distraction eliminated as far as possible to aid his concentration. Even then learning will continue to be slow and he will not achieve normal goals within the usual span of schooling to sixteen years of age. Consequently his curriculum priorities will require careful planning and revision in the light of his school progress[22]. Here is an extreme contrast: severe physical handicap with little or no curriculum consequence; mild physical handicap with severe implications for curriculum and teaching. Robert's mild physical handicap involves some central nervous system dysfunction, and indeed may be caused by the latter. But that interplay of cause and effect is of no consequence in curriculum terms. Robert's curriculum is not about the past: it is concerned with his contemporary situation and his future.

Contrasts similar to the above could be advanced from within any group of special needs – the case studies would make a book in themselves. Another way of illustrating the different levels which may exist in special needs is to examine the variety of arrangements considered necessary for delivering the curriculum in schools. The following list is taken from the Warnock Report[23] and represents what is required rather than what is available in every local education authority.

Provision for special needs

(i)   full-time education in an ordinary class with any necessary help and support;

(ii) education in an ordinary class with periods of withdrawal to a special class or unit or other supporting base;

(ii) education in a special class or unit with periods of attendance at an ordinary class and full involvement in the general community life and extracurricular activities of the ordinary school;

(iv) full-time education in a special class or unit with social contact with the main school;

(v)   education in a special school, day or residential, with some shared lessons with a neighbouring ordinary school;

(v)   full-time education in a day special school with social contact with an ordinary school;

(vii) full-time education in a residential special school with social contact with an ordinary school;

(viii) short-term education in hospitals or other establishments;

(ix) long-term education in hospitals or other establishments;

(x)   home tuition.

The implication is not only that different levels of need will require curriculum delivery in different situations, but also that for some needs it will not be practicable to provide for the whole curriculum in a single situation. Where the pupil is being taught in more than one situation there must be close co-operation between the teachers concerned; a degree of continuity is essential for curricular cohesion, not only in terms of what is taught, but how it is taught, and also about the planned and hidden curriculum. The situations should not be identical, however, for that would defeat the purpose of the movement and reduce the value to the pupil.

Another point to note about the above list is the assumption that 'necessary help and support' are required only for education in an ordinary class, presumably following a normal school curriculum. The next examples illustrate the inadequacy of the assumption:

Mary

Mary is deaf. When she was assessed, her poor intellectual performance was attributed to her difficulties with communication, and she was first placed in a unit for partially hearing pupils where she failed to progress. Subsequent time in a school for deaf pupils was no more successful. On reassessment it was decided that Mary had moderate learning difficulties of a permanent nature quite apart from any hearing loss. She was then placed in a special school for pupils with moderate learning difficulties where she is beginning to make progress in a curriculum appropriate to her needs. But to remain in that curriculum she still requires her hearing aid while she (and her teachers) are supported by regular visits from a peripatetic teacher of deaf pupils.

William

William is blind and is making satisfactory progress in a school for blind pupils. But he is also severely physically handicapped and has mobility only in a wheelchair. To remain in his curriculum William must be pushed around the school so that he is in the right place at the right time. This support would be necessary wherever William was educated, but for a blind pupil in a blind community it is more than ever essential.

James

James requires education as a pupil with moderate learning difficulties and is following appropriate curriculum in a special unit of a comprehensive school. But James has a severe specific difficulty with reading which is a barrier to progress. On three occasions each week James presents himself in the school centre for learning resources where he follows an individual programme designed to reduce or erradicate his reading difficulty. Without the learning and the confidence which the programme generates James would have great difficulty in maintaining progress in his special curriculum.

These examples could be multiplied, or the situation could be examined from the point of illness like epilepsy or diabetes. Both these conditions require continuous medication to establish the control necessary to allow children who suffer from them to be educated. The control is necessary at whatever level of curriculum appropriate for individual pupils – from the academic classes of the secondary school, to the classroom for young severely mentally handicapped pupils. To take account of the above discussion, it is possible to formulate an addition to the Warnock list:

> full- or part-time education in a special unit or class, or day or residential special school, with the necessary help and support.

Special educational needs and curricula interact in a complex manner. The interaction arises from the demands made upon curriculum by the range and level of special needs, by the multiplicity of special needs presented by some children, and by the help and assistance required if pupils are to be maintained in appropriate curricula and educated efficiently.

The time factor

Where there are special needs, consideration of the time available for education becomes important in arriving at decisions about the priorities that are to regulate both curriculum content and exclusions. Decisions affected by the time factor include those relating to learning, to intrusions and to the future.

Learning Sensory handicaps of blindness and deafness make it essential that teachers and pupils become involved in alternative methods of communication; and for blind pupils there is the additional complication of mobility. Physical disabilities raise mobility problems of a different kind, as well as those concerned with posture, personal hygiene and the management of written communication. Pupils with emotional disorders affecting behaviour face the task of eliminating the maladaptive patterns and replacing them with more acceptable behaviour. Intellectual limitation is usually associated with inefficient or ineffective perception which affects incidental learning and requires curriculum inclusions not necessary with other pupils. All these circumstances result in additional learning tasks for the pupils affected by them and the tasks must be accommodated within the time available in school, even if some support may come from learning outside the school.

Other factors extend required learning periods. General intellectual limitation slows up the pace of learning and the associated stress may reinforce the tendency to slowness. Stress of a different kind arising from emotional disorders or the tensions of social confrontation often has a significant effect on the learning of maladjusted pupils on tasks well within their intellectual capacity. Where these pupils are controlled through drug therapy any improvement in behaviour may be accompanied by lowered learning efficiency and a similar effect frequently follows the administration of drugs to control epilepsy. Specific learning difficulties, of whatever kind, disrupt the pattern of learning, extending the time required for mastery in areas otherwise within the pupil's capacity.

The above factors frequently overlap. The necessary additional learning required by a pupil may be complicated by the fact that associated conditions extend the time required to establish it. Even without that complication establishing the additional knowledge or skill may have the effect of lowering learning efficiency in other areas. The pattern of learning may also be influenced. For example, a physically handicapped pupil may be establishing walking skills at, say, seven years of ages. At that point, scholastically, he may be on the threshold of breakthrough into formal reading skills. Often the concentration on the physical task can cause temporary delay in the scholastic task, though the deficit may be eliminated once the physical stress disappears. Similarly, less clearly related perhaps, the learning patterns of maladjusted pupils may vary according to the degree of emotional or social tension which they are experiencing. All these factors which affect the rate of learning must be taken account of when reaching decisions about curricula involving special educational needs.

Intrusions into curriculum Many of the intrusions into the curriculum and teaching of children with special needs are essential, contribute to their future well-being, and indeed may be considered part of the pupil's overall curriculum. Nevertheless they occupy time and reduce that available for other essential learning. That is why the intrusions require careful evaluation in terms of curriculum balance.

What are the intrusions to be considered? And who is to decide what the balance should be? In the circumstances of most schools, following a curriculum necessitates movement around the school; from art room to laboratory, from form room to subject location, or from school hall to primary school classroom. Outside the curriculum, movements between classrooms and cloakrooms or meal locations are also required and generate no difficulty for children without special needs. But what about pupils who are physically handicapped or blind? They cannot be expected to move as quickly or efficiently as children without their disabilities. A special school timetable allows for the difficulty with more time between lesson periods: but that changes the balance between moving-time and learning-time to the disadvantage of the latter. Similar problems surround any question of movement within the school. In ordinary schools the problems posed by blind or physically handicapped pupils are more complicated, not because the nature of the problem changes, but because it must now be resolved within a regime designed for pupils without those special needs – i.e. balanced not only between movement and learning but also between the claims of pupils with disabilities and those without them.

If pupils with reduced mobility take longer to move between lesson locations than other children involved, are the intervals to be extended? If so, that wastes the time of other pupils. Are the less mobile pupils to be allowed to arrive after the lesson has started? If so, they will have less time for learning, and the learning of other pupils may be disrupted. The provision of more assistance to move handicapped pupils around the school may resolve the problems of time and disruption but it will deny the pupils the experience of coping unaided, overcoming their disability and achieving the positive effect of maximum independence: important aspects of their wider curriculum. These are not merely organizational problems, but affect curriculum directly, they are given added importance for ordinary schools by the Education Act 1981. Where a child with special needs is educated in an ordinary school, the act requires compatibility with:

(a) his receiving the special education that he requires;
(b) the provision of efficient education for the children with whom he will be educated . . .[24]

So the law itself requires that a balance be held.

Other intrusions into curriculum present real if less complicated problems. Physically handicapped pupils and those with poor health or medical problems require time out for medical treatment, physiotherapy or hospitalization. Maladjusted pupils may be in psychotherapy or visiting child guidance centres. Socially disadvantaged children may have periods in social service care. Any special need may interfere with school attendance and a high proportion of handicapped pupils require speech therapy. Essential though they may be, the time taken for these support services is time taken away from learning in the school curriculum.

It is essential that all the situations described above are taken into account when arriving at curriculum decisions. Correct decisions will require interdisciplinary co-operation, but during the child's school years education should be the central discipline, and the task of reaching a balance should rest with those responsible for the child's education.

The future   Attempting to relate the curriculum to the future of any pupil is hazardous at best. It requires sensitive appreciation of the pupil's potential together with intelligent analysis of current situations and future trends; only rarely is it achieved with complete success. When the pupils concerned have disabilities which result in special educational needs the task is more important and more difficult. There are three main factors to consider: changes in the pupils, changes in external factors, and the possible development of new techniques, medical, social or educational, which may affect the life pattern of the pupils.

First, possible alterations in the pupil's potential. The process of maturation and development is continuous, and qualitative changes in interest and attitudes often follow from it which have marked effects on willingness and ability to learn. It is one of the things good teachers attempt to foster and to make use of. On the other hand, the reverse may occur with deterioration in the pupil's performance. A similar situation may arise where extraneous stress is reduced or intensified. Planned medical treatment, physiotherapy or surgical intervention may alter the status of the pupil, often over considerable periods of time, and the altered potential should be planned for in educational terms. In some cases schools may be working with a current curriculum which is being implemented, but with medium- and long-term alternatives which take account of the possible outcomes of planned intervention and their relationship to the pupil's educational potential and possibilities, and even to his future career prospects. With maladjusted pupils this aspect of change is of special importance. The common feature of maladjusted pupils is that their behaviour is maladaptive, causes extreme difficulty in their relationships with other people, and creates severe obstacles to learning, especially where accuracy or sequence are important. An important part of their rehabilitation rests on interpersonal counselling or guidance supported by continuing and consistent school relationships. Success here is essential if there is to be progress in learning, but learning itself is therapeutic and contributes to positive relationships and adaptive behaviour. The process should be understood by teachers and taken account of in developing curriculum and teaching which keeps pace with and contributes to the improvement of the pupil.[25]

Second, changes in external factors which affect the pupil may have implications for curriculum planning. Brennan[26] described a pupil with a mild congenital heart condition allied to frequent chest infections who gained considerable benefit from a change of school and curriculum though her disability remained unaltered. Improved pupil–teacher ratios, better qualified teachers, provision of classroom and welfare assistants, enhanced capitation allowances, closer involvement of parents in the education of their children, improved medical, paramedical or social service support to the schools: all or any of these make possible improvements in curriculum and teaching. Conversely, deterioration could adversely affect what the school is able to offer. The development of further education facilities, with assurance of continuity for pupils with special needs, would open up rich possibilities. Assurance of continuity would have an immediate effect on curriculum in the schools, for it would no longer be necessary to include in the final years knowledge or skill for which pupils were not ready because of the fear that if not attempted by the school the pupils might be denied the opportunity to learn. Consequently, the school curriculum could be more closely related to the developmental needs of pupils, the time acquired could be devoted to necessary preparatory learning, and the excluded knowledge or skill might be established more efficiently with maturity in further education. Those pupils with intellectual or learning disabilities, or those with emotional or social immaturity, would gain most from the development described. But all would gain from the general further education curriculum with its increased element of work preparation, vocational training and student self-reliance and involvement.

These educational developments could be related to and anticipate any changes in the pattern of local industries. Industrial innovation could dramatically alter the employment possibilities for disabled young people, but to gain maximum benefit any changes should be related to school and college curricula in order to establish the general learning which would support later, specific industrial or on-the-job training. The loss of local industry without replacement, a deteriorating national economy and the prospect of increasing unemployment would create an adverse situation. But this, too, has potentially positive implications for curriculum of the kind indicated in Chapter 1 where economic influences were discussed.

CHANGES IN ATTITUDES   All these external changes take place against an important background: the attitude to disabled people which operates throughout society. This has changed and may be expected to go on changing. It influences the reality of the curriculum in many ways. Partly it influences the facilities available for the curriculum and the support services discussed above, but it also plays its part in shaping the educational philosophy of those responsible for developing curriculum for special needs. The operation of the general ethos is clearly seen in the belief that pupils with special needs should be educated alongside pupils without special needs. This is a distinct change from the separist view which supported the development of special schools for handicapped pupils, and it is clearly expressed in the Warnock Report. The change will not influence the curriculum directly, for it does not alter the kind of special need which pupils will present. But in time it will dramatically alter the background against which curricula for special needs are conducted. It will also extend curriculum possibilities by creating opportunities for some special educational needs to be met through the normal curriculum and in association with normal pupil groups. There is still a long way to go in establishing this in schools, and there is as much to be done in wider society to which education and the changes in the schools may contribute – for the curriculum is not merely a recipient of the changes; properly conceived, it may contribute to the changes.

TECHNOLOGY   Finally are changes which may follow future development in educational and other techniques. There was a time when schools generally did not have slide or film projectors, tape recorders, television or video-recorders, duplicators and photocopiers. Now they have, and each acquisition has extended the possibilities for curriculum and teaching. Now the era of microelectronics is here. In terms of curriculum and special needs, development has only begun. There are exciting possibilities for enabling disabled pupils to do things which once were beyond them, of increasing access to normal curriculum, and of learning skills and techniques which have economic value in areas where their disability does not constitute a handicap. Nor are the possibilities confined to occupations. Teletext for the deaf pupils and the newly introduced Braille printing press for the blind are examples that may extend curriculum over wide areas. Medical advances may have similar effects. Heart and limb replacement, electronically controlled artificial limbs and advances in the regulation of debilitating illness all suggest increasing hope for the disabled and extended possibilities for curriculum and teaching. Those concerned with curriculum for special needs must be aware of technological possibilities and constantly monitor their significance for curriculum development.

Summary of implications

The implications of special needs for curriculum are now becoming clear. Specific aims directed at meeting special needs must be consistent with the common aims of education. Factors influencing general curriculum considered in Chapter 1 continue to have influence, but the special needs themselves create additional pressures – largely due to the wide range and differing levels of need, to the extension of required learning time arising from them, and to the time absorbed by the additional support services necessary for pupils with special needs in any curriculum.

Special needs requirements
1. Clear identification of the special needs.
2. Extra-careful planning of curricula to meet them.
3. Continuous reassessment of need related to revision of curriculum.
4. Planning of interaction between normal and special curriculum where appropriate.
5. Individualizing of curriculum aims and teaching where necessary.
6. Careful preparation of teachers with the sensitivity and insight required for the tasks.

Developing and delivering curriculum for special needs make additional demands on teachers. They require clear concepts of the aims appropriate for their pupils in the absence of special needs. They must be equally clear about the aims required to meet the special needs themselves. At that point the teachers are in a position to decide to what extent meeting the special needs may be accommodated within the normal curriculum and to identify the support necessary to achieve that objective. Where special needs must dominate the curriculum because of severity or multiplicity, then decisions are required about what contribution is possible from the normal taught curriculum, or to what extent the planned or hidden curriculum may operate through social interaction between handicapped pupils and others. Where sensory loss or moderate or severe learning difficulties are involved, or where emotional disturbance may distort the pupil's perception, decision will be required about the extent to which the benefits of hidden curriculum must be planned for or the planned curriculum incorporated in the taught.

Decisions such as these demand 'intimacy of knowledge' on the part of the teacher.[27] Knowledge about the pupil's home and neighbourhood background; about his or her patterns of motivation, interests, and learning potential; about health and physical status; and about current special needs and the way they may develop: all these must be related to existing and potential facilities and professional skills in reaching decisions about curriculum. The intimacy of knowledge possibly exists only within the pupil's school, through continuous contact with him by sensitive teachers. It is there that the curriculum decisions must be made after all other factors have been considered. Special needs are personal needs, and personal knowledge of the pupil concerned is essential for appropriate and correct curricular decisions. That is why the responsibility must remain in the school.

Assessment of current provision in schools

It is not easy to present an overall assessment of current schools' provision for special needs and there is a danger that generalization will involve distortion. The most comprehensive survey is that of the Warnock Report, though the wide nature of the enquiry relegated curriculum to a minor feature. The evidence presented to the committee indicated a widespread belief that many special schools underestimated their pupils' abilities at all levels, and across all disabilities. The curriculum was also considered too narrow, mainly due to concentration on basic subjects to the neglect of wider aspects of English, mathematics, science and environmental studies. On the other hand, the strength of social training in the schools was generally recognized. While the committee found some evidence that the wider curriculum was neglected, evidence to the contrary is given greater stress in the report.[28]

In a Schools Council survey of 123 special schools for pupils with moderate learning difficulty, 61 per cent were rated as providing successful curricula. This tends to support the Warnock position: there are successful special schools in the system but there are also many in which curriculum is ineffective and the education of the pupils less efficient than it might be.[29] The authors of the Schools Council survey agreed with the Warnock view of the strength of social training, to the extent that they held that concern for *welfare* was outstanding and in danger of ousting some specifically educational objectives. Wilson and Evans report a similar concern with welfare and personal growth in the education of maladjusted children. But they comment on the many successful cases in which a high value was placed on scholastic progress, not only for itself, but because of its contribution to the self-concepts of maladjusted pupils. The progress was usually assessed through basic skills and achieved as a result of 'remedial' teaching. Fundamental skills, as the report calls them, occupied 39 per cent of timetables in the schools of the survey and the concentration was identified by Wilson and Evans as one reason for the narrowness of curriculum revealed in their study.[30]

All the sources noted above make the point about the narrowness of curricula in special schools, and there is no doubt that the urgent need to ensure pupils achieve some mastery of basic skills before leaving school plays some part in that narrowness. Yet it is not the whole story. Most special schools are small and do not have the range of specialist facilities provided in secondary schools,[31] a combination which makes them less attractive to specialist teachers who are looking to teach a full timetable in their own subject. Teachers who are attracted tend to be good general teachers with primary school backgrounds so that the lower part of the special school offers a broad primary curriculum. It is at secondary level that the curriculum narrows, due to the absence of facilities and restricted teaching skills at that level.

Assessment of curriculum provision for special needs in ordinary schools is more difficult than in special schools. One reason is that surveys tend to concentrate on 'integration' and, thus describing organization rather than curriculum, interaction becomes the main feature of assessment.[32] The Warnock Report says little, though it does identify the modification considered necessary if pupils with special needs are to be efficiently educated in ordinary schools. Modification of materials for pupils with sensory or physical disabilities may enable them to follow the normal curriculum; in addition children with mild or moderate learning problems may require modification of teaching objectives; the organization of the school must be assessed in relation to children with special needs; and particular attention will be required where these children are taught in mixed ability groups. The tone of the paragraph suggests that these modifications were not common in the schools.[33] That was certainly the position in a survey which included 91,527 secondary school pupils among whom 12,807 were regarded as having special educational needs.[34] Only 6,892 pupils were in schools where an attempt was being made to meet their special needs (54 per cent) and of these, 2,300 pupils (33 per cent) were in schools where their special needs were judged as being provided for in a satisfactory manner. Comments from the HMI are equally revealing:

> Uncertainty of aims, objectives and methods for the slow learners was immediately apparent in many – indeed the majority – of the schools visited.
> The needs of slow learners are seen in terms of basic skills . . .
> Little provision is made apart from slight modifications to existing schemes of work.
> Little evidence exists of suitably planned and integrated courses adapted to the needs of slow learners and designed to discover their interests and develop their strengths.

Some teachers were seen to triumph over unpromising curriculum, and HMI commented that to ignore the influence of such teachers would be to ignore 'an intangible of major consequence'. One school was described which showed great compassion and warmth, where the slowest pupils were welcomed and encouraged and were happy, but where their limitations and needs appeared unregarded and there was failure to offer them realistic learning experiences.

A survey of 98 special classes of 11 LEAs had little direct comment to offer on curriculum[35] though, by inference, the situation appeared far from satisfactory. Half the pupils were either intellectually retarded or impaired; one in five emotionally disturbed; one in eight socially deprived; and there was a wide scatter of other disabilities so that overall the groups consisted of pupils with more than one adverse condition. As with special schools some successful special classes were observed but they did not appear to represent the general case, which was one of 'teachers functioning largely in isolation, feeling the need for a greater measure of advice and support in providing for what were in many cases difficult groups of children'. Interaction with the main school curriculum was limited and the survey comments on the 'constant vigilance and careful planning' necessary if this was to be achieved. Without the interaction pupils and teachers were working in isolation, the education offered was narrow, the regime could be dull and undemanding, and 'special help given in reading seemed rather less effective and certainly less imaginative than that given in the rest of the school'.

Cope and Anderson[36] found similar difficulties when they studied the interaction with main curriculum for physically handicapped pupils in primary schools. They also found a lack of support for teachers and some lack of planning in establishing the classes rather unexpected in classes with a high degree of LEA involvement. As with most other studies of integration they pay little attention to broader aspects of curriculum evaluation. However, they compare attainment of the unit children on reading and number with those of similar pupils in special schools. The differences were not great, a fact held to the advantage of the units. But close study of the data reveals an important difference between units and special schools in the size of the teaching groups: junior units, 7.6 pupils – junior special school 13.1; infant units, 6.9 pupils; infant special school, 12.4. The range of class sizes also showed up the differences, with junior units ranging from 6 to 10 pupils compared with a range of 8 to 18 pupils for junior classes in special schools, with similar differences for infants. Insofar as the curriculum is reflected in behaviour, social adjustment or choice of friends there was little difference between unit and special school pupils. One inference from the study is that physically handicapped pupils appear to be as well educated in units as in special schools where the teaching group in the unit is half the size of that of the special schools. What would happen if units had to work at the special school level, or the special school to the unit level, remains an open question.

Perhaps the most comprehensive examination of curriculum provision for special needs was the Schools Council project, *The Curricular Needs of Slow Learners.*[37] Overall the report supports the inferences from the above studies that the general state of curriculum in special and ordinary schools was less than satisfactory; across the whole of curriculum studied satisfactory cases rarely exceeded 50 per cent of the total. However, within the successful groups were examples of both types of school operating at the level of real excellence. This is important; it means that there is sufficient excellence in the system to demonstrate that given adequate facilities and people the curricular problems presented by slow learners can be resolved successfully. It means, too, that resolution of problems does not depend on finding revolutionary new approaches; it is, rather, finding means of bringing more schools to the level of excellence demonstrated by the best. In all probability this is true of the whole of special education and, indeed, of the whole of education.

Other aspects of the Schools Council report may also apply more broadly than just to the group from which they were derived. The warm and necessary concern with welfare operating to the detriment of scholastic learning has already been mentioned, as has the concentration on basic skills to the reduction of humanities and science in curricula. Equally disturbing is the low status of music and the arts in the assessment of successful curricula and the even lower status of religious and moral education. More successful, comparatively, were the school leavers' and parenthood courses which indicated concern for the post-school world in secondary and special schools, a fact also suggested by environmental studies and social service schemes. Most disturbing was the attitude to curriculum found in a sizeable minority (about one third) of teachers who rejected the concept of a curriculum on the basis that the individual differences of the pupils made it inappropriate. In general the project workers found that attempts to totally individualize curriculum were not successful, primarily because the work involved was too extensive to be handled efficiently. The report argued that the case for a curriculum in special needs does not depend on the proposition that it is possible to construct a curriculum that will meet the special needs of all pupils. That is not possible. What is possible is the construction of a curriculum structure capable of meeting the main special needs of pupils, though it will not and is not intended to meet all. If the curriculum structure is related to the known developmental patterns of the pupils, and if it is related to a well-designed system of recording progress, then the structure becomes diagnostic, the failure of a pupil to meet the specified aims at the specified time identifying one for whom individualization is necessary if his or her education is to proceed efficiently. By this technique, it was claimed, most needs could be met with most economy of teachers' time, thus liberating them to work with individuals or small groups when modified curriculum, in-dividualized teaching or both, were required.

The report identified strong areas of excellence in the pattern of curricula observed in the schools. Statements of aims, identification of appropriate curriculum content, and outlines of teaching methods appropriate to pupils' special needs reached a high standard and wide application. There was, however, little evidence of attempts to define the outcomes of teaching and learning in terms of the knowledge, skills and attitudes which pupils should possess on leaving the curriculum. As a consequence recording of curricular progress lacked detail, and evaluation was in very general terms. The report regarded this pattern as a result of the system of education and the training of teachers rather than one for which individuals in the schools should be held solely responsible. In other words, at the time of the study the curriculum was largely lacking any concern with behavioural objectives. It was the precision which the behavioural approach could bring to basic knowledge and skill areas found difficult by the slow learners that led to its proposal by the project team. Increased efficiency here might release time for more attention to the wider areas of curriculum which were tending to be neglected, and where the learning required was of a nature which made behavioural teaching inappropriate, for example in the humanities, the arts and moral education. As the project saw it, the behavioural approach would be effective within a balanced curriculum which did not neglect personal and aesthetic development.

The Schools Council study has been summarized at length because slow learners are to be found among children with almost every kind of primary special need while others have learning difficulty generated by the primary need itself, and these situations are identified with the most serious problems encountered when developing curriculum to meet special needs. In terms of Wilson's groupings the problems cluster round the educationally disadvantaged pupils, those with significant learning difficulties, and the emotionally or behaviourally disturbed, together with those pupils with multiple disabilities. It is in these groups that the problems of modification or individualization of curriculum, teaching or both loom largest, and it is here that the challenge of a common curriculum creates most difficulty.

Common core curriculum

The idea of a common curriculum in the schools, or at least a common core of essential skills and knowledge for all children, is a logical continuation of the philosopy and social ethos which brought about mixed ability teaching, comprehensive secondary education and the demand that wherever possible children with special needs should be educated in ordinary schools with the fullest interaction with other pupils. The 'great debate' and the documents which followed from the DES[38] cast the concept mainly in terms of primary and secondary schools, though *The School Curriculum* briefly indicated that special schools should be involved in local dialogues and noted the need for continuity where pupils moved between special and ordinary schools. A publication from HMI made the important points that a common curricular experience meant much more than subjecting pupils to identical curriculum, that it could not be 'a prescription for uniformity' and, by reference to the Warnock Report definition of aims of education, brought children with special needs within the operation of the concept.[39] The Schools Council report quoted above concluded with a discussion of a common curriculum noting twelve points from which implementation might start, and quoting Professor Hirst on the common curriculum that there are 'no adequate grounds for saying it is impossible when we have in fact spent so little of our effort in trying to achieve this'.[40] The question of a common curriculum and how it might be achieved will be returned to later. It is an important part of general thinking about the curriculum in schools which cannot and should not be evaded in any discussion of the design and development of curriculum for children with special educational needs.[41]

Notes and References

1. BRENNAN, W. K. (1982) *Changing Special Education*, Milton Keynes, Open University Press.
2. Department of Education and Science (1978) *Special Educational Needs* (Warnock Report), London HMSO.
3. Education Act 1981, London, HMSO.
4. The Education Act 1981, sec. 1(4), lays down that a child is not to be regarded as having a learning difficulty solely because the language or form of language in which he will be taught is different from any which is used or has been used in his home.
5. Education Act 1981, sec. 2(3).
6. Warnock Report, para. 3.40.
7. The Warnock Report refers to pupils with special educational needs which have been 'recorded' by the LEA. In the Education Act 1981 these become children for whom the LEA has made a 'statement of special educational need'. See BRENNAN, W. K. (1982) op. cit., Ch. 4.
8. Warnock Report, paras. 4.35–47.
9. Ibid., paras. 3.17–18.
10. Ibid., para. 1.4.
11. YOUNGHUSBAND, E. *et al.* (1970) *Living with Handicap*, London, National Society for Co-operation in Child Care, now National Children's Bureau.
12. GULLIFORD, R. (1971) *Special Educational Needs*, London, Routledge & Kegan Paul.
13. Warnock Report, paras. 11.21–64.
14. BRENNAN, W. K. (1982) op. cit.
15. WILSON, M. (1983) 'The Curriculum for Special Needs', *Secondary Education Journal*, V.13.
16. CAVE, C. and MADDISON, P. (1978) *Survey of Recent Research in Special Education*, Windsor, NFER.
17. DES (1964) 'Survey of Children Born in 1947 who were in Schools

for the Deaf in 1962–3' in *Health of the School Child 1962–3*, London, HMSO.
18. WILLIAMS, P. (1966) 'Some Characteristics of Educationally Subnormal Children', *Br. J. Psychiat.* V.112.
19. McCONKEY, R and JEFFREE, D. M. 'Pre-school Mentally Handicapped Children', *Br. J. Ed. Psych.*, V.45.
20. RUTTER, M. *et al. Education, Health and Behaviour*, Harlow, Longman.
21. —. (1975) 'Attainment and Adjustment in Two Geographical Areas', *Br. J. Pschiat.*, V.126.
22. These boys were first described in BRENNAN, W. K. (1981) op. cit.
23. Warnock Report, para. 6.11.
24. Education Act 1981, sec. 2(3).
25. For a general review see GUILLIFORD, R. (1971) op. cit.; also DEVEREUX, K. (1982) *Understanding Learning Difficulties*, Milton Keynes, Open University Press; STOTT, D. (1982) *Helping the Maladjusted Child*, Milton Keynes, Open University Press.
26. BRENNAN, W. K. (1981) op. cit., Ch. 1.
27. BRENNAN, W. K. (1979) *The Curricular Needs of Slow Learners*, Schools Council working paper No. 63, Ch. 7, London, Evans/Methuen Educational.
28. Warnock Report, para. 11.13.
29. BRENNAN, W. K. (1979) op. cit., Ch. 6.
30. WILSON, M. and EVANS, M. (1980) *Education of Disturbed Pupils*, Schools Council working paper No. 65, London, Methuen Educational.
31. BRENNAN, W. K. (1979) op. cit., table p. 20.
32. The most comprehensive survey is in HEGARTY, S. and POLKINGTON, K. (1981) *Educating Pupils with Special Needs in Ordinary Schools*, Windsor, NFER. A more limited survey is BRENNAN, W. K. (1982) *Special Education in Mainstream Schools*, Stratford upon Avon, National Council for Special Education. See also various titles in DES, Aspects of Education: Education Surveys, London, HMSO.
33. Warnock Report, para. 11.10.
34. DES (1971) 'Slow Learners in Secondary Schools', *Education Survey 15*, London, HMSO.
35. — (1972) 'Special Classes in Ordinary Schools', *Education Survey 17*, London, HMSO.
36. COPE, C. and ANDERSON, E. (1977) *Special Units in Ordinary Schools*, Windsor, NFER.
37. BRENNAN, W. K. (1979) op. cit.
38. DES (1980) *A Framework for Curriculum*, London, HMSO; (1981) *The School Curriculum*, London, HMSO.
39. DES (1980) *A View of the Curriculum* in Matters for Discussion series, London, HMSO.
40. HIRST, P. H. (1969) 'The Logic of the Curriculum', *Journal of Curriculum Studies*, V.1; reprinted in Goldby, M. *et. al.*, eds. (1975) *Curriculum Design*, London and Milton Keynes, Croom Helm and Open University Press.

41. The most recent survey of curriculum is in HEGARTY, K. *et al.*
    (1982) *Curriculum Development in Special Education*, London and Harlow
    Schools Council/Longman. It usefully describes some curriculum
    approaches but offers little evaluation of quality. A final section
    briefly outlines six school approaches to curriculum development.

CHAPTER 3

Design of the curriculum

Design for special needs

There are pupils with special educational needs who do not
require special curriculum; that does not mean their main
curriculum should not be scrutinized in terms of their special
needs. There are other pupils for whom special curriculum is
essential, but it does not follow that they are unable to participate
in main curriculum. A minority of pupils may be unable to
participate in main curriculum; that does not necessarily mean
that they cannot gain from the planned or hidden curriculum
through interaction with other pupils. Such is the complexity
encountered when considering design for special needs with the
wide range and differing levels already discussed. Some of the
problems are now examined in the context of Wilson's four groups
from Chapter 2 before passing on to a general consideration of
curriculum design for special educational needs.

Defects of hearing, vision or mobility

In this group the assumption is that there are no complicating
factors of serious intellectual or emotional problems, though
there may be some retardation of educational progress and
tension due to frustration arising from the additional learning
demanded by the disability. Because their problems are considered
to be the easiest the school may fail the pupils through too easy an
assumption that they can find their own level in the main

curriculum. In fact the answers to many questions are required if the balance of their curriculum is to be appropriate to their potential and realistically related to their anticipated future needs.

Critical questions
1. What would be the main curriculum balance in the absence of the disabilities?
2. What are the additional learning tasks involved in the management of the disability?
3. Does the disability involve any communication difficulty in the classroom?
4. How will the disability affect the time taken to complete any necessary written or practical work?
5. Will there be any problem of movement between learning situations?
6. What are the implications of questions 2, 3, 4 and 5 on the time available for learning the main curriculum?
7. If the time available involves main curriculum limitations, what is the possibility of restoring balance through extended education in school or college?
8. What are the long-term prospects for individual pupils in terms of career opportunities and are they likely to alter?
9. In the context of the answers to the above questions, what is the most desirable and practical curriculum balance?

A process of analysis similar to the above is essential if pupils in this group are to be appropriately and effectively educated. It is necessary at two levels – first in terms of groups of pupils with similar needs, so that there is a framework available in the school; and second, in terms of individual pupils so that the necessary modifications of the framework may be identified relevant to each pupil. Some of the information required to answer the questions will be found in the records which follow pupils through education. Otherwise consultation may be necessary with previous schools, psychologists, specialist teachers, doctors or social workers, for good quality information is essential if the questions are to be answered in a manner which will contribute to the formulation of an appropriate curriculum balance for each pupil.

Educational disadvantage

The psychological and social effects of the disadvantage are stressed for this group. However, the effect of inappropriate, inefficient or intermittent teaching cannot be overlooked as a source of educational failure which may also adversely affect attitudes to school. Specific teaching in basic subjects should attack the retardation and success there make a contribution to improving attitudes, though the latter will probably require attention to the organization and tone of the groups in which curriculum is delivered. Again there are questions which require answers.

Critical questions
1. What is the precise nature of the disadvantage and for how long has it operated?
2. How does it affect basic learning and what are the areas in which special needs are evident?
3. How are attitudes to school, teachers, learning and other pupils affected?
4. What previous efforts have been made to overcome the disadvantage and what was the degree of success?
5. What are the implications of answers to questions 1–4 for basic subject teaching and to what extent will it require withdrawal from main teaching groups?
6. If withdrawal is necessary, how is it to be organized and how will it affect time available for main curriculum?
7. What is the arrangement necessary in order to secure the best balance between special needs teaching and main curriculum?
8. What changes, if any, are required in the organization or tone of teaching in order to improve attitudes to school?
9. What arrangements are necessary for monitoring or modifying curriculum and who is to be responsible for them?

The outcome of the analysis must gain the confidence of these pupils and demonstrate that they can be successful. To do this, basic teaching must be efficient as well as appropriate and must have the support of the broader planned curriculum if it is to succeed. Hidden curriculum may have little influence at first, becoming influential only as the pupils' attitudes begin to change, self-concepts improve, and as they start to identify with the school and assimilate its values.

Significant learning difficulties

Pupils with significant learning difficulties may be usefully considered as two sub-groups with different curricular needs. First, pupils with extensive learning difficulties associated with general immaturity which require a curriculum continuously related to their developing special needs throughout their time in school: and *adaptive–developmental* curriculum.[1] The final part of this chapter applies directly to that kind of curriculum, but what must be noted here is the importance of working out that special curriculum in detail so that it may be carefully related to main curriculum in order to identify special objectives attainable through main activities. The concept of a common core curriculum makes this procedure essential. Second, there are pupils without the immaturity of the first group and with normal or near normal intellectual potential who are at risk through specific difficulties affecting progress in basic academic skills or communication. Theirs is not the problem of educational disadvantage with psychological or social overlay, more a question of *learning disability*. Once that is realized, the questions posed for the educationally disadvantaged pupils are relevant to the needs of these pupils. In seeking the answers, the school will require access to refined assessment techniques closely related to specific, structured teaching techniques the definition of which should be the main purpose of the assessment. Most schools will require outside assistance with the assessment and possibly with the teaching procedure but the responsibility for ensuring that specific teaching is conducted within an appropriate and balanced curriculum must remain within the school. Securing interaction with main curriculum should not be a major problem with these pupils, though in the early stages modified teaching may be required making allowance for their specific difficulties with reading and writing.

Emotional or behavioural difficulties

Pupils with emotional or behavioural difficulties raise the most serious problems for education because of the variety of causation, teaching and prognosis which they present. In terms of curriculum this is most marked, and it accounts for the limited literature on this aspect of their education.[2] More than any other pupils these maladjusted children require what the Warnock Report identified as 'particular attention to the social structure and emotional climate in which education takes place'. Initially it is the extreme difficulty, if not impossibility, of teaching the pupils within the constraints of the ordinary classroom without detriment to other pupils which has led to their identification as pupils with special educational needs. At the heart of their problem is the degree of individualization necessary to meet their needs – individualization of adult – child relationships, of teaching methods, of disciplinary demands, of pace and pattern of learning – yet within a context which maintains a sense of group cohesion sufficiently flexible to accommodate the changing moods of individual pupils. In this the teacher is paramount. Adults who can accommodate to pupils without loss of control and guidance; be firm within friendship; chastise without rejection; apologize without loss of face; laugh without loosing their sense of purpose: these qualitites are essential if curriculum is to succeed. Whether or not the curriculum requires the same degree of individualization will depend on the range of learning potential and academic ability within the group, though there will be educational retardation at all levels. Even where a group curriculum is possible, fluctuations of mood and behaviour among pupils will require individualization of curriculum delivery and demand. Yet, even in the most varied and disturbed groups, there will be periods of relative calm and cohesion, however short, when pupils may be engaged in communal activities that contribute to group feeling and allow a gradual introduction of the kind of situation to which pupils must learn to accommodate if they are to participate in main curriculum.

The curriculum problem for these pupils is twofold, involving the objective of personal, emotional and social stability and the elimination of educational retardation. At one time it was thought that the personal – social aspects had to be resolved before basic learning could be attempted. More recently the therapeutic effects of successful learning have been recognized and the result has been a broader approach to curriculum involving specific structured teaching.[3] Thus the taught curriculum will concentrate on a carefully worked-out approach to basic skills utilizing small steps in order to ensure success, taking account of the short concentration periods of many pupils, and allowing work to be undertaken as and when individual pupils are receptive. It will go further: many pupils lack very basic, interpersonal social skills either because they fail to perceive other people in sufficient detail, or because their perception is fluctuating and determined by their shifting moods. Perception can be improved and the basic skills can be taught through task analysis and prescriptive teaching of the type successful with basic academic subjects.[4] In extreme cases the technique may be used to modify behaviour to the point where more open teaching and learning may begin. The scholastic and social skills established must then be generalized by the pupils in broad, open situations.

These are tasks for the planned curriculum and for the aesthetic experiences of art, craft, music and movement, and the inspiration of the humanities and literature. Here, too, inputs may need to be of short duration and the background organization sufficiently flexible to allow teachers to take advantage of receptive phases of individual mood and group morale. Essential in this type of teaching is the accumulation of a wide variety of material for use in the classroom, in structured teaching or in more open sessions.

The hidden curriculum also presents problems when educating maladjusted pupils. The egocentricity of individual pupils, together with fluctuating group morale, may introduce so great a lack of cohesion as to make the concept of a hidden curriculum inappropriate. Nevertheless the hidden curriculum can be a powerful influence for good which must not be abandoned. It may have to be planned for deliberately, either initially, or following breakdown of morale, or when new admissions to the group bring about qualitative changes. The probability is that the ethos of the group at any time will owe more to the adults involved than would be required or occur in a normal adult–child group. Consequently the pattern of adult relationships and behaviour will require close attention and analysis as part of overall curriculum input. Identical adult behaviour is not the objective – but adult consistency is necessary. Pupils should see adults behaving differently and yet become aware of consistent attitudes and values. Such a general model of relationships among adults may begin to transfer to the pupils, but it is also required as a consistent feature to which specific learning by the pupils may be referred as part of the process of generalization.

It is often argued that the wide individual differences among maladjusted pupils makes the concept of the curriculum inappropriate. This is true only if the curriculum is seen as a structure determining the work of the teacher as he or she interacts with the pupils. If, on the contrary, the purpose of the curriculum is seen as ensuring the teacher is clear in mind about the aims and objectives appropriate for the pupils, then it assists the teacher in behaving with freedom in the classroom. It is the teacher who is clear in mind about what the pupils are to learn or assimilate who is best placed to react to their moods, motivations and interests in selecting appropriate materials and approaches while moving to the clear objectives. With maladjusted pupils this is essential for successful education. Without it individualization loses its purpose and activity may lead nowhere.

Multiply handicapped pupils

The above groups are not independent or mutually exclusive. Blind pupils can have emotional or behavioural difficulties; pupils who require adaptive–developmental curriculum may also have specific learning difficulties; and among any of the major disabilities there will be pupils who are also educationally disadvantaged. Almost any serious disability generates secondary difficulties for the pupil which, though not sufficiently serious to rate as disability, interfere with learning to an extent to be taken account of when planning curriculum and teaching. The grouping of pupils is useful in facilitating discussion and in the development of general curricula, but the interaction of disabilities and the secondary conditions generated by them make it essential that individual needs are carefully considered before curriculum is finalized and at each review.

Curricula intended to meet special educational needs must take account of different kinds of learning. Some learning can be considered as basic, essential and capable of definition in the precise terms that make it suitable for a behavioural approach. Other learning is more subtle, involving the emotions, judgement, or thought sequences leading to the solution of a problem. These are not simple 'can or cannot' entities but require to be approached, established, refined and generalized through interaction of mind and personality between the teacher and the taught. Other learning cannot be approached directly through the taught or indirectly through the planned curriculum: it must be assimilated through the pupils' total experience in the school, involving the hidden curriculum.

In relation to these varied forms of learning, pupils with special educational needs are no different from others. Where they differ is in the time taken from main curriculum by the necessity of meeting their special needs and the importance of maintaining a balance between these two aspects of curriculum. Further, because special needs are *personal*, meeting them shifts the balance between the personal and social aspects of curriculum, reducing the time available for the latter. So the special problem for teachers of pupils with special needs is one of how to establish and sustain the balance between main and special curriculum and between personal and social curriculum aims plus, for some pupils, the question of ensuring that the hidden curriculum operates effectively. How this problem – one of curriculum priorities – might be approached is considered in the following section; a single solution is unlikely to be appropriate for all areas of the curriculum. The kind of learning required in different curriculum areas must be taken account of and may be an important factor in the identification of those areas where participation in main curriculum presents least problems. Among the areas identified will be those where mixed ability teaching is a viable proposition presenting opportunities for full interaction between pupils with special needs and other pupils.

General design

Three approaches to general curriculum design are relevant to curriculum for special needs: the objectives model, the process model, and a model based upon situational analysis.

The objectives model

This model is based upon behaviourist psychology. In the model an intervening step is considered necessary if the aims of education are to be successfully translated into curriculum transactions in the classroom, and for this purpose objectives must be defined. The objectives consist of the knowledge, skills, attitudes and values which must be established by the pupil if the aims of his education are to be satisfied. Objectives need to be precisely defined in a manner which will allow the teacher to assess, through observation of the behaviour of the pupil, whether or not they are established; hence the frequently used term 'behavioural objectives'. Observation includes objective measurement where-ever possible and the precision of the process not only benefits the pupil but also allows for improved evaluation and refinement of the curriculum itself. In the curriculum model, *terminal objectives* are first defined as the end products of the curriculum; from these, *intermediate objectives* are proposed which accord with the development of the pupils and their acquisition of knowledge, skill, etc. as they move through the school. Curriculum *content* and *learning experiences* are selected appropriate to the objectives, and a *recording system* is designed through which the progress of the pupils may be monitored. The record is the basis of *evaluation* and ideally it should be possible to modify objectives, content or teaching methods at any point where the evaluation shows it to be necessary for individual pupils or groups of pupils. The process of curriculum or teaching modification is often referred to as 'feedback'.[5]

The objectives model is not without its critics.[6] In its extreme behaviourist form it is regarded as narrow, relevant only to instruction in rote knowledge or the teaching of basic scholastic, physical and social skills. There have, however, been modifications which move the model away from the extreme. Eisner saw behavioural objectives as limited to direct instruction, proposing *expressive objectives* which were to describe situations calculated to evoke personal responses from pupils without defining the response in advance, and what he named 'type III' objectives where pupils were placed in open-ended problem-solving situations.[7] The broadening of the objectives approach opens considerable curriculum possibilities, as follows.

Behavioural (instructional) objectives These are the objectives that seem to be most widely referred to in the schools. They are concerned with the details of what the pupil has achieved as a result of the teaching received. The outcome of the pupil's learning is specified *before* the learning is undertaken, in detail. The exact nature of the response, the conditions under which it is obtained, the standard to be achieved, and the number of trials that must produce the correct response are all specified in advance. The terms of specification must make it possible to observe and, ideally, measure the response on the basis of the pupil's behaviour. The objective *is* the specified behaviour and the teacher knows in advance what to look for from the pupil. To operate in these terms complex behaviours must be broken down into constituent subroutines by task analysis, and the intermediate behaviours must be defined and organized in a correct sequence. Terminal and intermediate behavioural objectives may be broadly specifed in curriculum structure, but for teaching in the classroom specific definitions are required free from any ambiguity.[8]

Expressive objectives Expressive objectives describe educational encounters. Teachers organize situations that have within them the possibility of worthwhile experience for the pupil, but there is no attempt to define or prescribe the outcome for the pupil. The pupil acts freely, the thinking or feeling emerging being of his own making. The situation is evocative, *not* prescriptive. In the expressive objective part of curriculum, the pupil has the opportunity to make personal use of skills learned through instructional objectives or type III objectives, and these free, personal outcomes constitute the expressive objective *for that pupil.*[9] At the level of curriculum structure there will be broad descriptions of situations selected for the possibilities that they hold for pupils, and these should be related to the development of the pupils and the organizational phases of the curriculum. Situations that gain more as pupils develop may be repeated in curriculum. At classroom level teachers will select and modify situations on the basis of their knowledge of the pupils.

Type III objectives   These objectives focus upon problem solving by the pupils. In setting out the problem the teacher provides a high degree of structure in identifying the situation, defining the conditions and parameters within which the pupils must work, and indicating the kind of problem to be resolved. Ideally the situations should lend themselves to more than one solution, but however much information is given to the pupils it does not include solutions. Pupils approach the problem freely, working things out for themselves. The teacher does not assess pupil performance on any predetermined relationship between the problem and the solution but on the ingenuity of the solution worked out by the pupil.[10] Curriculum structure could include problems with variables progressively increasing to match the development and maturity of the pupils and to embrace different subjects or experiences, as well as collective group approaches to problems. Again this will be a broad structure, offering guidance to teachers about the type of situation to be presented yet allowing the teacher to shape the details to interest and motivate pupils. In these problem situations there will be opportunity for pupils to apply knowledge acquired through the instructional objectives curriculum in ordered and applied thought processes, which could assist in integrating their knowledge and extend and enrich their insights.

The three types of objective imply different kinds of curriculum activities, creating a variety which acts as a safeguard against the limitation of curriculum through excessive or 'trivial' use of instructional objectives with behavioural outcomes. They go further: the teacher becomes involved in different kinds of evaluation, in the process observing wider aspects of the pupils' learning. Many of the skills and procedures that make thinking and problem solving possible are established through instructional objectives and the same is true about many means of self-expression. Using the skills in those ways gives retrospective purpose to the learning of them, motiviating the pupils for further instructional learning. Positive feelings which accompany the resolution of problems or satisfactory self-expression incorporate the purpose of expressive objectives.

What, it may be asked, is the principal contribution of the extended objectives model? The answer is *precision*. Instructional behavioural objectives alone establish precision only in a narrow band of curriculum activities. With expressive and type III objectives, the precision applies in the construction of the situations selected and prepared for the pupils, though outcomes are left open. The curriculum constructor is compelled to plan more rigorously, as a result of which curriculum becomes more effective, better sequenced and more attractively varied.

The process model

In the process model there is no attempt to define the outcome of the curriculum in behavioural terms. Curriculum is shaped by the selection of content as knowledge which is intrinsically worthwhile and such that will facilitate the procedures, criteria and concepts appropriate to the particular kind of human experience it represents. If this is achieved, it is argued, no other extrinsic justification is required. The aim is that pupils should think themselves through to positions of understanding, insight and appreciation, establishing forms of discussion appropriate to situations under consideration. Planning the curriculum involves selecting the content and devising teaching methods to achieve the aims; evaluation becomes part of the process, not dependent on behaviour specified in advance. The model was worked out through the Schools Council Humanities Curriculum project which had a topic approach, for example 'war', 'poverty', 'relations between the sexes'. Pupils discussed the material presented with a teacher-chairman who sought to play a neutral role in the enterprise, free from any particular point of view which might influence the conclusions of the pupils. Broadening of view, tolerance of opposition, critical attitudes to evidence and deepening of insight were to emerge from the experience of the pupils.[11]

In one sense the model does seek ends, though in process rather than behavioural terms, and one criticism has been about the difficulty of assessing pupils' work and the value to them of the experience. The concept of teacher impartiality has been challenged on the basis that teachers should have positive attitudes on moral questions. Another limitation arises from the sophistication of the humanities materials, in terms of reading level and procedures. If the basic skills do not exist then the material is not necessarily the most efficient approach to teaching them. The technique has validity for pupils with special needs, though it may require the production of appropriate presentation material.[12]

The situation model

This is not so much a model as a way of approaching the curriculum in schools which takes account of the kinds of influence discussed in Chapter 1.

The starting point is an *analysis of the existing situation* on the assumption that something is going on which it may be possible to improve – not unusual in schools. External factors for assessment include: social changes and ideological shifts; parent and community expectations; development in academic disciplines; the level of support available for the teachers. Internal factors such as pupil attitudes, teaching staff skills and interests, availability of resources and school ethos are examined in order to identify possible problem areas.

Next comes *goal formulation* though not necessarily in behavioural terms. Statements of teacher and pupil actions desired are related to the situational analysis in areas where change or modification might operate.

From here arises *programme assembly* involving selection of subjection matter and arrangement in teaching sequence related to organization of materials and equipment and the deployment of staff. At this point there can be a survey of *application and interpretation*, including identification of any practical problems likely to arise from the introduction of new procedures or modification of existing practice, with forward planning calculated to overcome the problems.

Finally there is *operational assessment*. This is broad and ongoing, related to classroom experience, recording the responses of pupils and teachers, determining the extent to which curriculum objectives are achieved, and concerned also with wider issues such as school organization, morale of staff and pupils, and possible implications for future situation change. If necessary this leads to re-analysis of the curriculum situation or parts of it.[13]

These features of general curriculum design appear most directly applicable to curricula for special needs. The situational model highlights the importance of a broad analytical approach to curriculum that would include the factors considered in Chapter 1. Behavioural objectives are efficient in the learning of physical and social skills and in the rote aspects of basic subjects. The process model stresses the need for logical and sequential thought in approaching problems and for the education of the emotions, though without the concern for precision which is a feature of Eisner's expressive and type III objectives. No one of these approaches will meet all curricular needs. They must, therefore, be combined in designing a balanced curriculum for special needs.

Approaching the balance

Teachers of children with special educational needs face the problem of accommodating within a limited time both the learning made necessary by the special needs and the broader aspects of education through which the pupil is enabled to relate to the natural and social environment. The more time consuming the special curriculum, the less time is available for the wider curriculum; the more personal the special needs, the more difficult it becomes to provide a balance through the social objectives of curriculum. For teachers of pupils with learning difficulties the problem is the more serious. They work with pupils whose special needs affect learning over *the whole of the curriculum* with time and balance as ever-present, continuing pressures. It is not surprising, therefore, to find that the literature on curriculum for special needs abounds with work relating to pupils with learning difficulties, which is heavily drawn upon in the following discussion.[14]

An instructional approach

The instructional approach arises from a combination of traditional curriculum organization into subjects allied to teaching methods based upon a class or group and is usually associated with specialist subject teaching. The subject matter to be taught is considered in relation to the time available for teaching it and the assumed learning potential of the pupils who are to be taught.[15] On this basis curriculum content is organized according to a hierarchy of importance into three categories.

> **The instructional priorities**
> 1. *Must* be learned. This is the core of the curriculum, the imperative essential minimum to be mastered by the learners.
> 2. *Should* be learned. The next category of importance; content in this category is to be learned only if the *must* category learning is firmly established.

3. *Could be learned.* The least important category, to be
attempted only by learners who master the content of
the *must* and *should* categories.

The three categories constitute the whole curriculum to be
learned by those in the group with normal learning potential. For
these pupils, and where subject matter is consistent with the logic
of the hierarchy, the approach may be relatively efficient. But
where there are special needs that impede learning the result is
frequently ineffective. Such pupils may learn the core in a
satisfactory manner only to be left in possession of knowledge or
skills which they are unable to make use of outside the learning
situation due to their inadequate frame of reference and inability
to generalize to everyday situations.

The instructional approach has a heavy responsibility for many
pupils with learning difficulties who leave school with very few
mathematical concepts; the result of time expended on a core
imperative of the four basic rules of number. On the practical side
are boys who have not experienced all woodworking tools because
they failed to work through models designed to provide the
experience in the time available, or girls who did not know how
their cheese straws were to be cooked because they had not
finished their preparation in time. In a science lesson slower pupils
listened to the lecture and demonstration, but while others then
engaged in individual experiments they were set to copy notes
from a blackboard as 'otherwise they will not finish them', to quote
the teacher. These situations are still far too common; they occur
most frequently in mixed ability classes in ordinary schools but are
not unknown in special schools, from which two of the above
examples are taken. In part they result from teaching methods
where a single curriculum meets the needs of most of the class but
has little logical basis for others. Yet, as will be shown later, the
categories of the instructional approach may be useful in another
context.

An experience approach

The experience approach starts from the premise that in the
limited time available the priority rests with bringing the pupils in
contact with the maximum number of 'experiences' likely to be of
value to them in 'life' or in the post-school world. The curriculum
tends to be outward looking and organized on topic or centre-of-
interest lines with emphasis on what can be done outside the
school. It is often assumed that the interest generated by the

activity will be sufficient to ensure learning in basic subject skills, and as a consequence direct teaching of these may not form part of the curriculum. The assumption may be justified where the pupils have established early skills, have no learning difficulties and are subject only to time limitation. But where the learning is not established, or there are general or specific learning difficulties, the assumption does a disservice to the pupils. The situation is often encountered in the higher classes of junior and secondary schools where the emphasis is on providing common experience. Children with special needs for whom special curriculum or teaching has been arranged in the lower part of the school are often 'integrated' into classes in the upper school without continuation of the special arrangements; so for some pupils the foundations of learning are not developed, while for others established learning is allowed to deteriorate. Even where the experience approach is appropriate it does not evade the necessity to select carefully the experiences to be included in the curriculum.

Neither of the above approaches alone will sustain a balanced curriculum. The instructional approach is adequate for basic skills but may establish them without the necessary transfer to open situations, while the experience approach ensures that the pupil has a broad background, but may generate interest and motivation in pupils not utilized in the learning of basic skills. One approach is too 'closed' to provide a basis for broad and rich education; the other is too 'open' to provide the structure required by some pupils if they are to master the basic skills. However, both approaches share a limitation, for neither considers 'levels' of learning when establishing the priorities which govern curriculum selection. They both assume a constant level of learning in the curriculum and there seems little place for the concept of differential learning according to the nature of subject material or the needs of individual pupils.

Core and periphery

This approach was developed by Tansley and Gulliford[16] in their work with slow learners. They postulated a curriculum based upon (i) a central core of language and number and (ii) a periphery of useful knowledge about the environment, aesthetic activities and practical interests:

> As the core develops, so the periphery widens, and as the child achieves command of the essential tools of learning he realizes their usefulness. The interplay between core and periphery becomes more sensitive and apparent[17].

There is fluidity here, interaction between the areas; skills are applied in the periphery with the excitement feeding back to motivate learning in the core; the instructional closed approach increases potential in the open experience area while gaining purpose from it. Also present in this approach is the beginning of differential learning with the idea of 'awareness' in the periphery, especially 'social awareness'. Later work by Ainscow and Tweddle[18] developed a more precise approach to the core or closed curriculum by applying behavioural objectives methods in the area, thereby improving the model, though their work adds little to the concept of the periphery or 'open curriculum' as they termed it. This aspect of the approach was elaborated by Tansley and Gulliford:

> The periphery subjects can be integrated or correlated and used at all levels to encourage the development of basic subjects. There is no need for detailed syllabuses which so often result in an atomistic, subject-centred approach to learning. What is wanted is an approach which emphasises the relationship between the various elements in knowledge and results in broad rather than detailed experiences.[19]

The curriculum was to be approached from three points of view: the logical, based on the internal logic of subjects and order of presentation; the psychological, taking account of child development and pupil motivation; and the social, contemporary in terms of the pupils' relationships but also taking account of the social demands to be made in the future. Both core and periphery were to be subjected to this analysis and from the balance among the viewpoints would emerge the priorities governing curriculum selection and presentation. In what manner was the curriculum to be organized and presented – subjects or experiences? The answer was a compromise, or in terms of this discussion, a balance.

The core and periphery approach has much to commend it and has been widely applied in the education of children with learning difficulties, but there are limitations. As stated, it is biased to knowledge rather than skill and the concept of differential learning is only beginning to emerge in the reference to social awareness. Nor is it made clear what the relative importance is between core and periphery curriculum or whether expansion in the latter is to be entirely governed by progress in the former.

Broad based approach

The broad based approach has emerged from a Schools Council seminar on curriculum for special schools reported by Wilson.[20] In figure 2 the rectangle represents the whole of the curriculum with the different aspects represented by the capitalized (upper-case) labels on the diagonals.

As knowledge is wider than subjects it has been inserted in brackets on the original SUBJECT diagonal. Looking at the diagonals in figure 2, it is possible to conceptualize the areas between them as representing combinations indicated by the lower-case labels. Thus a combination of knowledge and skill is seen as technique; skill and experience as judgement; experience and attitude as values; and knowledge and attitude as interest. The left side of the figure (knowledge, skills and techniques) would certainly focus on the core curriculum involving the instructional approach and use of behavioural objectives. Experience, attitudes and values (the right of the figure) offer scope for the process model, expressive objectives, and the experience approach. The areas of judgement and interests may be regarded as operating over both sides of the figure, and though this takes the figure beyond its original purpose it appears consistent with the broad based approach.

These are helpful techniques of curriculum survey which stress the broader aspects of school subjects and should prevent the common weakness where knowledge is allowed to dominate teaching. They are a logical outcome of the broad based

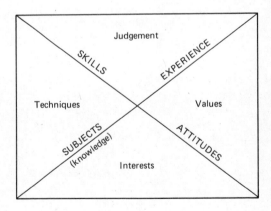

Figure 2 Broad based approach to curriculum balance

The range of the broad based approach is seen if the skills and attitudes to be established by the pupils are set against the experiences and subjects that are to form the curriculum.

Broad based curriculum

Skills	Attitudes	Experiences	Subjects
Perceptive	Self-confidence	*Aesthetic/creative*	Arts
Seeing	Self-awareness	Appreciative	Crafts
Hearing	Self-discipline	Expressive	Music
Touching	Honesty		Home economics
Smelling	Integrity	*Ethical/spiritual*	Dance and
	Sensitivity	Humanitarian	movement
Manipulative	Consideration	Religious	Drama
Dexterity	Compassion		Literature
Agility	Adaptability	*Social/political*	English
Handwriting	Perseverence	Historical	Second language
Tool/material	Initiative	Contemporary	Religious
control	Imagination	Projective	education
Movement	Objectivity		History
	Concentration	*Physical*	Geography
Communication	Helpfulness	Individual	Social science
Listening	Accepting of	Collective	Physical science
Speaking	help	Cooperative	Arithmetic
Reading		Competitive	Mathematics
Writing			Physical education
Using technical		*Communication*	Health Education
equipment		Receptive	Preparation for
Non-verbal/		Expressive	work and leisure
artistic		Face-to-face	Preparation for
expression		Distant	family/
			community life
Intellectual		*Mathematical*	
Observing		Computive	
Investigating		Conceptual	
Estimating			
Measuring		*Scientific*	
Computing		Physical	
Assessing		Social	
Problem solving		Proof/	
		hypothese	
Social			
Self-care		*Industrial*	
Self-regulation		Working	
Accepting others		conditions	
Assisting others		Work procedures	
Interaction		Work choice	
Travelling		Worklessness	
Using leisure			
Working		*Leisure*	
Caring for living		Range	
animals and		Assessment	
plants		Choice	
Aesthetic		*Economic*	
Judging		Income	
Discriminating		Expenditure	
Selecting		Budgeting	
Conserving			

Another way to analyse and assess the broad based approach is to chart curriculum subjects against aspects of pupil development as in the following profile.

Broad based curriculum and development

Development	Arts	Crafts	Music	Home economics	Dance/movement	Drama	Physical education	Literature	English	Second Language	Religious educ.	History	Geography	Social science	Physical science	Arithmetic	Mathematics	Health education	Work experience	Leisure experience	Community experience	Preparation for family life	Gardening/rural studies	Safety/traffic education	Disability Management	Disability support
Personal																										
Physical	x				x	x	x											x					x		x	
Self-concept				x	x	x			x	x	x	x	x	x				x	x	x	x	x		x	x	x
Self-regulation	x	x		x	x	x			x									x	x			x	x	x	x	
Independence				x		x			x															x	x	x
Moral behaviour							x				x	x	x									x				
Social																										
Perspective					x			x	x		x	x	x	x	x			x	x	x	x	x			x	x
Competence								x	x																	
Judgement						x			x			x	x					x	x	x	x	x		x	x	x
Intellectual																										
Perception	x	x	x		x	x	x								x	x									x	x
Observation	x	x				x	x							x	x	x		x	x	x	x	x	x	x		
Memory	x	x	x		x	x			x																	
Problem solving	x	x		x	x				x	x					x	x	x	x							x	x
Language	x	x	x	x	x	x	x	x	x	x	x	x	x	x	x	x	x	x	x	x	x	x	x	x	x	x
Reading			x					x	x	x	x	x	x	x	x	x		x	x	x	x	x	x	x	x	x
Writing																										
Numeracy/maths		x												x	x	x	x		x		x	x	x			
Social concepts																										
Environmental concepts	x	x		x								x	x	x	x			x	x		x	x	x	x	x	x
Objectivity																										
Aesthetic																										
Artistic	x	x	x	x	x																					
Musical			x		x			x										x								
Dramatic																										
Literary							x		x	x	x	x	x													
Imaginative	x	x	x		x	x		x			x	x						x		x						
Practical																										
Dexterity	x	x	x																							
Agility				x		x																				
Craft/domestic			x																							
Handwriting			x					x	x	x	x	x	x	x	x	x										
Vocational/leisure																										
Attitudes									x	x		x	x	x					x	x	x	x		x	x	x
Knowledge																										
Skills																										

curriculum, one advantage of which is that they are aimed at broadening work in special schools, thus acting on the Warnock Report criticism that special school curricula were generally too narrow.

The weakness of the broad based approach is the absence of any indication of priorities among the aspects of curriculum considered. Nor does it take into account that there might be different levels of learning in the curriculum. Consequently the approach offers little guidance towards a solution of the time limitation problem so central for children with special educational needs. Such a solution requires the establishment of curriculum priorities in all the attributes of the broad based approach – not just in skills and knowledge, where it is not possible to include everything desirable in the time available; the same is true of the more intrinsic attributes of values and judgement. Without such priorities there is danger that the broad approach may dissipate effort over the whole curriculum without bringing any aspects to an operational level in the behaviour of the pupils. The priorities themselves will not resolve the time dilemma unless they can be associated with the idea of levels of learning appropriate to the needs of the pupils. This is attempted in the next approach to balanced curriculum.

Differential learning

The differential approach has been gradually developed out of the idea of social awareness suggested by Tansley and Gulliford.[21][22] Though worked out mainly in curriculum for pupils with learning difficulties, the principles apply wherever the time available for education imposes upon teachers the task of curriculum selection in order to ensure that what the pupils are required to learn will be relevant to the tasks and roles of later life.

Knowledge and skill The problem of securing balance in the curriculum is approached in differential learning by stipulating that knowledge and skills may be included at two levels, designated as 'function' and 'context', as illustrated in Figure 3.

FUNCTION LEARNING. This is essential learning which must be established in the behaviour of the pupils if they are to face the problems of later life with a reasonable level of success. Learning at this functional level must incorporate some critical qualities: it must be accurate, permanent, integrated and generalized. Accuracy and permanency require no comment. Integration is necessary to ensure that knowledge and skill do not consist of isolated, splinter achievements, while generalization ensures that they operate in the everyday behaviour of the pupils.

CONTEXT LEARNING.   This does not require the precise, thorough qualities defined above, for it serves a different purpose. Context learning is the assimilated learning which is the background or context of pupils' behaviours and allows them to relate to and maintain contact with the natural, social, emotional and aesthetic aspects of their environment. Through it pupils are aware of or familiar with many things which they may be unable to make explicit.

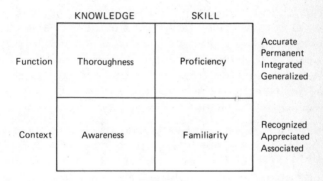

Figure 3 Differential learning approach to curriculum balance— knowledge and skill

Function level in curriculum The term *thoroughness* is used for knowledge at the functional level, with *proficiency* identifying that level of skill. In considering pupils with special needs, two factors are considered: first, what is entered in the curriculum at the functional level must be learned with the qualities noted above; second, the time it will take to establish that level of learning is such that it must be limited to absolute essentials if broader aspects of curriculum are to be negotiated successfully. It will be possible to design general curricula at this level where there are pupils with similar special needs, though it will always be necessary to make evaluation of this aspect of curriculum in terms of the needs of individual pupils, individualizing curriculum and teaching for small groups or single pupils whenever that is seen to be necessary.

This part of the curriculum has about it some aspects of the 'core' discussed earlier. Large parts of it will consist of basic subjects and social skills for some pupils, with for others the essential foundation knowledge and skill for a wider range of studies where higher order learning is seen to be possible and appropriate. For example, except for pupils for whom the study of chemistry to higher level was a feasible and appropriate curriculum possibility, there would be little point in entering the table of elements and laws of proportion in the functional level; similarly, certain basic skills in arts or crafts would be appropriate at this level only where pupil aptitude and interest indicated a major curriculum component. As will shortly become apparent, exclusion of knowledge or skill from the functional level does not imply total exclusion from the curriculum. Conversely, for pupils with moderate or severe learning difficulties, the functional level will include fundamental linguistic, social and self-care knowledge and skills which other pupils bring to school with them and about which the school curriculum need not be concerned.

Context level in curriculum   At the context level knowledge is labelled by *awareness* and skill by *familiarity*. The key concepts at this level are recognition, appreciation and association, for the purpose of learning is that the pupils should acquire a broad background which will enable them to relate to people, conversation and events in the environment in a manner acceptable to other persons and within the broad norm of their social group. For pupils with moderate or severe learning difficulties it will be sufficient if the knowledge/background guards them against attracting unwelcome attention or ridicule through exposing ignorance of common topics, language, sport, entertainment or news items, and their contact with skills enables them to appreciate expertise when they see it and enter into everyday discussions about it. Other pupils will require wider backgrounds which include areas ranking for this level of curriculum only because shortage of time has excluded them from the functional level. This is made clear by considering the examples used previously in discussing know-ledge: pupils for whom tables of elements and laws of proportion are inappropriate will nevertheless need some context awareness of chemistry as a particular subject within a general classification of science, or as a way of dealing with the properties of substances, or even that some 'chemicals' are poisonous; and though functional skills of art or craft may be unsuitable for some pupils, there is no doubt that all should experience the activities, gain the satisfaction that comes from them and acquire familiarity which enables them to appreciate as many forms of artistic expression as possible.

An important aspect of the context curriculum is that it does *not* require the precision of the functional. It can be more relaxed, it is conducive to an activity approach, and it can gain greatly from the 'planned' aspect of the curriculum.

Relation of function and context The purpose of the differential learning approach is that of securing balance in the curriculum, so there is a continuing relationship between the function and context levels. The more restricted the functional curriculum, the broader and more important the context curriculum becomes if the pupils concerned are to demonstrate their limited function within a general awareness and familiarity that allows them to relate successfully to life around them. An extensive curriculum at functional level reduces the importance of the context but does not eliminate it. All normal people have areas of expertise where they operate at functional level but few maintain it over the whole of their behaviour, relying for general orientation on broad background at the context level. For example, most people today are aware that at a certain point in a space vehicle the occupants experience 'weightlessness' – yet they have never experienced it and would be unable to explain it; but for a limited number of people it *is* important that they should understand the physical laws which govern weightlessness at the functional level as a part of a whole complex of knowledge that has made possible the reality of the space vehicle. Knowledge at the latter level is clearly unnecessary for all people. In terms of skills, sports provide a good example, for it is the familiarity with sporting skills established in the physical education curriculum that allows a multitude of people to appreciate and enjoy the performance of those sportsmen and women who have established skills at the proficiency level.

The proposal that the curriculum should operate with different levels of learning for pupils with special needs, then, is perfectly consistent with the way that almost all normal people behave in our culture, where the astrophysicist requires a broad context background if he is not to make a fool of himself in more mundane political or social matters or be regarded as a philistine in the arts. There must be balance in the relative content of functional and context curricula for pupils with special needs which are similar, and the balance will require assessment for individuals within the groups. The *relative, complementary importance* of the two aspects of curriculum should not be overlooked: where the functional curriculum is limited, for whatever reason (sensory, social, emotional or intellectual), the context assumes more importance than the functional in enabling the individual to accommodate to his social situation. This is well known to teachers of pupils with moderate learning difficulties. They know from many research studies that where their pupils fail in the post-school world it is not usually because they lack the basic skills of the functional curriculum (which they often do), but because they are unable to relate in an acceptable manner to the everyday behaviours and topics of the workplace and the street which are the concern of the context curriculum. The implication is clear: if the balance between function and context is to be achieved, the relationship must be evaluated in terms of relative importance as well as in curriculum content, and to achieve this the needs of individuals must be taken into account.

Priorities in curriculum The differential learning approach has introduced the useful concept of different levels of learning in curricula, but it has not gone beyond this in terms of curriculum priorities. The problem remains that it will not be possible to include all beneficial learning at either of the levels, and therefore selection will continue to be necessary. Here a useful framework is provided by introducing the priorities defined above in the instructional approach, as illustrated in figure 4.

Figure 4 emphasizes that selection may be necessary in all areas of curriculum at both levels if a balance is to be achieved appropriate for the needs of individual pupils. In practice this may be approached through the construction of a general curriculum calculated to meet the needs of groups of pupils with similar special needs. The general curriculum has a number of advantages when seen in an appropriate context, as now set out.

Advantages of general curriculum
1. Provides purpose and direction for curriculum transactions.
2. Clarifies the teacher's role and contribution in curriculum.
3. Provides structure for observation of pupil progress.
4. Allows for rapid and accurate identification of failure to progress.
5. Information on breakdown becomes the starting point for modification of curriculum/teaching.

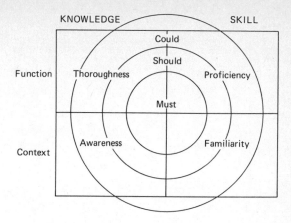

Figure 4 Differential learning – knowledge and skill – with priorities

Through this framework the general curriculum becomes diagnostic in the true sense as the failure of the pupil attracts attention and directs it to his special needs with a starting point for modification.

Experience and attitudes The principles of the differential approach may also be applied in the curriculum areas of experience and attitudes, as figure 5 illustrates. Because experience and attitudes are concerned with internalized matters, the figure lacks the precision of that for knowledge and skill. Nevertheless it is possible to stipulate levels of learning.

FUNCTION LEARNING. This is now postulated as the effects of experience and attitudes incorporated in the behaviour of the pupil.

CONTEXT LEARNING. This is not incorporated in behaviour but recognized by the pupil as a 'norm' or expectancy in his social situation.

The nature of the learning in this area of curriculum will also mean that criteria for curriculum inclusion will also differ from those of knowledge and skill. However, it would be wrong to consider the knowledge/skill and experience/attitudes aspects of curriculum as separate, for teaching in the former areas may make important

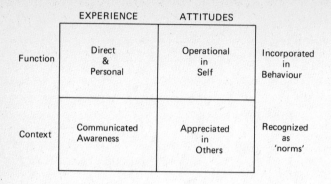

Figure 5   Differential learning approach to curriculum balance –
experience and attitudes

contributions to the latter – not necessarily in terms of what is
taught but more from the style of teaching and learning and the
relationships that inform classroom communication.

Experiences included in curriculum at the function level are
those which *must* be incorporated in the behaviour of pupils as
essential to their education. Time pressures make the restriction
necessary and the nature of the learning requires that the
experiences be direct and personal, the outcome of situations
planned for the purpose. Similar restriction will be necessary for
attitudes included in curriculum at this level. Those to be worked
for should be absolutely essential as support for appropriate and
acceptable behaviour to the extent that they constitute the moral
basis from which pupils will judge their own and others' actions.
Criteria for curriculum inclusion are not so rigorous at the context
level. Here the purpose is to establish a background that will
enable pupils to generalize and regulate established behaviour to
accord with the social environment. Thus experience may be
indirect, communicated through literature, drama, social or
religious studies, and through the planned and hidden curriculum.
From these activities pupils will also derive a general familiarity
with or awareness of attitudes – a context of expectancies wider
than the attitudes which inform their own functional behaviour.

Attitudes and experiences and the values which emerge from them are of particular importance in curriculum for children with special educational needs. The importance derives from their having more to contend with than their more fortunate contemporaries through the additional demands, constraints and frustrations generated by their disabilities. Pupils with special needs require a broader curriculum to compensate for the additional demands, yet it will not be possible to include all that is desirable in a curriculum limited by time. There is increased pressure on their teachers as they seek to achieve appropriate priorities for experiences and attitudes at both function and context levels in the curriculum. The priorities from the instructional approach again serve a useful purpose as they focus attention on the problem.

Figure 6 emphasizes that priority choices are necessary in all the aspects of curriculum represented by the quadrants, though there is not a fixed degree of importance between the function and context levels. The importance is relative and compensatory, and must be determined by a close study of the needs of pupils and an equally careful assessment of their life situations and the demands likely to be made on them in the future. Of first importance is knowledge of the pupils' previous experience and its effect on their

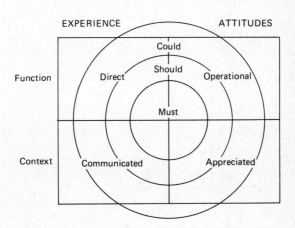

Figure 6   Differential learning – experience and attitudes 2 with priorities

contemporary behaviour, especially where special needs arise from emotional or behaviour difficulties – see the discussion earlier in this chapter.

The balanced curriculum

No single model or approach is capable of sustaining a full curriculum for children with special educational needs, though all have some contribution which is valuable. So here again pupils with special needs are *not* different from other pupils. In aspects of curriculum where learning with accuracy and permanency are necessary, the behavioural objectives model and the instructional approach offer a high degree of learning efficiency with optimal expenditure of time. The process model, together with expressive and type III objectives, combines with the experience or, better, broad based approach as the basis for those aspects of curriculum concerned with emotional and aesthetic development or knowledge utilized in the process of thinking and problem solving. The differential learning approach, growing out of the core–periphery concept, offers a structure able to accommodate the above curricular suggestions and adds to them the levels-of-learning idea which ensures that precision is achieved where necessary while maintaining a broadly based curriculum closely related to the needs of pupils. It also offers a useful approach to the problem of a common or core curriculum, as will be shown later. Situational analysis directs attention to the many factors, in school and in the broader environment, which must be examined and taken account of in reaching the necessary decisions about curriculum priorities and their implications for curriculum development.

Notes and references

1. BRENNAN, W. K. (1974) *Shaping the Education of Slow Learners*, London, Routledge & Kegan Paul; (1979) *The Curricular Needs of Slow Learners*, London, Evans/Methuen Educational.
2. WILSON, M. and EVANS, M. (1980) *Education of Disturbed Pupils*, London Methuen Educational; contains an excellent review of literature. See also DAWSON, R. L. (1980) *Special Provision for Disturbed Pupils*, London, especially Ch. 5 'Educational programmes'.
3. HARING, N. G. and PHILLIPS, E. L. (1962) *Educating Emotionally Disturbed Children*, New York, McGraw Hill; HEWETT, F. M. (1968) *The Emotionally Disturbed Child in the Classroom*, Boston, Allyn & Bacon.
4. LASLETT, R. (1977) *Educating Maladjusted Children*, Crosby, Lockwood

& Staples; TOWER, P. *et al* (1978) *Social Skills and Mental Health*, London, Methuen Educational; ARGYLE, M. (1972) *The Psychology of Inter-personal Behaviour*, Harmondsworth, Penguin; FLAVELL, J. H. (1968) *The Development of Role-taking and Communication Skills in Children*, New York, Wiley.

5. There is an extensive bibliography on the objectives model, e.g. TYLER, R. W. (1950) *Basic Principles of Curriculum and Instruction*, Chicago, University of Chicago Press; TABA, H. (1962) *Curriculum Development: Theory and Practice*, New York, Harcourt Brace Jovanovich; POPHAM, W. J. (1977) 'Objectives 72,) in Rubin, L., ed. *Curriculum Handbook: The Disciplines, Current Movements and Instructional Methodology*, Boston, Allyn & Bacon; yes, the approach does seem to have been generated in the USA.

6. STENHOUSE, L. (1971) 'Some Limitations on the Use of Objectives in the Curriculum', *Paedagocica Europaea*, 78–83; MACDONAL-ROSS, M. (1973) 'Behavioural Objectives: A Critical Review', reprinted in Golby, M. *et al.* (1975) *Curriculum Design*, London, Croom Helm.

7. EISNER, E. W. (1969) 'Instructional and Expressive Objectives', reprinted in Golby, M. *et al.* (1975) op. cit.

8. AINSCOW, M. and TWEDDLE, D. A. (1979) Preventing Classroom Failure: An Objectives Approach. Chichester, John Wiley.

9. EISNER, E. W. (1969). op. cit.; (1972) 'Emerging Models for Educational Evaluation', *School Review*, August.

10. EISNER, E. W. (1972) op. cit.

11. STENHOUSE, L. (1970) *The Humanities Project: An Introduction*, London, Heinemann Educational; (1975) *An Introduction to Curriculum Research and Development*, London, Heinemann Educational.

12. GULLIFORD, R. and WIDLAKE, P. (1975) *Teaching Materials for Disadvantaged Children*, London, Evans/Methuen Educational.

13. SKILBECK, M. (1976) 'The Curriculum Development Process: A Model for School Use' in *Styles of Curriculum Development*, Unit 8, E203, Milton Keynes, Open University Press; see also SOCKETT, H. (1976) *Design in the Curriculum*, London, Open Books.

14. TANSLEY, A. E. and GULLIFORD, R. (1960). The Education of Slow Learning Children, London, Routledge & Kegan Paul; STEPHENS, T. M. (1977) *Teaching Skills to Children with Learning and Behaviour Disorders*, Columbus, Merrill; LERNER, J. W. (1976) *Children with Learning Disabilities*, Boston, Houghton Mifflin; BRENNAN, W. K. (1974/79) op. cit.

15. TAYLOR, P. (1970) *How Teachers Plan Their Courses*, Windsor, NFER.

16. TANSLEY, A. E. and GULLIFORD, R. (1960) op cit.

17. TANSLEY, A. E. and GULLIFORD, R. (1960) op cit.

18. AINSCOW, M. and TWEDDLE, D. A. (1979) op. cit.

19. TANSLEY, A. E. and GULLIFORD, R. (1960) op. cit.

20. WILSON, M. D. (1981) *The Curriculum in Special Schools*, London, Harlow and Longman for Schools Council.

21. TANSLEY, A. E. and GULLIFORD, R. (1960) op. cit.

22. BRENNAN, W. K. (1974/79) op. cit.

CHAPTER 4

Aspects of curriculum for special needs

The importance of clarity and organization

The Warnock Report considered that aims and practices should be clear in order to provide the framework within which flexible curriculum arrangements could be made for individual children. It also identified consistent features of high quality curriculum:

> First, well defined guidelines for each area of curriculum have been drawn up, which enable teachers to plan their own work and relate it to that of colleagues and other professionals. Secondly, programmes have been planned for individual children with clearly defined short-term goals within the general plan.[1]

The report also adds: 'We regard these strands as important criteria of effective special education'. Nor is there any mistaking the call for precision as the report identifies the interrelated elements which contribute to curriculum development:

> They are: i. setting of objectives; ii. choice of materials and experiences; iii. choice of teaching and learning methods to attain the objectives; and iv appraisal of the appropriateness of the objectives and the effectiveness of the means of achieving them.[2]

Also recognized was the teachers' need for a starting point for curriculum:

> One starting point is the detailed specification of each child's attributes and needs. Another is experience and knowledge of the problems faced by children with different disabilities, at home, in

the neighbourhood and as young adults in achieving the maximum degree of independence.[3]

Realistically the report adds: 'In all cases the available premises, resources and staffing will set limits to what is possible.'

An impetus to re-examine these aspects of curriculum was certainly one of the effects of the Warnock Report, and there has been an increase in developmental activity concerned with curriculum for pupils with special needs – both in LEAs and within individual schools. However, only 53 out of 102 LEAs replied to a Schools Council follow-up survey and from 169 non-maintained and independent schools only 44 replies were received.[4] It may well be that action on the curriculum is occurring in only about half of the LEAs and the non-maintained and independent schools, and much needs to be done to extend the activity throughout the system wherever children with special needs are receiving education.

The advantages of clear and well-organized curriculum, which assume increased importance for pupils with special needs, are easily summarized.

Advantages of well-organized curriculum

1. Assists efficient integration of main and special curriculum.
2. Fosters flexibility required to meet intrusions required by special needs.
3. Allows modifications to offset absence caused by special needs.
4. Facilitates observation and recording of pupil progress.
5. Is a basis for curriculum/teaching modifications to promote progress.
6. Enables pupils to see the plan and purpose of their learning.
7. Clarifies the concepts of teachers about the purpose of their teaching.
8. Is a basis from which teachers can make full use of pupils' interests and motivation.
9. Facilitates communication with parents.
10. Assists in communicating school policy in community.
11. Is a basis for continuity into further education.
12. Allows for evaluation by teachers, parents, LEA and community.

The clarity and organization bring further benefit because they create a positive situation which encourages involvement. Involvement of staff, pupils, parents and community should broaden the experience base from which curriculum is developed, refined and communicated.

Comments on curriculum structure

Aims in curriculum

The aims of education are the same for all pupils. Where pupils have special needs, some aspects of aims merit special stress. It is not good enough merely to re-state general aims – they should be thought through and reformulated in the context of special needs, as in the following instances.

Educational aims and special needs
1. Respect for human worth and dignity persists however disabled or deviant the individual.
2. Freedom of thought, speech, writing and worship persists whatever the level at which individuals can exercise it.
3. Equal opportunity for personal development exists independent of the ability, potential or competence of individuals.
4. Disability does not reduce individual differences.
5. Continuous learning must be allowed for, however slow the progress.
6. Social relevance of aims must be evaluated in terms of individual special needs.
7. Special needs add to the individual needs that aims must allow for.
8. Special needs make acceptance by others an even more important part of personal security.
9. Special needs make success even more important — assessed within the capabilities of individuals.
10. Autonomy is needed by everyone — each within individual capability.
11. The individual's right to learn and develop at one's own pace also includes the disabled and deviant.
12. Some special needs may make it more difficult to achieve harmony of physical, intellectual, emotional and moral development.

Educational aims have a supreme importance in that they should reflect the values of society and the aspirations which it has for the young. Where the young have needs which make them special, the importance is enhanced. That is why aims in special education should be subjected to critical questions.

Aims in special education: critical questions
1. Do the aims take account of individual needs – emotional, social, intellectual, physical and special?
2. Will they promote social interaction and allow individuals to relate to society?
3. Are they calculated to promote individual moral development?
4. Will they release individual potential and allow it to be realized?
5. Will the realization include judgement and adaptability as well as knowledge and skill?
6. Are potential and its realization seen as open-ended for all pupils?
7. Are aims specific to special needs compatible with aims in mainstream curriculum?
8. Are aims for special needs formulated in a manner that will positively encourage interaction with main curriculum where appropriate?
9. Are aims stated in clear and direct language that will make sense for parents and people in the community?

Parents, school governors and appropriate community representatives should be involved by the school as active participants in the formulation of aims. The resulting statements, however clear, are unlikely to be directly applicable to classroom transactions. For that purpose objectives must be defined which have meaning in terms of the learning of pupils in the classrooms.

Objectives in the curriculum
The objectives model of the curriculum was outlined in Chapter 3. During the 1970s, and following earlier work in the USA, the behavioural version of the objectives model began to take a firm hold of special education in England. The movement centred upon pupils with learning difficulties and those with behaviour disorders, where it took the form of 'behaviour shaping'. There are a number of reasons to account for the phenomenon.[5]

Reasons for extension of behavioural objectives curricula
1. Pressure for increased precision and accountability.
2. Desire to correct over-concern with pastoral aspects of teaching.
3. Efficiency in enabling pupils to establish skills.
4. Efficiency in dealing with specific learning difficulties.
5. Efficiency in eliminating or changing unacceptable behaviours.
6. Suitability for observation and recording of pupil learning.
7. Contribution to the evaluation of pupil learning.
8. Facility afforded to relate established pupil learning to the objectives forecast in curriculum.

These are valid reasons for the use of behavioural objectives, and in areas where it is appropriate the technique has much to commend it. There are, however, two dangers. First, the technique is often used inappropriately; and second, over-extension tends to limit curricula to overt behaviours and learning that can be externalized.

There has always been a tendency to over-use or over-elaborate behavioural objectives in curriculum, particularly in the literature from the USA which has dominated the field. Popham,[6] a leading authority in the USA, regretted what he termed the trivialization of the technique, or the unnecessarily fine analysis of simple behaviours leading to absurd steps on the way to the final skill, or the neglect of higher order cognitive or affective objectives. Wheeler[7] was aware of this difficulty, arguing that there is a point beyond which the *curriculum* should not attempt to analyse behaviour. The curriculum should be concerned with statements of the behaviours to be established by pupils as the end product of the teaching received. Within these terminal objectives it would be possible to define broad intermediate objectives to be achieved by pupils at critical points in the curriculum selected to accord with the development of the pupils and the ordering of material to be learned. To go beyond this point involved the definition of *specific objectives* which required classroom knowledge of the pupils for whom they were intended, knowledge that could not be assumed at the level of the curriculum. If this is true of the main curriculum, about which Wheeler was writing, it applies even more to curriculum for special needs, where the individual differences among the pupils are greater. The position was adopted by a Schools Council project with the concept of 'a curriculum which stops at the classroom door' and the idea that the selection of specific objectives, teaching methods and learning experiences was the responsibility of the classroom teacher exercising the 'intimacy of knowledge' of the pupils derived from continuous contact.[8]

When seen in this perspective the curriculum objectives of the classroom derive from a process of decreasing generality culminating with a precision relating to the needs of individual pupils.

The curriculum framework

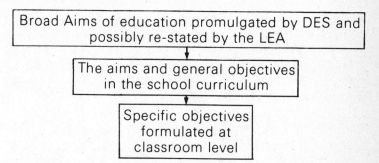

Starting at the school curriculum level, here is an example:

Extract from reading curriculum
Objectives for word recognition:
1. Recognizes and reads by sight 150 words.
2. Uses context clues to solve unknown words.
3. When necessary uses structural analysis to solve unknown words.
4. Uses phonic analysis appropriately for unknown words.
5. Is aware of range of word-attack strategies and uses appropriately.
6. Recognizes when assistance is required and seeks willingly.
7. Within vocabulary reads orally with acceptable phrasing.
8. Reads silently at a speed appropriate to recognition skill.
9. Has grasp of meaning when answering questions on reading.
10. Shows evidence of independence in reading by using skills without prompting and reading outside school.

In this extract, the objectives of word recognition are stated in general terms of what the pupil must be able to do, so the class teacher has a clear framework of the behaviours to be established. At the same time the teacher is not restricted. He or she is free to choose books and materials from those available; content and methods may be closely related to the interests of individual pupils; and it is the teachers' responsibility to translate the general objectives of the curriculum into the specific objectives that will best meet the needs of the pupils in the class. The teacher is also the person who will decide the level of accuracy required from individual pupils before the specific and general objectives are regarded as achieved.[9]

The above principle also applies to expressive and type III objectives. The purpose here is to construct learning situations with precision while leaving open the outcome for the pupil. Here are some examples from a special school curriculum.

Extract from an art curriculum
Texture
In addition to colour and form pupils should explore texture widely through *touch, sight* and *sound*. Combination with colour and form should also form part of their experience.

Categories of experience
Natural texture: grasses, leaves and barks of trees, soils, rocks and minerals, timber, animal coats, etc.
Man-made texture: cloth, decorative finishes, building materials, floor coverings, worked art materials, etc.
Changes in texture: worked material (e.g. rough and sawn timber), the effect of weathering, wear, polishing, brushing, etc.
Texture and touch: pupils to have experience of 'feeling' textures and opportunity to recognize by touch.
Texture and colour: explore texture in relation to different intensity and direction of light; note the effect of cast shadow and the differences between different texture on the same background colour.
Texture and sound: this combines with touch through listening to texture stroked; extend it by stroking with different materials; consider texture and reflected sound.

Methods
Discovery: pupils explore environment to discover texture; arrange situations where they are set to discover precise texture; arrange classroom experiments with lighting

---

then arrange for pupils to discover natural changes
through cloud-shadow, altered position, etc.
Problems: matching textures; predicting effect of different
light intensity and direction; predicting effect of texture
on colour, or polishing, brushing on texture, etc.
Expression: creating pattern and pictures using textural
aspect of materials; using texture in picture-making by
using different materials, altering consistency, or adding
texture; describing in words or writing the sight and feel
and sound of textures.

Note how the curriculum establishes the general purpose of the
activity for the teacher, gives adequate direction, suggests the
range of activities in which pupils should engage; and offers some
structure on methods. Though the words are not used, the
structure almost ensures that expressive and type III objectives
will feature in the activities. Note also how the teacher is left free.
Within the broad framework, content and situations can be
defined which are shaped by the teacher's knowledge of the
experience, interests and motivation of the pupils. For many
pupils, in particular those with learning difficulties or behaviour
disorders, successful learning may depend on the efficiency with
which the class teacher establishes and uses his or her unique
knowledge about the pupils.

In contrast with the above example, an art curriculum for pupils
with moderate learning difficulties included twenty 'experiments'
each employing behavioural methods. The intention was to teach
techniques in order to extend the palette to which the pupils had
access, as it was contended that lack of technique was a major
element restricting their self-expression. Here is an example of
one 'experiment'.

Colour mixing
Materials: paper, water, brushes, yellow, blue, black and
white paint. Set out before each pupil.
Method: ensure that pupils know names of the colours.
Instruct them to paint an area of yellow colour on their
paper. Next have them run blue paint into one half of the
yellow. Have pupils describe what happens. Try to elicit a
clear statement. Repeat the experiment as yellow onto
blue.
Reinforce: on the next use of the experiment, have pupils
predict the outcome before the experiment.

This type of experiment was repeated using primary colours and also using white and black paint to experiment with tints and shades; paint was thickened for textures; applied with different brushes; applied to wet and dry paper; other implements were used to apply paint; and dry brushes were drawn over wet paint, etc. Pupils experimented, observed and drew conclusions in 'experimental' sessions within art periods. The teaching was kept separate from the pupils' expressive work, though when problems were met in that work, teachers would remind pupils of relevant experiments that might assist towards a solution, encouraging them to try out solutions away from their expressive work. Many pupils were observed to have generalized this procedure, using it of their own initiative without prompting by teachers. This is an excellent example of the interplay between different objectives, with instructional (behavioural) objectives contributing to and enhancing both expressive and type III (problem-solving) objectives.

The interaction of different objectives in the same learning activities is a sure sign of a mature curriculum as shown in our next example, an environmental studies curriculum. The visits organized in the curriculum were seen as open-ended situations to be freely explored by the pupils. But teachers were briefed to ensure that among the exploration each pupil looked, touched, smelled or listened to certain things or observed certain procedures. These were points subsequently picked up in school using photographs, slides and film and made the basis of a selection of problem-solving and expressive exercises. There was ample scope allowed for the expression of personal aspects of the visit and for further investigation of points of interest to individuals. This was a very positive, well-planned curriculum. Of particular interest was the way broad 'context' learning was encouraged without neglecting the precision required for objectives at 'function' level.

Selecting curriculum objectives The selection of curriculum objectives is at the heart of the problem of curriculum priorities. Approach to the problem is from three bases that must be analysed and related in any attempt to reach a solution.

The curriculum bases

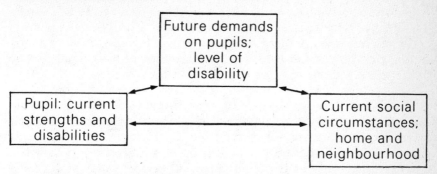

In considering the bases there will always be a lack of certainty and a necessity to make 'best possible' decisions according to the information available. Changes in any of the bases may affect decisions at any time, through either developments that extend possibilities or regressions that narrow possible choices. Some demands and the behaviours required to meet them may be ruled out by the pupil's disabilities; others may be found inappropriate for the school curriculum, requiring the maturity reached in further (or even adult) education; while others may be ruled out or accorded low priority by family aspirations or social or industrial conditions. Any of these may be changed over a period of time; that is why the school must always have access to current good quality information and advice about prospects from doctors, family, social workers and youth employment officers if curriculum choices are to take full account of the pupils' special needs.

The range of special needs, their combinations, and the distribution of severity of disability within any group of needs make it impossible to consider here the selection of objectives in detail. At one extreme are pupils who are able to follow mainstream curriculum where the problem is providing the support that enables them to achieve the objectives specified for all pupils. The support may take the form of medical or paramedical supervision, alternative systems of communication, alterations to buildings or furniture, or special arrangements for practical periods in craft, housecraft, science or physical education. Close co-operation between teachers and supporting specialists will be necessary if mainstream objectives are to be achieved. However efficient the arrangements, it is unlikely that the pupils will be able to sustain the range of objectives projected for their non-handicapped peers. The support they require will make inroads on learning time and more time will be taken up in the management of disabilities. So there will be additional problems in the selection of curriculum objectives. This is a problem for teachers, though they will require advice from colleagues in the supportive services.

At the other extreme of disability are children with such grave disabilities, illness, behaviour, or combination of needs that part or all of their education requires the formulation of specific, often individual, curriculum objectives. Now another qualitative difference intrudes: the care and maintenance of the pupils may have to take precedence over their education if they are to benefit from it, and teaching may have to be 'fitted in' to other services. Inter-service co-operation will still be required, though here the teacher may not have the leading role. Objectives may be severely limited by advice from other workers and those formulated by the teacher may have to be achieved within arrangements that are not exclusively educational.

Between these two extremes are multitudinous combinations of disability and need distributed over a range from mild to severe. No general statement of objectives could possibly encompass such a divergence of needs, and the individual school curriculum is the first place in which it may be attempted with success. Nevertheless, it should be possible to establish useful guidelines. Schedules such as those appertaining to broad based curriculum in Chapter 3 are a useful approach to selection of objectives at curriculum level. Another approach takes general statements about pupils and relates them to knowledge, skills, attitudes and values essential to their achievement.

Components of personal needs

Personal needs	Components			
	Knowledge	**Skills**	**Attitudes**	**Values**
Self-knowledge				
Self-maintenance				
Self-expression				
Interaction with others				
Earning a living				
Maintaining a family				
Civic responsibility				
Appreciating environment				
Appreciating the arts				
etc.				

A similar approach with slow learners in a secondary school (described in more detail in Chapter 5) based initial selection on what were termed human universals, defined as: food, shelter, clothing, heat and energy, communication and transport.

Schedules such as these focus upon the end result anticipated in the school curriculum, and there remains the need to indicate some idea of progression in the curriculum outline. A useful example is taken from a primary school curriculum, part of the curriculum concerned with communication.

Extract from primary curriculum

Area: Communication.

Section: Communication Services.

Year 1 The Postman. Children will study the work of the *local* postman. At the end of the year they should: recognize the postman's uniform; know where the post office is situated; be able to describe the postman's work; address a letter; have posted a letter to themselves and received it.

Year 2   The Local Post Office. Children will study the work of the post office. At the end of the year they should: name the parts of the office and identify the names in print; do the same with different kinds of workers; do the same with PO services; explain how letters are sorted into rounds.

Year 3   The Postal Services. Children will study the arrangements for the transfer of mail. At the end of the year they should: know the relationship between local and central PO; have seen the main sorting office; be able to use and read the vocabulary of the services; be able to specify how letters travel between areas; know the significance of post codes; have experience of a range of PO services.

Year 4   The Communication Services. Children will study alternative means of communication. At the end of the year they should: use a telephone; send overnight communications; use and read the relevant vocabulary; have seen local phone junction boxes and visited an exchange; state generally how telephones work; know the difference between line and radio telephone; know about satellite communication, computer nets, telex, etc. and describe them in general terms.

This extract illustrates the developmental aspects of curriculum. Experience, awareness and knowledge are fostered progressively to enable learners to acquire rich concepts over a period of time. For the teacher the structure is positive as both the progression and relationship of objectives are clearly indicated, though in a manner that does not impose restrictions on skilful classroom choices. Specific objectives, content and teaching methods remain within the responsibility of the classroom teacher and may be shaped by his or her knowledge of the pupils.

Sequencing curriculum objectives   The above example raises one of the most difficult problems in the construction of curricula. It is not sufficient that terminal objectives be devolved into intermediate objectives or stages; these must be arranged in a learning sequence that facilitates the development of the pupil. Logical development of subject matter is but one consideration, for account must also be taken of pupil interests, the psychology of learning, school organization and the styles of teaching available. The learning potential of the pupils is also important, and where there are specific learning difficulties, or behaviours that affect learning, appropriate sequencing of objectives may present problems. Easy solutions are not to be looked for, while first attempts at curriculum sequencing rarely offer once-and-for-all solutions. The attempt must be accompanied by careful observation of pupils' progress allied to intelligent and sensitive modification of objectives and sequences to develop them to a point compatible with pupils' needs. As the needs themselves are in constant change, the process must be continuous. At any point, existing objective sequences may be tested by the following criteria.

Criteria for objective sequences
Sequence must:
1. Accord with accepted divisions of subject matter.
2. Allow variety of learning experiences.
3. Be compatible with pupil development.
4. Make pupils aware of their own progress.
5. Be compatible with school organization.
6. Assist teachers to observe pupil progress.
7. Form the basis of a recording system.
8. Form starting points for modification where necessary.
9. Allow breakdown to more detailed sequences where needed.
10. Be within the competence of the teachers.

The purpose of objectives Structure of the curriculum has a clear purpose, to ensure the teachers responsible for special needs are thoroughly briefed about the learning that should be established by the pupils when they leave the curriculum, are aware of the stages through which that situation is to be approached, and accept their personal responsibility for the part of curriculum they teach. In discharging that responsibility each teacher should understand that the formulation of specific objectives, the selection of content and learning experiences, and the choice of teaching methods form part of the task of classroom teaching exercised within the broad guidance of the curriculum for special needs. The objectives structure provides a basis for the individualization of teaching for pupils with special needs; the creativity of the teacher within that structure makes individualization a reality for the pupil. That kind of creativity cannot operate where the curriculum is restricted by over-emphasis on behavioural objectives. That is why the objectives approach must be extended as suggested above. As will be shown later, teaching methods themselves are main contributors to expressive and type

III (problem-solving) objectives, as are personal relationships in the classroom. In such situations the objective itself becomes the pupils' experience of being involved in the type of teaching and learning described as the 'process model' in Chapter 3.

In this context, the objectives structure of the curriculum does *not* limit the professional freedom of the teacher. On the contrary, it provides the broad framework that enables the teacher to operate freely and effectively in exercising teaching skills in the classroom.

Curriculum content

Traditionally, content has formed a substantial part of curriculum in schools of the UK. Wheeler[10] makes the point:

> This third phase of the curriculum process (content) bulks large in educational thinking today, so the selection of subject matter or content tends to become the principal concern of many curriculum-makers. Indeed, in some countries, particularly those with well established systems of external examinations, the selection of content by bodies outside the school (even though teachers are represented on these bodies) determines the experiences undergone by the students, that is, the curriculum. This is both logically and educationally wrong, but such is the pressure of educational tradition that errors are not always perceived nor the consequences inferred.

This connects with the discussion in Chapter 1 of examinations as an influence on curriculum, but it also brings to attention that the main curriculum, through which it is intended that some special needs should be met, may have content determined by sources far removed from the special needs of pupils. This is not an argument against interaction, though it does suggest that those who plan it should be aware of the fact. There is also evidence of the dominant place of content in special education:

> Specification and description of the content of the curriculum form the major part of the curriculum documents submitted to the project. There is little variation in this between primary, secondary and special schools, the more competent submissions from all sources being remarkable for the care with which the content has been selected, the detail of its organization and the clarity of its presentation.[11]

A recent Schools Council curriculum publication[12] suggests that the situation has not changed. Out of twenty-two examples of curriculum for special needs, fifteen appear to be dominated by curriculum content without attempting to outline objectives, in a sample that covers eight different kinds of special schools.

Content and learning experience The content of the curriculum invariably takes the form of the specification of traditional school subjects. For pupils with learning difficulties the organization may apply only to the basics of numeracy and literacy, the rest of the curriculum being organized in terms of broad subject fields, topics or centres of interest.[13] However, in bringing together content and learning experiences there is a tacit assumption that curriculum for special needs cannot be described adequately in terms of subject divisions or even broad subject fields, topics or centres of interest. Most subjects interact with others and contribute to numerous different learning experiences; and most learning experiences, when examined, are found to include contributions from more than one subject. Currently fashionable 'subjects' such as personal adequacy or social competence defy precise definition, appearing as applications of almost everything that could be included in curriculum. Subject content appears to promote logically organized curriculum formally taught, perhaps efficient with many pupils but failing to capture the interests of those with special needs and creating problems of generalization for those with learning difficulties. Centres of interest or topics capture interest and promote concepts but may override the need which some pupils have for continued learning of basic skills:

> If the curriculum content is compartmentalized into subjects, it is less easy to provide those broad experiences and real life situations which are so necessary. The importance of social education may be overlooked. If correlation is emphasized the basic subjects are likely to suffer because of difficulties of control and continuity; teaching may tend to become subservient to the project and not related to the individual.[14]

This is the point from which Tansley and Gulliford developed the core and periphery approach described in Chapter 3 and now widely used in special education. Although the approach goes far to resolve the problem of maintaining balance in curriculum for special needs, it only partially allows for the combination of content and experience. That requires an even broader approach which anticipates the discussion of teaching methods.

The broader approach involves consideration of the total learning situation:

Content in the broad approach
1. Definition of content essential for the establishment of objectives at the function level.
2. Definition of content relevant to the context objectives.

---

3. Establishment of content in 1 and 2 at priority levels determined by the needs of the pupils.
4. Organization of teaching strategies through which content will enable pupils to achieve objectives.
5. Promotion of interaction between learning at both levels in order to motivate and reinforce learning.

Content priority should rest on the perceived needs of the pupils rather than upon the level specified. Then, given appropriate selection and organization of content, it must become part of a 'shaping' approach to the pupils' learning in which the simultaneous operation of the constituent factors influences the outcome.

Content and experience in a 'shaping' approach
1. The factual content, illustrations and materials with which pupils are required to operate.
2. The process of communication between teachers and pupils that guides the pupils' operations.
3. The level of knowledge to be acquired through the process and its manipulation in thought and language.
4. The skills to be established or practised.
5. The attitudes which pupils bring from the total situation and experience together with associated values.
6. The extended social and verbal interactions that are incidental to the activities.

The simultaneous operation of the factors constitutes the total *learning experience* for the pupils. It is a 'shaping' situation precisely because the outcome is open, can be evaluated by the teacher for *individual pupils* according to the level of objectives rather than committed to their absolute achievement. What is achieved then becomes the basis for further learning.

Criteria for content and experience
The broad, shaping approach that unites content and experience is compatible with other aspects of curriculum discussed above. It allows for differential learning, accommodates the three types of objective, is compatible with a 'process' approach and is appropriate at any level of priority necessary to meet special educational needs. The critical point for its realization is in the classroom and requires intimate knowledge of the pupils to be taught. There content and learning experiences must be combined and organized to give pattern and direction to activities while providing flexibility to allow the interests, motivation and

learning potential of pupils to be fully utilized in the attainment of curriculum objectives. Such classroom intimacy cannot be defined in detail, but it is possible to suggest criteria by which it may be monitored.

Criteria for content and learning experiences
Relevance: register with meaning for the pupils.
Validity: move learning towards curriculum objectives.
Suitability: appropriate to developmental patterns of pupils.
Continuity: foster concept growth and link areas of knowledge.
Variety: allow multiple learning, alternative presentations.
Flexibility: allow for classroom adjustment, changes in pupil needs and teachers' skills.
Balance: between personal/social and main/special curricula.
Repetition: for reinforcement, concept development, generalization.
Broad based: has involved staff, advisers, parents, governors and relevant local organizations.

Though classroom detail cannot be specified from outside, the question remains as to whether there may be broad, national guidelines within which schools and classes may operate. That question is taken up in Chapter 6 in the discussion of a common curriculum.

Teaching methods

In discussing the broad shaping approach to curriculum content and the association of content and learning experience, the question of teaching method has been anticipated. If there is to be unity of curriculum this is as it should be. Aims influence the definition of objectives, these in turn shape the choice of content, and the delivery of content through learning experience intimately involves the development of teaching methods. Method, then, is about the manipulation of the learning in which pupils are involved; but learning is not confined to the taught curriculum in the classroom, as the discussion of the planned and hidden curriculum indicated. So what is commonly termed method may be said to involve the total complex of relationships and communication existing in the school, since it is through these that pupils assimilate important attitudes and values that affect their behaviour and, indeed, the kind of persons they are or are becoming. As was pointed out in Chapter 1, it is within this very complex that there is a danger that ideology may operate unseen in opposition to the overt values to which the school is committed. In this broad sense method could be considered as concerned with the shape and the shaping of the curriculum itself; for it is, or ought to be, an important instrument in establishing the complex of relationships and communication within the school.

Wilson and Evans have emphasized the importance of method in their conclusions from a survey of disturbed children.[15] They asked how the curriculum for such children should differ from the curriculum in ordinary schools:

> we have been compelled to the conclusion that method is more important than content: what matters is the way in which teachers generate enthusiasm and plan the programme.

Primacy of method is associated with a planned programme. Brennan[16] made a similar point following a study of curriculum for slow learners. He was discussing objectives involving sensitivities, attitudes and values (areas in which disturbed children have difficulties) and he concluded:

> objectives which reside in the areas of sensitivities, attitudes or values will depend for their attainment more upon *how* the pupil learns than upon *what* he learns. In other words, there are circumstances in which method becomes more important than content.

A similar relationship between aims and methods was noted in a Schools Council project report.[17] Teachers stressing as their aims pupil self-control or self-regulation tended to adopt formal teaching methods, with informal methods used by teachers aiming at self-realization or self-expression for their pupils. In schools considered to have balanced aims the tendency was for basic subjects taught by formal methods, with child-centred methods operating in other areas of curricula.

Teaching methods are of the utmost importance, for through them the school achieves objectives, satisfies aims and makes a reality of the individualization of curriculum and teaching for pupils with special educational needs. Teaching methods should be subject to continuing discussion and evaluation, but it should be discussion with a purpose. Theoretical contemplation and analysis must be closely related to actual work in classrooms in which new ideas or modifications of those existing are tested and evaluated with the pupils they are intended to benefit. Ideas from sources outside the school should be welcome, as should constructive criticism, though neither should be allowed to operate as edicts.[18]

Criteria for teaching methods

Except where there is major sensory loss, children with special educational needs learn through methods appropriate for children without special needs, though, for most, some modification will be required. The nature of the modification varies according to the individual special needs of pupils, so once more the critical factor is the teacher's continuous relationship with the pupil. It is not possible to detail all the modifications that may be required in classrooms, but we can establish the criteria by which proposed modifications may be assessed.

Criteria for modified teaching methods

Relevance: utilizing the pupil's strengths and avoiding any limitations imposed by special needs.

Individualization: meeting individual and social needs and special needs consequent on disability.

Motivation: involving the pupil in planning, goal setting and self-assessment.

Integration: relating areas of knowledge and skill in appropriate behaviours and attitudes.

Generalization: using knowledge and skill in a variety of situations on personal initiative.

Linking: subjects and experience, main and special curriculum, physical, intellectual and aesthetic activities.

Reinforcement: overlearning in critical areas, especially of precise behavioural objectives.

Responsibility: of pupil, class-teacher and special needs teacher for the achievement of curriculum objectives.

Communication: of the means and ends of methods, to the pupil, his parents and family, and care workers.

Sources: use of texts, advisers, teachers' centres and courses to improve and refine methods.

The criteria themselves are not special. What is special is the care required in applying them to methods for special needs, especially where there are discrepancies in physical, mental, emotional or aesthetic development. It is too easy to allow special needs to distract attention from common needs.

Record keeping

Records may be kept for a variety of purposes. Some records have
a statistical purpose, for example when an LEA wishes to establish
local norms for comparison with national standards or as a
benchmark for local schools. Other records are concerned with the
achievement or attainment of individual pupils in order to
evaluate their learning or their progression through the
curriculum. Then there are teaching records. These are the
records that operate within the intimacy of the classroom,
providing the information upon which the teacher bases the
daily decisions shaping his or her work to the needs of the pupils.[19]
This section is concerned with those records which monitor
curriculum progress and shape teaching in the classroom:

> To know what work is planned and what has actually been done at
> each stage of a pupil's progress through school are minimum
> requirements for avoiding wasteful repetition and vital
> omissions.[20]

The important point Wilson has made here is the concern with
what has been planned and what has been done; in other words,
with the curriculum and its delivery in the classroom.

Equal importance is accorded by the recommendation of *The
School Curriculum* on the assessment of aims that have been set
down in writing:

> Such assessments should apply not only to the school as a whole but
> also to each individual pupil, and need to be supported by the
> keeping of adequate records for each pupil's progress. The
> assessments will help schools to plan effectively and to give, both to
> pupils and their parents, a clear account of what the school is
> offering.[21]

Records in curriculum   The records written into the curriculum
documents should be those required to chart the progress of
individual pupils through the curriculum objectives. So the
objectives should come first; put another way, if the record is to be
that of progress through the curriculum then there must first
exist a curriculum through which progress may be charted. Given
the curriculum, then the pattern of intermediate objectives
leading to terminal objectives provides the framework of charting
the *behaviour* of each pupil. The framework should be more than a
mere checklist. The record should identify the situations and
experiences designed into the curriculum for the purpose of
facilitating expressive or problem-solving objectives, not in the
detail in which they appear in the curriculum, but in a clear
manner so that a pattern of progression can be seen. The **exact**

format of the record may vary to suit the purpose of the school or unit, though some common points may be identified.

Common points of individual records

1. These records are individual and should be in each child's folder.
2. The pattern of progression should show in the form of the record.
3. Entry in the record should be by a date-mark to reduce the demands on teachers.
4. There should be categories of response so that the record shows:
   - What the pupil is working on with date started.
   - What the pupil has achieved with date.
   - The date when achievement was checked and confirmed.
   - The date revision was started where necessary.
   - A category of alternative or coloured marking by which a revision progress may be charted.
   - Space for any special notes by the teacher.
   - An arrangement for the teacher to initial his or her review of the pupil's progress.
   - An arrangement for initialling by the headteacher or teacher responsible when there is overview of progress.
5. For expressive and problem-solving situations the record should show:
   - The date when the pupil was in the defined situation.
   - A subjective assessment of his response.
   - An indication of whether or not repetition is advisable.
   - If so, any suggested alterations to the situation.
   - A note of any behavioural or other learning applied in the situation.
   - The arrangements for initialling reviews as noted above.
6. There should be arrangements for the entry of any routine standardized tests used in the school or unit.
7. A prominent panel should allow for entry of any disability or limiting factor which may be relevant to assessment of the pupil's function or progress with arrangement for periodic review and initialling.

---

8. There should be entry on the form of the pupil's attendance each term so that it may be taken account of in any review of progress.
9. Classroom or responsible teachers should be identified by name with dates of beginning and end of responsibility.
10. There should be arrangement for a summary sheet to be completed by the pupil's responsible teacher whenever there is a change and responsibility is passed on. The sheet should be countersigned by the headteacher, head of department or teacher with oversight of curriculum.

The purpose of the above record is twofold: it charts continuity in the sense that no objective or experience planned for the curriculum is omitted; progression in that the quality of the pupil's execution, concept formation, thinking and aesthetic expression or appreciation can be seen to mature as he passes through the curriculum. These are the things to be looked for by classroom teachers on review and by other teachers who oversee the record. Except when being overviewed, the record should be with the teacher currently responsible for the pupil, though it should be identified as a school record that moves with the pupil. Whenever a pupil is involved in main and special curriculum, and particularly in secondary schools where specialist subject teachers are contributing, it will be exceptionally important that the responsible teacher for special needs is identified and his or her role unambiguously defined and understood by all concerned.

Access to individual records   There is advantage to be gained from allowing pupils and parents to have access to the above record. Access by the pupil to his record creates an opportunity for educational guidance that brings scholastic progress within the counselling policy of the school and widens the base from which pupils may be assisted towards maturity. Out of the interaction with teachers, pupils reach understanding of the purpose of their curriculum, and the possibility is increased that they will incorporate its objectives as their own with positive effect on their motivation. Similarly with parents: in their scrutiny of the record they should have opportunity to interact with a teacher who knows their child and is able to interpret and answer their questions. Both sides may gain insight and understanding of their complementary roles in the common purpose of the pupil's education. The quality of interaction with pupils will be shaped by their age and maturity, which will also affect communication with parents. With young pupils, there may need to be separate discussions, but as the pupil matures the objective should be to move towards joint discussion with parents and pupil, so that, with the teacher, there is a trinity for progress, a sharing of aspirations and endeavour. Involvement and co-operation of this kind not only make good curriculum practice, they carry forward the principles of the Warnock Report and the legislation of the Education Act 1981.

Teaching records   Teaching records consist of intimate information about the learning of individual pupils and curriculum presentations in the classroom. They are the working notes of classroom teachers. It must not be expected that the notes will be identical in form, for they will reflect the personality, background and professional style of each teacher. Nevertheless they are more than personal notes, and it is essential that the information they contain is made available to teachers who will subsequently teach the pupils, so the record should indicate broad categories of content and sequence of presentation.

First there should be relevant and useful details of the pupil's history and background. These will include educational status of parents and type of home area, occupations of members of family, a note on home language, membership of churches or youth groups, etc., hobbies and interests, places visited and holidays, newspapers and magazines seen by the pupil, library membership and favourite reading, and a note on television watching, radio and films. Previous schools should be noted together with any relevant information on the pupil's attendance and learning. This section should be organized to allow for development as the pupil passes through the school, so that growing and changing interests may be added – including those introduced and fostered by the school.

The next section will consist of cumulative notes on the pupil's learning and interim assessment of progress. Here will be the teacher's observations on the outcomes of learning situations and suggestions for modification, re-presentation and development as necessary. With young or immature pupils, or those with learning difficulties, there will be a running record in basic subjects or even perceptual-motor learning with the intermediate objectives of the curriculum analysed into smaller and finer steps. This will produce a supplementary curriculum for which a checklist type of record may be designed and included as part of the pupil's record.[22] At these early levels there is advantage in keeping a running record of each pupil's word recognition vocabulary which later doubles as a spelling curriculum and record.[23] A similar system may be helpful for basic number to cover number combinations in the four rules.[24] These notes should also contain cumulative teachers' comments on the pupil's reactions to different approaches; his demonstrated interests through activities, books read, etc.; his aesthetic sensitivities; relationships with other pupils and teachers; and observations which suggest emerging values behind behaviour that are almost impossible to note in any manner other than the subjective. As the notes build up throughout the pupil's school career the contributions of different teachers increase the reliability of the value judgements.

A final section covers the content of curriculum; the presentations which the teacher has chosen to make in class or group situations as a means of assisting pupils to achieve curriculum objectives. For pupils following special needs curricula, especially those with learning difficulties or emotional or behavioural problems, this record is of the first importance to achieve curriculum continuity and progression. Its importance may justify the design of a special record booklet and there is advantage if the format promotes planning or forethought by the teacher as well as being a record of work covered with pupils. One successful format for this purpose was as follows.

Forecast record in a secondary school

1. At the end of a term the teacher entered an outline forecast of the work proposed with classes or groups during the following term, noting the materials, equipment, visits, etc. required for the work.

2. The forecast was checked with the headteacher or responsible teacher to establish suitability, viability and availability of the teaching materials.

3. During each week of the next term the teacher made a forcast of the work to be undertaken with each class or group during the following week and this, too, was submitted to the responsible teacher. There was here an assurance that teachers were thinking and planning ahead in a responsible manner. The forecasts were brief but meaningful. They included the content to be covered and its purpose, outline of the proposed approach, and indication of work to be set for and completed by the pupils.

4. Forecasts were made in a looseleaf book. During the week of operation the teacher made working comments on a facing page, assessing the work and the response of the pupils; noting any need for repetition, reinforcement, or alteration for subsequent presentation. Absent pupils were also noted.

---

5. There were occasions on which work was not carried out, not completed, or even changed by the teacher during the week. Whenever these occurred the entry in the forecast was underlined in red and an explanatory note added on the comment page. Incomplete work was carried forward and entered in the forecast for the next week, as was omitted work unless covered by an alternative appearing in the notes. Most frequent reasons for alterations appeared as misjudgement of time allowance, intrusions into teaching time, diversions or extensions resulting from pupils' interests, availability of more topical and relevant materials, abandonment or substitution through failure to capture pupils' interest or misjudgement of their readiness for the learning involved.
6. In addition to assessment of weekly work, the teachers wrote a brief assessment of work at the end of each term.
7. The curriculum forecasts/records were filed in school under the year-group and were available for consultation by members of staff. They were held on file for three years or for one year after the pupil left the school.

A system such as this allows the record to show what was planned and what was done at each stage throughout the school, and also provides information about how it was done and through what contents, as well as ensuring that teachers think and plan ahead in their work.

If the education of children with special needs is to be both appropriate and efficient then each school or unit must develop a sensitive and effective means of recording curriculum and pupil progress. The recording is not an end in itself; the purpose of the record is to enable teachers to make evaluations of the curriculum process and the outcome established by the pupils.

Evaluation

The purpose of evaluation is more easily understood if the nature of the curriculum is kept firmly in mind. The curriculum can only *anticipate* learning. To convert the anticipations of the curriculum into real established learning by the pupils, efficient teaching is necessary. In evaluating the curriculum the actual learning established by the pupils is compared with the learning anticipated in the curriculum. The clearer the definitions of objectives, the easier it becomes to observe whether or not they are achieved in the behaviour of the pupils. So defined, evaluation is an ongoing process concerned with the achievement by the pupils of the sequential intermediate objectives postulated in the curriculum as leading to the terminal objectives.

Evaluation asks a series of questions:

- As a result of the teaching received has there been any change in the behaviour of the pupil?
- If so, in what direction is the change and what is its magnitude?
- Is the behaviour now established that which was anticipated in the curriculum for this point in the pupil's learning?

These questions are about measurement, assessment or observation, and from these come the data necessary to answer them. At that point another question is posed:

- Is the behaviour established by the pupil to be regarded as satisfactory or unsatisfactory?

Now the real process of evaluation begins. The learning established by the pupil must be considered in the context of all that is known: the amount of teaching received; its quality; the pupil's motivation; the appropriateness of content; the suitability of the objectives for the pupil; any factors concerning the pupil that may have affected learning and so on. Learning failure or even regression may be temporarily accepted if stress or trauma in the pupil's life are sufficient to account for it. Advancement of learning may be considered unsatisfactory where it does not reflect the amount and quality of teaching that the pupil has experienced.

Where there is unsatisfactory learning, evaluation looks further. The quality and appropriateness of the teaching must be assessed; the suitability of the objective for the pupil's point in development must be examined; and the relevance of curriculum content must be questioned. The cause of the pupil's failure may be in the arrangements made for his learning, in curriculum and teaching, and these must also be assessed. Evaluation, then, is a complex process concerned with the appropriateness and suitability of curriculum objectives and the sequence in which they are presented; with the delivery of the curriculum in the classroom in terms of content and learning experience; and with the progress in learning established by the pupil.

Evaluation has a purpose beyond that of judging the progress of the pupil. It is a 'formative' process shaping every aspect of curriculum from the formulation of objectives and their intermediate sequencing to classroom organization and presentations, in a continuous search for improvement and refinement. In this search, evaluation must follow the curriculum beyond the confines of objectives that are overtly behavioural in order to accommodate expressive and problem-solving objectives and that part of the curriculum concerned with context learning and awareness. Though outcomes in these areas are not predicted in advance and may differ for individual pupils, teachers should still be concerned about what the outcomes are and their quality. Caution is necessary in going 'beyond behaviour' in this way but it is possible to do so if some behaviours are regarded as reflecting inner states or processes that cannot be directly observed.[25]

A dual role of behaviour in evaluation		
Observed pupil behaviours	Direct: the behaviour is the objective	Instructional, behavioural objectives; function learning
	Indirect: the behaviour reflects an inner state or process	Expressive and problem-solving objectives; context learning

The subjectivity introduced into evaluation by these procedures cannot be denied, but it is necessary to monitor and assess important aspects of education in the areas of attitudes and values. The curriculum is not merely about what people know, or can do; it is about the kind of people they are, or are becoming. This is just the area in which there are many differences of opinion without objective basis for their reconciliation, so the best safeguard may be to broaden the basis of participation in curriculum evaluation to include parents, governors and representatives of the community in a manner to be discussed later. From this involvement a consensus may emerge which protects pupils from the more unacceptable idiosyncrasies of their elders.

Criteria for evaluation

Useful guidelines for evaluation have been proposed that have particular relevance for curriculum concerned with special educational needs.[26] Though intended primarily for the evaluation of curriculum objectives, they may with modification be equally applied to the evaluation of curriculum content or learning experiences, to the whole curriculum or any part being reviewed.

Guidelines for curriculum evaluation

Is it real?

Does what the pupils are being required to learn relate to the wider world outside the school? Is there a point of register that may be used?

Is it relevant?

Does the point of register have meaning within the outside world as perceived by the pupils? Will curriculum experiences broaden the pupils' perceptions and extend the area of relevance?

Is it realistic?

Is the learning required achievable by the pupil given his or her potential for learning and a degree of effort of which he or she is capable? Are the proposed stages in the learning appropriate for the pupil? Is any necessary pre-learning firmly established?

Is it rational?

Is the purpose of the learning clear to the pupils? If not, can it be explained to them in a manner compatible with their stage of personal development and intellectual competence?

All these questions are important in evaluation, but the question 'Is it realistic?' is the most critical where the curriculum is concerned with special needs. That is because it focuses on the individual pupil, on his or her needs, strengths and limitations, and is the starting point for individualization of curriculum. It also requires critical judgement from the teacher, who must pitch demands on the pupil at just the right level. Over-demanding curriculum faces the pupil with the frustration of failure; when under-demanding, it deprives him or her of the excitement and satisfaction of success as a result of personally recognized effort.

The purpose of evaluation

Evaluation is not something which operates at the end point of the curriculum only. It is an intrinsic part of the curriculum process. Consideration of any part of the curriculum has implications for other parts, such is its essential unity. The same is true where alterations or refinements are concerned. This feedback or modification constitutes the real purpose of evaluation. Yet organization is necessary if modification is to be achieved. A decision to modify the curriculum should involve identification of the person to be responsible for it and indication of how the modification is to be communicated to the appropriate teachers in the school. This is also necessary if teachers are to be well motivated. Evaluation involves considerable time and discussion, and if teachers are to consider these worthwhile then it is important that the practical effect on curriculum and teaching should be plain to see. Otherwise evaluation may become a mere academic exercise.

Notes and references

1. Department of Education and Science (1978) *Special Educational Needs* (Warnock Report), 11.15, London, HMSO.
2. Ibid., 11.15.
3. Ibid., 11.6.
4. HEGARTY, S. *et al.* (1982) *Recent Curriculum Development in Special Education*, York, Longman for Schools Council.
5. DES (1978) op cit.; LEEMING, K. *et al.* (1979) *Teaching Language and Communication to the Mentally Handicapped*, London, Evans/Methuen Educational; BRENNAN, W. K. (1979) *Curricular Needs of Slow Learners*, London, Evans/Methuen Educational.
6. POPHAM, W. J. (1977) 'Objectives 72' in Rubin, L., ed. *Curriculum Handbook*, Boston, Allyn & Bacon.
7. WHEELER, D. K. (1967) *Curriculum Process*, London, University of London Press.
8. BRENNAN, W. K. (1979) op. cit.
9. For examples of objectives stated at curriculum level see (1978) 'Reading for Slow Learners – A Curriculum Guide', *Curriculum Bulletin 7*, London, Evans/Methuen Educational.
10. WHEELER, D. K. (1967) op. cit., p. 37.
11. BRENNAN, W. K. (1979) op. cit., pp. 70–72.
12. HEGARTY, S. *et al.* (1982) op. cit.
13. BRENNAN, W. K. (1979) op. cit., p. 70.
14. TANSLEY, A. E. and GULLIFORD, R. (1960) *The Education of Slow Learning Children*, London, Routledge & Kegan Paul.
15. WILSON, M. and EVANS, M. (1980) *Education of Disturbed Pupils*, London, Methuen Educational, p. 185.
16. BRENNAN, W. K. (1974) *Shaping the Education of Slow Learners*, London, Routledge & Kegan Paul.
17. BRENNAN, W. K. (1979) op cit., p. 74.
18. On teaching methods for pupils with learning difficulties, see TANSLEY, A. E. and GULLIFORD, R. (1960) op cit., WILLIAMS, A. A. (1970) *Basic Subjects for the Slow Learner*, London, Methuen Educational; BELL, P. (1970) *Basic Teaching for Slow Learners*, London, Muller Educational; AINSCOW, M. and TWEDDLE, D. A. (1979)

Preventing Classroom Failure, Chichester, Wiley; McCREESH, J. and MAHER, A. (1974) *Remedial Education: Objectives and Techniques*, London, Ward Lock Educational; HINSON and HUGHES, eds. (1982) *Planning Effective Progress*, London, Hulton. More general books but still useful are: WATERHOUSE, P. *Managing the Learning Process*, New York. McGraw Hill (1983); KERRY and SANDS (1983) *Handling Classroom Groups*, Basingstoke, Macmillan Educational; BRADLEY, J. (1983) *Inside Staff Development*, Windsor and Walton-on-Thames, NFER/Nelson; BOLAM, R. (1983) *School Focussed In-service Training*, London, Heinemann Educational.

19. A more extensive discussion of record keeping is in: (1978) *Reading for Slow Learners*, London, Evans/Methuen Educational.

20. WILSON, M. D. (1981) *The Curriculum in Special Schools*, York, Longman for Schools Council.

21. Department of Education and Science (1981) *The School Curriculum*, London, HMSO.

22. With very young or immature pupils the curriculum may focus at this level; see (1978) *Reading for Slow Learners*, op. cit., pp. 76–84; (1981) *Handbook for LOOK Perceptual Materials*, Basingstoke, Macmillan Educational.

23. (1978) *Reading for Slow Learners*, op. cit., pp. 63–5, 95–7.

24. Inner London Education Authority curriculum guides *Checkpoints 1978* and *Checkpoints Assessment Cards 1979*, London, ILEA Learning Materials Service.

25. For further discussion of these points, see WHITE, J. P. (1971) 'The Concept of Curriculum Evaluation', *Journal of Curriculum Studies*, V.3 No. 3; also SCRIVEN, M. (1967) 'The Methodology of Evaluation' in AERA monograph No. 1, *Perceptives of Curriculum Evaluation*, Chicago, Rand McNally.

26. BRENNAN, W. K. (1979) op. cit., pp. 89–91.

CHAPTER 5

Resources

The curriculum needs people

Pupils

The special needs of the pupils are constraints on the curriculum. Their effects may be reduced by skilful design and teaching, and that is the purpose of special education. On the other hand, no disability is absolutely total, and strengths may be found upon which curriculum may focus in order to achieve fulfilment and satisfaction for the individual as near to normality as possible. That, too, is achieved through the exercise of skill by teachers; it has been referred to as individualization of curriculum and teaching and is also what special education is about. So the pupils themselves are a curriculum resource though they are also the reason for its existence, and the quality of their learning is its ultimate purpose.

Teachers

The teachers are a supreme curriculum resource, not only in terms of professional skill in the taught curriculum but because of the kind of people they are and their contribution to the planned and hidden curriculum of the school. It is doubtful if any curriculum would be successful if it required skills or personal qualities not present in the group of teachers who were to teach it.

The need for additional teaching resources in special education has long been recognized, at first through a low statutory maximum size of classes for handicapped pupils.[1] Later, as increased multiple handicaps led to recognition of the desirability of flexible teaching arrangements, class size gave way to suggested teaching ratios as the basis of staffing classes for handicapped pupils in special or ordinary schools.[2] The new pupil–teacher ratios also improved staffing standards as the following examples illustrate: blind pupils, class size 15 – ratio 1:6; maladjusted pupils, 15 – ratio 1:6; pupils with moderate learning difficulties, 20 – ratio 1:11. It was specified that the suggested ratios should apply to special classes because, though pupil disabilities were less severe than in special schools, the classes would have a wider range of age and ability, more individual and group work would be required of the teacher, handicapped pupils in ordinary classes would require support and their teachers need to be kept informed of their needs.[3] For the first time, pupil–teacher ratios were related to classroom support staff:

> The staff ratios suggested in the preceding paragraphs are based on the assumption that adequate numbers of suitable ancillary staff are available. With very severely handicapped children it may be desirable to have as many ancillary staff as teachers.[4]

The Warnock Report welcomed the staffing ratios and recomended that they be regarded by LEAs as the minimum standard to be achieved[5] and applied also in special classes.[6] More important, the report expressed concern about the disruptions experienced by children in special classes when staff absence or changes, or other crisis, affected the ordinary schools:

> we recommend that local education authorities should ensure that a school with a special class or unit is allocated an extra specialist teacher to its staffing complement . . . the number of teachers in the special classes . . . attached to a school should always exceed the number of such classes.

Besides the assurance of continuity for pupils with special needs, the recommendation was justified as allowing for the release of teachers to attend in-service training or other activities to extend their professional competence.[7]

Some important principles may be established about teacher resources for pupils with special educational needs. First, the learning problems created by special needs require for their solution pupil–teacher ratios more favourable than those considered necessary for pupils without special needs. Second, the non-teaching support required by the pupils should be provided through suitable ancillary staff so that teachers may concentrate on their main educational task. Third, as the professional responsible for the pupils' learning, it is the teacher's responsibility to ensure that the work of ancillaries is incorporated in classroom activities in a manner compatible with pupil learning and if possible contributory to it. Fourth, the security of the pupil and the essential continuity in his learning is firmly focused on teacher continuity.

Teacher training

A reality to be faced when considering the teacher resources for curriculum for special needs is the low percentage of special training among the teachers who must develop and operate the curriculum. Even in special schools for blind and deaf children, where specialized training within three years is a requirement for continued employment, only 57 per cent of teachers of blind pupils and 67 per cent of those teaching the deaf have completed specialized further training.[8] Of all teachers in special schools in England and Wales only 22 per cent have additional training, with the figure for Scotland 50 per cent. Among pupils with learning difficulties the percentage of teachers with additional training were: in secondary school special classes 28 per cent; in primary schools 4 per cent; and in special schools 44 per cent.[9] Wilson and Evans[10] were informed by the DES that only one fifth of teachers of maladjusted pupils could be expected to have additional training for their work – though the authors comment on the experience and skill of teachers working in special units and classes for pupils with behaviour difficulties, the so-called 'disruptive units'.

This last point is important. Most surveys refer to teachers with additional one-year courses, ignoring shorter courses, often part-time, through which many keen teachers improve their professional competence. Nevertheless the Warnock Report considered the general position of training for special educational needs unsatisfactory, particularly in view of the proposal to educate more pupils with those needs in ordinary schools. A special education element was proposed for all students in initial teacher training with the aim of making them aware of special needs and resources for meeting them.[11] As 40 years would elapse before all teachers in schools had taken such an initial course, the conclusion was that a massive in-service effort was required to ensure all teachers in post followed such a course within four years.[12] Other in-service courses were to be continued and expanded with special attention to working with parents, working with non-teaching assistants, peripatetic teaching, work with pre-school pupils, and the principles of guidance and counselling.[13] It is possible to allow this lack of training too much influence, overlooking the fact that almost all teachers of children with special needs are trained teachers, many with years of rich and successful experience behind them. The value of experience was recognized in the Warnock Report suggestion that, where relevant and successful, it should be allowed to count towards any new qualification for teachers of children with special needs.[14]

Teachers' role in curriculum

When curriculum is to be constructed, or existing curriculum modified, analysis of the teacher-resource is essential. The principle should be to use the strengths of individual teachers, if necessary safeguarding them from their weaknesses. Where this is sensitively carried out and intelligently related to curriculum and timetable, teaching staff frequently complement each other in a manner that tends to eliminate individual gaps or weaknesses and results in an acceptable level of competence across the curriculum. Where that does not emerge, then the analysis provides the basis for the development of strengths through school or other in-service work or identifies skills, interests or experience to be looked for when new teaching appointments become possible.

The precise role of the teacher is worked out within individual schools to accord with the pattern of curriculum and the style of teaching developed in the school. Where curriculum responsibility is within the school it could not be otherwise, but decisions taken directly affect the quality of curriculum, and some general principles merit consideration.

The teacher in the curriculum

1. *Teachers should be involved in curriculum development.* They should not be regarded as mere purveyors of curriculum but as central figures in its development, operation and refinement. The continuous face-to-face involvement of the classroom teacher gives a special quality to his or her contribution not available from any other source.

2. *Teacher involvement should be planned.*
   All teachers should have the right to participate in curriculum development without compulsion and it may be necessary to guard against the overcommitment of some arising from their enthusiasm. Planning involves sharing the work so that none are overburdened and as far as possible each contributes in an area of interest. A

useful technique is that of curriculum working parties which harness enthusiasms but carry the danger of generating factions. Members of working parties should be free to discuss work in progress with colleagues not involved, as this is often a source of important ideas and inputs as well as a safeguard against the faction danger. Invited contributions from LEA advisers or others with relevant expertise or experience serve a similar purpose.

3. *Teachers should be involved in operating curriculum.* Operating the curriculum involves the teaching materials in use and the methods through which learning is shaped in the classroom. Reviewing materials and teaching equipment forms a part of curriculum development, a particularly practical part which may be of special interest for some members of staff.

4. *Teachers should be involved in curriculum communication.* Curriculum communication has two main aspects both concerned with evaluation. One aspect is the dissemination of information about curriculum changes and the action required to implement them. The other is monitoring individual pupil progress through curriculum and communicating information about modifications where they are required. A school or department policy is required for both aspects, and teaching staff should be involved in its framing and operation. This arrangement may incorporate the requirement of the Education Act 1981 that each school shall have a 'responsible person' for pupils with special educational needs.[15]

5. *Teachers should bring life experience to curriculum.* The contribution of teachers to curriculum should not be limited to their professional perspective. Outside school most live a rich life, are members of many groups and experience the pressures of life in the community. Each teacher's life experience is a legitimate base from which to criticize, assess and evaluate all aspects of the curriculum offered to pupils in the school, and, provided there is critical awareness that the life situations of the pupils may differ from those of teachers, a worthwhile reality may be brought to curriculum transactions.

6. *Teachers should have contact with school governors.* The Education Act 1981 places a responsibility on school governors by defining their *duty* in relation to pupils with special educational needs.[16] Governors need

> to be fully aware of school principles and arrangements. There should be formal reports to governors' meetings about teaching pupils with special needs, the reports being made by teachers who are doing the teaching.

Procedures involving the above or similar principles form a base from which teachers may develop a broad curriculum role, both as individuals and as a co-operative staff group. The role generates the interest and commitment necessary for the teacher-resource to be fully used in the curriculum, at the same time promoting the good staff morale necessary as the procedures can make heavy demands on the out-of-school time of the teachers. Currently the demands are met through the goodwill of the teachers concerned but, as the task of curriculum development increases, the time required for it may have to be taken account of in arriving at staffing levels for special schools and classes.

Headteacher's role in curriculum

The responsibility of the headteacher for curriculum matters also involves the school governors and the LEA in a relationship set out in the instrument of government for the school. In addition, the head may have (one hopes has) been nominated as the 'responsible person' for pupils in the school who have special educational needs. Professionally the ultimate responsibility for curriculum remains with the headteacher, a fact not always appreciated by the staff.

The headteacher in curriculum
1. Create opportunities for teachers to discuss their *personal* teaching role in curriculum on a regular scheduled basis. This avoids the negative situation where teachers tend to seek discussion when there are problems.
2. Be liberal with credit but make sure it is justified – also make sure that others are aware of the individual's credit.
3. Operate in the same way with encouragement, though possibily more in private.
4. Maintain general staff interest in curriculum matters, encouraging informal discussion and assessment.
5. Demonstrate interest and awareness across the curriculum without claiming expertise.
6. Use the discussions in 1 above to expand documentary information about staff strengths and weaknesses,

patterns of interests and particular skills.

7. Make sure teachers are working in curriculum areas of interest to them, that work is equitably shared, and that schedules and times are established well in advance and known to all concerned.

8. Take a fair share of work in a curriculum area of interest but do not necessarily lead the group.

9. Occasionally attend the various curriculum working party discussions to show and maintain interest.

10. Bring teachers to governors' meetings to present and discuss their curriculum work, using emerging governors' interests to develop school visits and association.

11. Encourage staff groups to make use of LEA and community resources in curriculum work and be prepared to act as a link.

12. Make sure that staff are contributing to *practical* aspects of curriculum maintenance and development – allocation of resources and facilities, financial planning, choice of materials, ordering, etc.

13. Develop a staff role in the routine review of curriculum.

14. When there are individual reviews of pupils, ensure there is consideration of the pupil's curriculum and teaching in which considerable importance is attached to input from classroom teachers.

15. Develop an association of non-teaching staff with curriculum in a manner which does not conflict with the role of teachers but makes classroom assistants aware of the work being done and the importance of their contribution.

16. Include curriculum discussion in the school policy for interaction with parents so they know what the school is attempting to achieve and are made aware of the amount of work staff contribute outside their classroom teaching. Encourage and accept parental suggestions, making sure they are appropriately shaped. Equally, make sure parents are aware that they are seriously considered, with explanation if they are not implemented.

17. Make sure there is adequate attention to the planned and hidden curriculum and to the relationship between these and the taught curriculum.

Ancillary staff

All ancillary staff in a school represent a potential curriculum resource in that all are links with the wider community and each has a special life experience which may be of value. How far the resource is utilized will depend on the enterprise and initiative of the teachers. Special schools, particularly boarding schools, are more likely to exploit the resource than the ordinary schools, possibly as a means of reducing the effect of segregation. More specifically, the ancillary workers most likely to interact with curriculum activities are classroom assistants and, in boarding special schools, child care staff.

The Warnock Report commented on the different standards of provision of classroom assistants among LEAs and suggested that for immobile children or those requiring regular training in feeding or self-care there should be one assistant to every four or five children. For special classes a firm recommendation was made:

> special classes for children of primary school age, whether in special schools or units attached to ordinary schools, and special classes for children of secondary school age with physical disabilities, severe learning difficulties or emotional or behavioural disorders, should each have at least one ancillary worker.[17]

As the report notes, classroom assistants are usually untrained (except where nursery nurses are employed in this capacity) and opportunities for training are virtually non-existent, so the workers must rely upon the teachers or upon any local arrangements for training in the LEA – a situation that still exists. Not surprisingly, the resource remains relatively little exploited in curriculum terms. Most classroom assistants in special education are facilitators, helping children with disabilities to do what other children do for themselves or relieving the teacher of classroom chores which interfere with teaching. These are not unimportant tasks, but better use could be made of the classroom assistants.

Classroom assistant in curriculum
1. Supervision of ongoing work to free teacher for individual or small-group work.
2. Supervision of repetitive work or practice.
3. Supervision of generalization of established skill or knowledge.
4. Conversation with disadvantaged or other pupils who need extended conversational experience.
5. Supervision of small groups on out-of-school projects.

6. Contribution of local knowledge in environmental projects.
7. Point of contact with local people who may contribute to curriculum.
8. Assistance with pupils who have problems with mobility.
9. As a 'reinforcer' in behavioural learning.
10. As a recorder in experimental teaching or in establishing behavioural base lines.
11. As a contributor of any personal skill in practical or artistic activities.
12. As a potential contributor of additional local knowledge in any relevant aspect of curriculum development.

Used in the way suggested, the assistants make two important contributions to curriculum. First, they enable teachers to individualize curriculum and teaching in a way impossible without them. Second, they extend curriculum possibilities, in particular in relation to the community and the environment. But they cannot do this themselves; the contributions are possible only as a result of professional planning and direction for which teachers are responsible.

Child care workers in boarding special schools stand in the place of parents in out-of-schoolroom time; they should have a similar relationship to the pupils' learning, and are in a position to support and reinforce what goes on in the classroom. They, too, offer possibilities for extending curriculum through out-of-schoolroom activities with – at least in theory – the prospect of greater unity then in a day school. In practice, caution is necessary. The two situations should complement each other for maximum effect; unity overdone may restrict the experience of the pupils and lower their motivation for learning, while the separation of teachers and care workers may go too far. Of necessity the latter take much of their free time while pupils are in schoolroom, but where flexibility exists it is possible for care workers to spend some of their working time assisting in the classroom, which gives them real insight into their role as supporters of it. This bringing together of house parents and teachers is a further bonus much appreciated where it occurs. The boarding-school relationship may also be used to reduce the time pressures on curriculum noted in Chapter 1. There are many aspects of art and craft, for instance, where once initial skills and techniques have been taught and learned the activity becomes one of personal self-expression. The early stage belongs in school taught by skilled teachers. But a point is reached where the activity may pass into out-of-schoolroom activities supervised and stimulated by child care workers or teachers in their extraneous role. This clears precious schoolroom time for other curriculum activities according to the needs of the pupils as well as being a further link between teachers and care workers. Many physical education and games activities adapt easily to this technique. Here too, the lead must come from the teaching side of the school, and it may involve some in-service training for the child care workers as only about one in ten of workers has any special training.[18]

Support staff and curriculum

Professional support staff may contribute to curriculum in two main ways: first, by advice from within their own area of competence; and second, perhaps more limited, by some special contribution to teaching. School doctor and nurse may assist in shaping health education and also make a contribution to it; speech therapists are a source of expertise on early language development and may work with teachers in classrooms; physiotherapists may be helpful for physical education for some children; while social workers or school welfare officers have much to contribute about the pupils' homes and neighbourhoods that is pertinent to situational analysis and the problem of ensuring that the curriculum is socially relevant. They can also be the source of follow-up information about former pupils necessary if the long-term effectiveness of curriculum is to be evaluated. In a category of their own are the advisers and teachers from the LEA Special Education Advisory Service[19] who should be in a position to provide or obtain any specialized assistance required by the schools.

Subject advisers employed by the LEA are also a source of support for curriculum though less likely to be involved in curriculum for special needs; this should alter as more pupils with those needs are educated in ordinary schools and the common core curriculum assumes its rightful place in the forefront of educational thinking. A special importance attaches to career officers. Apart from their services to individual pupils, they have experience valuable in shaping school leavers' curriculum and are well placed to provide the feedback of information necessary for its evaluation. Educational psychologists likewise have the training to advise schools on methods of assessment and evaluation – for curriculum as well as for individual pupils. They have a wider role, in relation to teaching and learning, assistance with individual programmes for pupils with special learning difficulties, and advice about pupils with behaviour or emotional difficulties. Psychologists should have useful things to suggest about interpersonal relationships and mental health calculated to maintain good relationships and benefit the planned and hidden curricula. However, these support workers have no personal responsibility for the curriculum nor authority for direct intervention, and the extent of their usefulness rests entirely on the initiative of teachers – in particular of the headteacher.

Parents as a curriculum resource

No substitute exists for the knowledge which parents possess about their own children. That is why the Warnock Report stressed the involvement of parents in the assessment of special needs and in education at every level. Equally, parents should be an important source of input to the development of curriculum, though one that is currently greatly neglected. Nor has past experience encouraged parents to contribute or teachers to seek their involvement. Both sides have much to learn about this important co-operation. So how could parents contribute to curriculum?

Parents in curriculum
1. Provision of information about their child's special needs.
2. Effective communication about home circumstances.
3. Communication of information about the child's out-of-school behaviour and attitude to school and teachers.
4. Alert school to any special interests or talents the child exhibits at home.
5. Communicate their ideas about the child's education, its relationship to potential and future plans.
6. Play their part in securing harmony of home and school.
7. Become active participants in the child's learning.
8. Organize family visits that contribute to curriculum.
9. Co-operate with other parents and teachers in discussion and evaluation of curriculum, school resources, etc.
10. Use their influence and experience to foster links between school and community.
11. Put any special knowledge or skill at the disposal of the school curriculum.

A number of significant inferences may be derived from this section. First is the extent and variety of the human resources needed to maintain curriculum for special educational needs. Second comes the premier position of the teachers, as a resource and as organizers of other resources. Third is the importance of adequate and suitable ancillary support if teachers are to individualize curriculum. And fourth is the need to improve the quality of all concerned through improved training in their own skills and in techniques of co-operation.

The school as a curriculum resource

Accommodation

Pupils with special educational needs almost always require additional accommodation. Wheelchairs and inadequacies of control over movement necessitate more classroom space for each pupil. Nor is this confined only to pupils with physical disabilities, for general clumsiness is a common feature of pupils with moderate or severe learning difficulties and of some with behaviour disorders. Allowance must also be made for the adult classroom assistance which the pupils may require. Some of the suggestions made earlier about more educative use of classroom assistants require additional classroom space to operate effectively. Storage is another problem. Children with special needs show greater variation in a class than other children: in age, ability, home and social background, patterns of interest, duration of attention to a task and degree of individual attention from the teacher. To meet these needs the teacher must have a greater variety of teaching material to hand than normally necessary. Furthermore the progress of the pupils tends to be slower and tasks take longer to complete – so there must be somewhere safe yet to hand for work in progress. Because of the need to individualize curriculum and teaching, classroom seating arrangements must be flexible – which again calls for adequate space as well as for attention to natural and artificial lighting. Visual disabilities also generate this need, along with the complication that levels of illumination may have to vary for different pupils. A different problem is posed by pupils with hearing loss for whom acoustic treatment of classrooms may be essential, as well as, for some pupils, electronic classroom equipment necessary for the use of spoken language. A point frequently overlooked is that of classroom temperature and the restricted range within which work is comfortable. The individual's physical activity is a factor here, and situations arise when there may be differences in the air temperature needed for comfort.

Other accommodation problems relate to the school as a whole. Among these is the suitability of the school layout for the necessary movement of *all* pupils, whatever their disability. The curriculum consequences of restricted movement were discussed in Chapter 2; the problem should be anticipated, identified, and if possible resolved when accommodation is planned. Storage also has a wider school aspect. Where do special chairs stay when not in use? What happens to large physiotherapy equipment in the same circumstances? Is the storage space required for any curriculum activity? If so, is the associated curriculum restriction acceptable? Or can it be avoided or reduced by changes in timetable? Overall accommodation also requires review in terms of the whole curriculum. It is not enough to know that pupils can move to any part of the school; once there, it must be possible to offer appropriate teaching in circumstances compatible with the pupils' learning needs. Furthermore, as the Warnock Report is implemented, these considerations will increasingly acquire another dimension in the employment of disabled persons as teachers.[20]

About one in three of special schools has no specialist teaching accommodation other than for woodwork or home economics. Thus their secondary age pupils are less well provided for than pupils in secondary schools, though their primary age pupils may gain from some contact with the specialist provision. Drama, music, metalwork, physical education and science are the main deficiency areas in special schools. Together with less adequate library facilities, this must have an adverse effect on secondary education in special schools.[21] [22]

It is possible that some of the additional difficulties in ordinary schools are overlooked as comparisons are made with special schools. Movement in ordinary schools tends to be over greater distances and is more likely to involve stairs or lifts; it often takes place in more crowded conditions among pupils able to move with greater speed and precision; and the frequency of movement (especially in secondary schools) exceeds that required in special schools: consequently the problems are greater. They involve more than pupils in wheelchairs or with restricted movement, for those with sensory loss or behaviour difficulties are also affected – albeit to a lesser degree. Where pupils who require additional space are included in ordinary classes it may be necessary to reduce the numbers in the class in order to accommodate them and to make sure the teacher is able to give adequate attention to *all* the pupils through available seating and working arrangements. Special attention will be required in workshops, kitchens, laboratories and gymnasiums where, apart from consideration of curriculum and teaching, questions of personal safety are involved. As the security and confidence of staff are important aspects of the curriculum context, the introduction of pupils with special needs in ordinary schools merits a full review of health, safety and fire arrangements followed by a full briefing of all staff and pupils.

The illumination and acoustic treatment of classrooms for pupils with visual or hearing disabilities also create a special problem. It is often considered sufficient to treat one or two rooms in the school – the 'home rooms' for the pupils with the special needs – a practice that may confine the teaching of some pupils to those rooms and restrict their curriculum. If the principle is that pupils with special needs should be taught in any part of the school required by their curriculum, then the 'home room' practice is not good enough. What is required in secondary schools is at least one suitably modified classroom in every subject department in the school, for it cannot be predicted with certainty where the facility will be required at any given time. These accommodation requirements will be expensive but are necessary if the resource is to be adequate. They are also required by the Education Act 1981 if the special education required is to be provided in a manner compatible with the efficient education of pupils without special needs.[23]

Whatever the state or status of the accommodation resource it is the responsibility of teachers in the school to make the best possible use of it. The principles to be observed are fundamentally those of good teaching, but they require more care when applied for pupils with special needs, most of whom have to cope with additional stresses in school. This is of special importance in relation to pupils with learning difficulties and those with emotional or behavioural problems, as good special schools demonstrate. It is there that one finds extra care about the school environment, about tidiness, cheerful colours, well-displayed work and exhibits, and a nice balance between permanent displays and changing elements. There is also understanding of the need of the pupils for security, reflected in some permanent arrangements of classrooms upon which pupils can rely, together with established routines of behaviour at critical points of the day like entering classrooms, leaving, attracting teacher's attention, changing books or activities, so that the pupils always have a point of reference which assists them in establishing self-control. Also to be seen is the skilful association of space, class size and activity.

Surplus of space is avoided as conducive to uncontrolled behaviour, with furniture and displays used to create appropriate places for group activities or individual work; overcrowding may be offset by the removal of doors and the use of corridors as work spaces. In a subtle way the teacher's manner, language and relationships may be observed changing to accommodate the situations and activities, and to cue appropriate behaviour in the pupils.

This kind of regime is also seen in good primary schools or special classes in secondary schools, where the common element with special schools is a high proportion of class teaching, which allows the teacher to have maximum control of the classroom environment and accommodation resource. Some problems will arise when pupils who require the kind of regime described above have curriculum which requires their presence in ordinary classes for specialist subject teaching in secondary schools. Both may be essential if the pupil is to be appropriately educated. Either some of the features described may be incorporated in the ordinary classes, or the pupil's needs are met by a balance between ordinary and special classes. Only specific experience will resolve such a problem; it should certainly involve the teacher responsible for special needs in the school.[24]

As the Warnock Report is implemented and the Education Act 1981 begins to operate, the kind of problem noted above will require careful thought if adequate provision is to be made available in ordinary schools for pupils with special educational needs. A publication from the National Council for Special Education has explored the issue.[25] The main problem is where pupils for whom the LEA has made a 'statement of special educational need' are to be accommodated in 'designated classes' within the ordinary school; that is, pupils who have been subject to multi-disciplinary assessment in the same manner as pupils placed in special schools. The first concern is with the quality of the ordinary school which is to host the designated special classes. Ten criteria are identified that ensure the host school is good of its kind and satisfactorily meeting the needs of pupils already on the roll. For a unit of 28 physically handicapped pupils, 4 teachers and 4 general assistants, the following accommodation would be required: three appropriately furnished teaching spaces; a central interaction space doubling for dining where necessary; interview space for visiting specialists; adequately equipped medical room; physiotherapy space with storage; administration space for the teacher in charge and clerical work; suitable toilet and hygiene accommodation with provision for wheelchairs; access for nonambulent pupils arriving in special vehicles; and access for physcially handicapped pupils to all areas of the school on a scale likely to rule out curriculum restriction. It is not assumed that all the accommodation would be separate, though shared spaces must be able to absorb the added demands of the pupils with special needs and those who work with them. The above is a maximum accommodation need, as other disabilities would require less extensive support provision. Also, with the 4 teachers the unit could take 40 pupils with moderate learning difficulties but only 22 with emotional or behaviour difficulties, or the same number with visual or hearing disabilities. The suggestion is also made that the number of pupils with special needs should not be more than 10 per cent of the school roll, which would set a limit to the size of the designated unit. As indicated, the staffing suggestions make allowance for the additional duties of teachers of children with special needs in ordinary schools and are consistent with the Warnock recommendation that there should be one special teacher more than the number of special classes.

Equipment

Some specialized equipment in use with pupils with special needs is almost entirely facilitating; its main use is to give the pupil access to a form of communication or an area of curriculum. A lift enables a child in a wheelchair to participate in curriculum on the second floor of the school, but it adds nothing to curriculum. More subtle is Braille. It must be learned by a blind pupil and is therefore an important part of the curriculum, but its curricular purpose is to give access to literature and to a means of 'written' communication. Recorded sound is in another category for the blind pupil, having all the importance it has for a sighted pupil with in addition an extended function in giving the blind pupil aural contact with aspects of his world otherwise denied to the blind. Illustrations, photographs, film and television serve a similar purpose for deaf pupils, while for some who are partially hearing the hearing-aid may facilitate access to normal curriculum and teaching. Spectacles serve the same purpose for many thousands of children with mild visual defects. Special chairs, walking aids, typewriters for pupils incapable of handwriting, microelectronics and even microcomputers: the list of facilitators is as long as a list of disabilities. The importance of ensuring that children with special needs have access to necessary facilitating equipment cannot be over-stressed; to those who need them they are as important as pens and pencils to pupils in an ordinary primary school. Without them curriculum restriction or limitation is inevitable.

The great majority of pupils with special needs do not require elaborate facilitating equipment. Children with learning difficulties, those with emotional or behavioural disorders, children with health problems, those with specific learning disabilities and many with physical handicaps need access to the visual, audio and audio-visual aids to learning used with all pupils – perhaps used by their teachers with special care and skill. There is a lack of comparative studies of access to aids across the handicaps and primary, secondary and special schools, except for the study noted above for slow learners.[26] The study listed 5 visual aids, 7 audio aids and 5 audio-visual aids in use in all three types of school with slow learners. In the primary and secondary schools there was a slight but general tendency for the aids to be used less with slow learners than with other pupils in the schools, which surprised the researchers, who expected the reverse. In terms of usage, overhead projectors led the visual aids, radio the audio aids and television the audio-visual aids in primary and special schools, though the radio was replaced by the tape-recorder for secondary schools. All the aids were used less with slow learners in primary schools than in secondary or special schools. Slow learners in secondary schools made more use than in special schools of all the aids except teaching machines, both manual and electronic, and radio. Of reproductive equipment in use, duplicators led the field though photocopiers were growing. Again least use was in primary schools, and secondary schools were superior to special in all except spirit duplicator. The data given applies to slow learners, but there are no strong reasons for assuming that it does not reflect the situation of the children identified in this paragraph. And though the data are about access, which does not of itself guarantee quality in use, without the access quality is difficult to achieve.

Are there any reasons why reproductive equipment and learning aids are more desirable for pupils with special educational needs than for other children? If so, what are they?

First is the compelling need to individualize curriculum and teaching to accommodate the pupils' special needs. Teaching individuals or small groups makes greater demands on school-produced material than does class teaching; and its presentation makes greater demands on equipment. Allied to this is the role of specially produced and presented material in allowing some pupils to have access to the normal school curriculum. In addition there are the learning delays occasioned by the combination of stresses and demands that many pupils face, or the high proportion of learning difficulties associated with other special needs. These often mean that pupils must learn at a level below that of their general maturity, which rules out much material at an appropriate level if the learners are to be motivated; specially produced material is a necessity if the problem is to be resolved. Similarly it may be necessary to produce material with exceptionally fine grading.

Second, the time pressures on curriculum and the restricted mobility of some pupils make it essential to use out-of-school experience to the full. Instant picture and video cameras, 35mm cameras and portable tape-recorders are essential if the link between classroom and environment is to have the immediacy which some pupils need as well as the continued access which optimizes learning. Projection equipment is essential on a scale that allows flexible use with individuals or small groups of pupils. Within the school, recording equipment also reduces unnecessary movement by allowing programmes or material to be taken to the pupils at an appropriate and convenient time.

The third point is that the use of recording equipment gives teachers control over the many excellent off-air programmes and courses available. Programmes may be re-viewed when necessary by just those pupils who require to do so; critical sequences may be immediately re-presented; at suitable points programmes may be stopped for added discussion, or for the presentation of additional material through slides, pictures, etc.; still-frame or slow motion may direct attention to important points; and in dramatic situations presentation may be stopped and pupils invited to anticipate development. These techniques may help to make programmes useful with learning groups other than that originally intended. For some pupils this may be their entry to normal curriculum through a change in the *pace* of presentation, while for others the level of objective may change with detailed thoroughness replaced by awareness in the vocabulary of differential learning.

Fourth, simple closed-circuit television recording has much to offer curriculum, particularly in motor skill learning and dramatic activities where pupils may observe and discuss their own performance and immediately review their attempts at improvement. Where progress is slow, the comparison of video-recordings may be the most effective method of assessment and evaluation for individual pupils, who may also find it a source of confidence and motivation. Wider use of closed-circuit recordings may be a means of explaining the school curriculum to parents and (with parental permission) to the community so that school policy may be comprehended and others become aware of how they might support or make a contribution to it.

Microelectronics

Micro electronic aids have been noted in passing and represent the most recent and growing development in teaching aids. The growth is rapid and information soon outdated, so Appendix 2 directs attention to sources of information beyond the data that follows.

In June 1983 the Microelectronics Programme[27] recorded 21 projects in special education curriculum development distributed across special needs as follows: severe learning difficulty 4; deafness 4; physical disability 3; mild learning difficulty 3; moderate learning difficulty 3; blindness 1; maladjustment 1; and of general application 2. Rearranging the projects according to curriculum area gave the following distribution: language 5; perception 4; remedial programmes 4; social skills 3; number 2; concept development 2; and individualization of curriculum 1. In October 1983 the same source[28] listed commercially available computer programmes which totalled 144, though of these 72 were listed as 'not seen' and only 18 had been subject to limited trial. This point is important, since very few available programmes are backed by reliable and objective information about their effectiveness. Then in November 1983 the DES sponsored a presentation of Microtechnology in Special Education.[29] Of the 59 presentations 36 appeared to be directly applicable to special needs, the rest having been developed for some other purpose, though they may have had limited application. The 36 distributed across special needs as follows: moderate learning difficulty 7; physical disability 6; mild learning difficulty 5; severe learning difficulty 5; deafness 5; partial hearing 2; language difficulty 2; visual handicap 2; assessment procedure general 1; and further education 1. Re-distributing presentations by curricular areas gave the following: language 12; reading 9; writing 9; non-verbal communication 7; spatial concepts 6; perception 4; number 3; problem solving 2; life skills 2; methods of recording 2; preparation for work 1; spelling 1 – a total of 58 programmes. In the description of the programmes only two indicated a design which would allow local insertion of data, while data base appeared in only two specifications, disappointing in view of the flexibility it gives in the use of classroom data.

Interestingly, the new techniques are being used with severe physical and learning disabilities, and the concentration on communication is welcome. It means, though, that basic elementary programmes predominate to the neglect of concept building, problem solving and social aspects. Quite possibly the elementary nature of many programmes is responsible for the emphasis on repetition and reinforcement which does give the impression that the field is dominated by behavioural objectives. Not that this is improper given the general type of programme, though it may be inhibiting more creative approaches to social and environmental studies, problem solving, etc. There are exceptions to the trend. One special school which had a fine reputation in the use of audio-visual aids before moving into computerized learning has harnessed the computer to the pre-existing techniques, using it to control and improve presentation.[30] The principle that the curriculum must determine programmes has been maintained; 35mm slides are still preferred to computer graphics; content-free master tapes allow teachers to select the most suitable format, synchronize voice-over and exercise keyboard control. There is both experience and awareness of the problems which follow when the number of computer terminals in the classroom is insufficient for effective use. This point is important at a time when most special needs use is limited to one or two computers. The idea of content-free programmes that allow local inputs has been taken up elsewhere[31] and appears to hold out promise in education for special needs as an additional means of individualizing curriculum and teaching.

There are applications of microelectronics more limited than the microcomputer but not less important for that. Optacon, which allows a blind person to 'read' printed text directly through the finger, could have a marked effect on education and expand employment prospects for blind people. Simple microswitches enable severely handicapped children to do what was impossible without them. Big Track and Turtle bring totally new concepts of direction and sequence for some children – and a lot of fun besides. The computer itself as a controller of environment stands to the older Possum as a transistor radio to a valve set. Electronic sophisticates may scoff at these limited applications, but to see the joy they engender in seriously handicapped children is to be filled with wonder; and to see retarded readers laugh at their mistakes and try again on the Walsall Village Board[32] is to witness a new dimension of reading.

Microtechnology in the education of children with special needs is still only beginning, at least in curriculum terms. While the techniques are giving many pupils broader access to curriculum, they do not yet broaden the curriculum for children with special needs. The signs of movement to the new dimension are there, though it requires more than new programmes. Equally important is the familiarization of teachers with the flexible technique at their disposal – and in some cases the eradication of their fears.

Organization

The organizational problem

The fact that pupils have special educational needs does not change the organizational problem; but it adds complications and increases the difficulties to be resolved. Pupils and teachers must be brought together for specified activities in suitable classrooms or elsewhere where there are appropriate materials and equipment for the intended learning, and time must be allowed for the learning to be established by the pupils. The problem is complicated by the range of experiences and subjects that make up the curriculum, so the 'bringing together' must be arranged in a manner that accommodates the variety within the curriculum. The emerging curriculum pattern must also allow for the differing interests of pupils as reflected in curriculum emphasis, particularly at the secondary stage of education, while attention must be paid to motivation in achieving a suitable balance and sequence in curriculum activities.

Within the curriculum pattern, special educational needs must be provided for, whenever possible through the normal curriculum, otherwise through special curriculum arrangements. For some pupils with special needs it may be necessary to arrange individual teaching, or teaching in a small group withdrawn from the regular classes. The attempts that most schools make to resolve the problems vary, first, in the way pupils are grouped for the purpose of learning and, second, through the timetable pattern adopted in the school. Both features reflect the educational philosophy prevailing in the school as much as the perceived curricular needs of the pupils.

The complication of special needs

The approach to organizing curriculum for pupils with special educational needs is mainly influenced by two sets of pressures, discussed in Chapter 1 and 2. On one hand, are the intrusions made necessary by support services, hospitalization or absence through poor health; on the other, associated with the above, are the gaps in learning, learning delay or learning difficulties concurrent with most disabilities. Together these amount to an inflation of the time pressures to which all curricula are subject. One response is to reduce curriculum to its essentials so that what is learned is critical and is learned well, even though the individual will have received a narrow, utilitarian education. The approach has its opponents, who regard the differentiated curriculum as a separatist device that cuts off the individual from the common culture and denies a main purpose of education, which is to contribute to social cohesion. They also ask by what right any child is denied access to any area of human knowledge.[33] This argument is about the organization of curriculum content. Though the utilitarian view may be explicitly neutral, it implicitly favours the known efficiency of special schools while its opposite is biased in the direction of meeting special needs in ordinary schools. It is also strongly on the side of a common curriculum. Both these arguments are in touch with reality and both have good reasons in support which make it difficult to choose between them. The alternative, to achieve a curriculum balance, is equally difficult but probably necessary, and the attempts to achieve it formed the final section of Chapter 3.

Organizationally the utilitarian approach has a long association with a subject-centred curriculum, formal teaching methods and the 'streaming' of pupils by ability, with the result that slow learners in the lower streams learn basic subjects relatively well though they fail to generalize the learning and make little use of the skill outside the classroom. Otherwise, subjects are not limited but what is learned is restricted across the range and remains without real meaning – the so-called 'watered-down' curriculum. In contrast, the broader approach has tended towards a curriculum organized around topics or themes, more informal methods and mixed ability groups. Unfortunately most mixed ability groups are following one curriculum which rarely meets the wide range of needs, does not have any 'planned' differentiation of objectives and requires methodological skills available only from the best of teachers; the results for the slow pupils are not markedly different from those described for streaming.[34] One attempt to break out from the pattern is based upon so-called 'remedial' groups, either as special classes or according to some withdrawal or extraction system. Often these groups, too, are treated as homogeneous, which is far from the reality as Warnock saw it:

> At present 'remedial' groups include children with a variety of difficulties which, though different in origin, are frequently treated alike. There are children who have been absent from school and need to make up work which they have missed; children with physical or sensory disabilities, sometimes temporary, sometimes permanent; children with varying degrees of learning difficulties and children who need to be temporarily withdrawn from the normal classes for specific purposes . . . Children in these so-called 'remedial' groups have a wide variety of individual needs, some linked to psychological or physical factors, which call for skilled and discriminating attention by staff – in assessment, the devising of

suitable programmes and the organization of group or individual teaching whether in ordinary or special classes.[35]

Taken together these arrangements cover most of the situations in ordinary schools. HMI surveys[36] indicate that about 95 per cent of children in primary schools are taught in mixed ability classes; in secondary schools the figure falls to about 35 per cent concentrated into the first two years of the course with a gradual decline thereafter. Not all the other schools are streamed by ability. Some have 'broad banding', others 'setting', and either of these may be combined with mixed ability teaching in limited areas of curriculum, with special or remedial classes for slow learners, or with a withdrawal or extraction arrangement. For many reasons – the developmental levels of the pupils, the nature of the curriculum and the class-teacher organization – the situation is least complicated in primary schools. It is most complicated in the early secondary years, becoming simpler as the mixed ability organization declines, though the need to individualize curriculum as well as teaching generates a variety of arrangements.[37] At present the response is primarily to the different learning potentials of pupils and to learning difficulties but it represents a complex situation which will have to accommodate a wider range of special needs at different levels as the Education Act 1981 is implemented.

Placement in the schools of pupils with special educational needs at a more serious level, those for whom the LEA has made a 'statement', will create three main curriculum problems. First will be the pupils who are capable of following the normal school curriculum if they have access to the non-teaching support made necessary by their disabilities; next will be pupils who require special teaching or curriculum in some areas but who may, with assistance, participate in normal curriculum to a limited extent; and finally there will be pupils who, because of extensive sensory loss, need for extensively modified curriculum or teaching, or major changes in the size or tone of teaching groups, require separate curriculum and teaching but benefit from the social interaction in the school. Put another way, some ordinary schools will be required to provide education for all the special needs defined by Wilson – see Chapter 2 – *in addition to* the range of problems for which they are currently responsible. The range will most probably be within one major disability such as blind, or deaf or physically handicapped pupils, because of the accommodation problems already discussed. The organizational problem will be formidable in an area where existing experience is limited. How is it to be approached?

The responsibility of the LEA
The organizational problem is not one to be resolved by individual schools. If schools are to be effective, they must operate within a policy related to the needs of the area and responsive to changes in those needs. It is the responsibility of the LEA to develop that policy and keep it under review, allocating roles to the individual schools and ensuring the governors and teaching staff are provided with the resources necessary to the fulfilment of the role. That achieved, the LEA is in a position to place children in schools where their special needs may be appropriately provided for and to ensure the provision is, and remains, efficient. From such a base individual schools are able to develop their precise role in the system of special education.

The responsibility of the schools
Within individual schools the organization must operate at two levels. The first is concerned with pupils who are able to follow the normal curriculum. The problem here is that of professional and non-teaching support which may be provided from within the school staff or from community resources on a visiting basis, the decision depending on the number of pupils with special needs and the local resources. This arrangement is particularly suitable for primary schools, rural areas or other situations where the concentration of pupils with special needs is low. Its special value is in enabling the pupils with special needs to attend their local school. The second level is necessary where there are concentrations of pupils with special needs, a particular feature of the secondary stage of education where school populations are concentrated by the operation of the system. It is here that organized support measures within schools becomes necessary. These are the 'designated classes', accommodation for which was discussed earlier.

DESIGNATED CLASSES. Three basic organizations are possible for designated classes or units, each reflecting a particular organizational philosophy. The first might be termed a teaching organization. Here it is assumed that the pupils with special needs will receive the greater part of their teaching in the designated class, most of their interaction with other pupils being in out-of-classroom activities. The arrangement may be suitable for a minority of seriously disabled pupils, but for others it implies a considerable and possibly unnecessary restriction of curriculum.

In the second organization the designated class is regarded as a support class. Here the assumption is that the pupils will receive by far the greater part of their teaching in the normal classes of the school, teaching in the designated class being restricted to that made absolutely necessary by the management of their special needs; the special education teachers are otherwise occupied in supporting their colleagues meeting special needs in ordinary classes. For many pupils the arrangement will be excellent but it limits the placement of pupils capable only of partial involvement in normal curriculum. More important, it may be a factor which determines that some pupils are placed in special schools when a more appropriate curriculum could have been made available through suitable arrangements in an ordinary school.

The third arrangement avoids the limitations of the first two. It is a response to a belief that the amount of time the pupil spends in designated or ordinary classes should be determined by the needs of the pupil and not by the particular organization operating in the school. Hence the designated class should be 'mixed', staffed to meet the needs specified by either the teaching or support classes.[38] Further, if the objective is to have an organization that will support the education of as many pupils with special needs as is possible in ordinary schools, then the flexibility of the 'mixed designated class or unit' is essential. Attention is also necessary to the needs of those pupils who spend the greater part of their time in the designated class. They, too, must have a sense of 'moving on' as their education progresses in the same manner as all pupils in the school. In practice this will rule out a single designated class in which some pupils may spend the whole of their primary or secondary education, a situation found unsatisfactory when providing only for slow learners:

> Observation in schools convinced project workers that the single special class in any type of school was rarely successful and usually took on the distressing features of a 'sink' class. A considered judgement was that the minimum was two special classes to cover the junior or secondary age range. Where numbers did not allow this it seemed preferable to seek other ways of meeting the needs of slow learning pupils.[39]

The most suitable organization is a designated unit of at least two 'mixed' special classes appropriately accommodated and staffed to provide special needs curriculum at any level and with the degree of association with normal curriculum indicated by the needs of individual pupils. The existence of such a unit has other advantages for the ordinary school.

Advantages of a mixed designated unit

1. Support for pupils with special needs following the normal school curriculum is available from the unit and therefore under direct school control.
2. The group of special education teachers in the unit are a source of support and generate confidence in colleagues who teach children with special needs in ordinary classes.
3. The presence of the unit makes possible wide association of all pupils and staff with children with disabilities.
4. When the interaction of ordinary and special curricula is under discussion and review, wide and balanced training and experience are brought to the task.
5. The same experience and training are available in the school for the development of school-based in-service work covering theoretical and practical aspects.
6. All staff have opportunities on hand to broaden their teaching experience; in particular the special education teachers are able to keep in touch with the teaching of pupils without special needs.
7. The interaction that is fostered enables the school to meet in a realistic and flexible manner the challenge of those pupils with special needs that operate in only limited areas of curriculum or for a temporary period in the process of education.
8. The composition of the school population is brought nearer to normality with the possibility of beneficial effects on the planned and hidden curricula.

Though the organization for pupils with special needs brings many problems it also opens out the possibility of many advantages if fully utilized. The question is how the situation can be most effectively handled within the school.

The task of developing special education in an ordinary school, of integrating it fully with the normal curriculum, and also ensuring that the presence has a beneficial effect on all aspects of the host school, is a task some hold to be beyond the resources of existing departments based upon the 'remedial' concept. It requires a trained and experienced head of special education in the school operating at the level next below that of the deputy headteacher.[40] His or her role would extend over *all* special needs in the school, including pupils with and without 'statements', wherever taught, and whether needs were permanent or temporary. The specialist teachers of special needs would form the nucleus special education team but should be joined by a teacher from each year or each subject department as active links with the main school organization and curriculum. This group, led by the head of special education, would formulate policy and curricula for special needs for submission to the school staff; be responsible for monitoring special needs curricula and the progress of the pupils receiving them; and operate the system by which alterations and modifications of special curricula were communicated to members of staff. They would, in fact, be responsible for translating into action in the school some of the principles discussed in previous chapters, including scrutiny and assessment of social interaction and the operation of planned and hidden curricula in relation to pupils with special educational needs. As will be discussed below, the point of contact with special schools and with the Special Education Advisory and Support Service would be within the team.

The special schools

What of the special schools? Nobody currently envisages their demise, and the Warnock Report regarded them as a permanent feature of the educational system, reduced in some ways but with their role extended in others and with closer links to ordinary schools.[41] From a curriculum point of view the special schools will still be limited due to the small number of pupils, restricted specialist accommodation, and lack of specialist subject teachers. The school population will gradually change as more special needs are provided for in ordinary schools. Pupils will concentrate more at the severe level of disability, the range of learning potential will narrow and consequently the curriculum limitations noted above may become of less consequence, with previously overlooked needs being perceived and the schools developing more specialized curriculum and teaching. There should not be any revolutionary change in the principles of curriculum and its development in the special schools and the procedures discussed above should remain valid. There will, however, be a need for a more experimental approach as new curricula are developed; for more able pupils, much more attention will be required to the points of contact between special curricula and that considered to be part of the common experience of all pupils. To assist in the latter special schools must become less isolated in the educational system, developing improved interaction with ordinary schools through links with designated classes in them.

Interaction between schools

The problem

It is not sufficient in itself that the system of special education should be capable of developing individualized curricula to meet different combinations of special needs. It must also exhibit flexibility in the variety of learning situations necessary if these also are to match the needs to the pupils. As it is unlikely that any single institution will produce the necessary variety, interaction between schools is a necessary condition if the system is to achieve maximum response to individual curricular needs. Current experience of interaction is not extensive and full-scale development is something for the future. Here the concern is with the curricular aspects of the interaction, including the flexibility that allows individuals to be in the situation most suitable for their curriculum at *any* point in their school career. As each institution has responsibility for its own curriculum, interaction must be based upon co-operation focused upon the needs of the pupils. There are three main levels at which interaction must operate: between pre-school situations and the schools; between the schools themselves; and between schools and colleges of further education. The first and last of these depend to some extent on inter-service co-operation, but there should be no administrative obstacle to interaction between schools.

Promoting interaction

Interaction between schools must be distinguished from integration. Integration usually means that pupils with special needs are placed for their education in ordinary schools. Interaction is about the movement of pupils and staff between schools and, equally important, the dialogue between schools as a result of which each is influenced and improved by the others' ideas on curriculum, teaching and organization. Integration and interaction may each exist independently, though each should tend to promote the other. The question is, what kind of organization will promote interaction as more pupils with special needs receive their education within the ordinary schools? One approach is the campus concept, the building of primary, secondary and special school on the same site and designed for interaction. When successful this achieves an intimate relationship between the schools in which many special school pupils are taught in the ordinary schools' curriculum.[42] However, only a few such sites exist, the future hardly seems conducive to their development, and in urban areas site difficulties may make provision impossible. Alternatives must be looked for that may operate with existing schools.

The development of designated units within ordinary schools provides a focal point for bringing together ordinary and special schools. As the units develop, the special needs teachers within them should achieve an intimacy and continuity with mainstream teaching and teachers impossible in separate schools. They should maintain their links and professional relationships with their colleagues still teaching in special schools. The existence of properly organized special needs provision in the ordinary school creates an entirely new situation, for previously the absence of such a facility was the main obstacle to the transfer of many pupils from special to ordinary schools. In curriculum terms, unit teachers should be looking for some continuity with the special school that will smooth the transfer of suitable pupils, and developing similar contact to promote curriculum continuity within the ordinary school. The outcome, where successful, should be threefold: first, an intimacy among three groups of teachers; second, points of continuity across curriculum; and third, the removal of obstacles to the smooth transfer of pupils.

In time another outcome should develop. The interaction between the teachers, together with their observation of other situations and practice, should broaden their thinking about curriculum. As a result they should begin to move beyond thinking about how pupils with special needs might participate in mainstream curriculum; they should begin to think positively about how that curriculum may be modified to allow more pupils with special needs to participate. The new thinking should also affect curriculum for those pupils whose education of necessity remains in designated class or special school. The pupils should not be denied the experience of as much of the common curriculum as possible, and their teachers should take account of mainstream curriculum and seek ways of replicating it in a manner appropriate for their pupils. The starting point is the fact that common curriculum is about common experience; it does not depend upon every pupil being educated in the same place and the same manner.

Teachers and schools cannot be 'instructed' to put such developments into operation. Attitudes require modification and new thinking promulgation before committed action can be expected. These are objectives for in-service education to be taken on board by the advisory and support service for special education in the LEA.

The administration contribution

In considering changes in administration and organization the starting point is in the 'broader concept of special education' developed in the Warnock Report.[43] In addition to the abolition of categories of handicapped children and their replacement by the concept of special educational need, the report also concluded that the differences that exist between 'remedial' education in ordinary schools and 'special' education in special schools should disappear and that all education designed to meet special needs should be special education, no matter where it might be delivered:

> Our view of special education . . . encompasses the whole range and variety of special help, wherever it is provided and whether on a full- or part-time basis, by which children may be helped to overcome educational difficulties, however they are caused.[44]

The view is supported by two other recommendations, first that every LEA should have an education officer responsible for all arrangements for children with special needs wherever the needs were being met, and second that the officer should work to a committee of the authority with a similar remit.[45] The Warnock Committee wished to see a unified approach to special needs, which is precisely the basis required for the achievement of maximum variety and flexibility in curriculum.

Administrative unity should end the practice of developing and staffing special schools and special classes in ordinary schools from separate sources. It should allow thinking about staffing areas of special need within which designated units and special schools are seen as complementary to each other and engaged in resolving different parts of the same problem. For example, in the area of moderate learning difficulties, a day special school could be grouped with, say, two designated units, one in a primary school and one in a secondary school. The three would be responsible to the same education officer, they would be staffed and resourced on the same basis, the teachers in them would be appointed to the group with a current allocation to school or unit but an understanding that they would work in either, and the school and units would have the advice of the same person from the advisory and support service. The interchange of teachers would give them experience at different levels of special need; and when working in units teachers could undertake some teaching in ordinary classes to maintain contact with mainstream education. Conversely, the flexibility should permit interested mainstream teachers to establish understanding and experience of teaching pupils with special needs.

These advantages could operate for any group of needs, physical handicap, sensory disability, even emotional or behavioural difficulty, though for the latter it may be necessary to exercise control over teacher exchanges to avoid unsettling pupils and make sure the experience was positive for both pupils and teachers. Careful management arrangements would be required. In designated units ultimate responsibility must reside with the headteacher of the school, though delegated to the teacher in charge of special need, and in curriculum matters these two would share the task of development. Between the three schools and the two units an additional arrangement would be required to develop and monitor continuity of curriculum, cross-transfer of pupils where required, and the interchange of teachers. For this purpose a suitable group might consist of the heads of the three schools and the teachers in charge of special needs in the ordinary schools, together with the adviser appointed for the special school and units.

Before suggestions such as the above can be implemented, much discussion and staff training will be required, since many new skills are needed in areas where there is little contemporary experience. Some of the skills will be learned only in the doing and some of the necessary experience only in the living. So the arrangements may have to operate at a more discrete level in the beginning with the objective to be achieved that of mature curriculum interaction. Ultimate excellence is not to be judged in special school or designated units or in mainstream curriculum; it will be seen in the quality of interaction and continuity between them and in the ease with which pupils are able to move to the provision most appropriate for them at any point in their school career.

Interaction and the special school
As it would be unrealistic to expect broad and rapid movement on the above lines, the problem of the isolated special school will remain, perhaps permanently in some circumstances. However, the circumstances are not sufficient to justify curriculum limitation for any pupil who is capable of more than the special school can offer. Nor is it sufficient that individual special schools offer isolated subjects at 'O' level, as these often reflect the interests and skills of teachers rather than the pattern of studies appropriate for the pupil's aspirations. If the curriculum problem is to be resolved, either the teaching must be brought to pupils or pupils taken to the teaching, though current experience of either is limited. Arranging for pupils from special schools to be taught in ordinary schools proves difficult in practice, particularly where there is no special class support-base to offer assistance. Special school teachers must spend time supporting colleagues doing the

teaching in the ordinary school; non-teaching support must be from the special school staff; transport absorbs time, an intrusion which often offsets benefit for the pupil; and time pressures often limit social interaction with pupils in the ordinary school.

None of these problems are incapable of resolution. They exist because neither special nor ordinary school has the staff to meet them, and if staffing is made available the problems will be resolved as the work develops. The same may be said about teachers from ordinary schools teaching pupils in special schools. It involves time-out from the ordinary school, support for the teacher in the special school and time-out of both schools while travelling. It probably requires more teacher time to provide an appropriate pattern of studies than would be required if pupils were taught in ordinary schools where they would also have the advantage of joining existing teaching groups.

Other techniques might be used to broaden special schools curricula. Joint appointments of specialist teachers would allow them to teach in more than one special school; the same kind of appointment could be made between a special school and an ordinary school; peripatetic specialist teachers could combine work in special schools with teaching sick or handicapped pupils in their homes where necessary; or distance teaching techniques could be adopted based upon specially produced 'teaching packs' including videotaped sequences, the packs designed for use in specialist areas by non-specialist teachers. 'Linked' courses with colleges of further education offer another means of broadening curriculum for senior special school pupils. They may also broaden the pupils' total perspectives and take them a step nearer to the post-school world. But they do need to be 'linked' and form part of the pupils' total curriculum, with close co-operation between the staffs of school and college. These or similar measures not only broaden the special school curriculum; they go some way to reducing the separation from other schools to which many people object. That will become increasingly important as the very ethos which demands that more pupils with special needs are educated in ordinary schools also demands that those who must be educated in special schools are not subjected to unnecessary curriculum restriction as a consequence.

Beyond the school

As was shown in Chapter 1, the curriculum operates in time, its ultimate concern being with the pupils as young adults in a world of the future. Hence the curriculum must be concerned with the outside world that pupils are to enter, and in seeking to prepare them for the transition it must look for resources in that world. Like school resources, those beyond the school also form two main groups: the human resources of the community and the material resources of the environment, whether man-made or natural. These differ widely between schools and are discussed here in general terms, the details being the responsibility, once again, of the teachers in individual schools.

Community resources

The community resources for the curriculum are the same for all pupils though their significance for those with special needs will be discussed later. Here they are listed under generalized functions.

Economic resources are those through which the community maintains itself, such as the factories, shops and offices in which people work; the job centres concerned with employment; the trade unions and employers' associations; the transport system and post offices concerned with travel and communication; the banks that deal with finance; the sources of heat, light and power; and the houses and homes through which individuals acquire shelter, food and clothing.

The *social–helping resources* include the Department of Health and Social Security through its doctors, hospital and social security arrangements; local council social services; voluntary organizations for the handicapped and disadvantaged; police; the churches and religious bodies; voluntary first-aid societies and local charities in some areas.

Social-entertainment resoures include private clubs concerned with games, physical activities, hobbies, etc.; cinemas, theatres, swimming pools, etc.; cultural societies, music, literature, drama, dancing, etc.; and voluntary groups which come together for specific purposes.

Educational resources include colleges and institutes for adult education; libraries, art galleries and museums; local voluntary societies concerned with education; and societies with a specific purpose, e.g. CND, anti-vivisection, ecology.

Environmental resources

Environmental resources are also the same for all pupils though their special place in relation to children with disabilities is discussed later. They include geographical and scenic aspects of landscape; features that offer leisure activities – coast, sea, inland water, mountains, nature reserves and centres, camping facilities; buildings of historic or other interest; evidence of past or current industry; areas of conservation; examples of improper use or neglect of natural features; and evidence of past methods of land usage.

Using the resources

The above examples illustrate the complexity and variety of curriculum resources that exist beyond the school. The classifications are non-exclusive and many resources interact, together with human endeavour, in the business of daily living within the local community. Such is the richness of interaction that some pupils may be overwhelmed, and part of the function of the curriculum is to bring an order that will give meaning to the activities and stimulate thoughts and feelings without being over-deterministic. Such a structure can be devised only by those who know their pupils. The outline of a successful example used with slow learners now follows.

EXAMPLE OF RESOURCE USE. The study of the community and the environment had been related to themes of universal individual need. These were: food, shelter, clothing, heat and energy, communication and transport. A rich variety of material had been assembled for each theme and link-points between themes as well as points for application of literacy, numeracy and artistic skills were indicated in the curriculum outlines. Starting points for themes were in the community and the environment as local studies which then went back to 'beginnings' before adopting a developmental treatment which emphasized historical aspects and linked with geography wherever possible. On the developmental side, 'change' was continually emphasized as a constant aspect of human experience which was tested in an interesting manner by requiring pupils to arrange in correct sequence pictures or slides of houses, tools, clothing, vehicles, etc. On the geographical side, the concept running through the themes was 'dependence', how the things around are shaped by land, water and climate, and how the food and goods used are dependent on the work of people in other parts of the country and the world. Local products for export had been identified together with their destination to illustrate interdependence. Here, too, concepts were assessed by the arrangement of pictures of goods and produce according to country of origin or climatic conditions required for growth.

Among the impressive features of the work were the following: the amount of time spent out of school looking, observing, improving perception; the simple scientific 'experiments' designed to go with heat and energy, industry, agriculture, etc.; and the effects of the work on the vocabularies of the pupils which reflected the broadening of concepts, even if at the awareness level. Also interesting was the longitudinal development of the themes using a 'spiral' approach, with themes returned to after an interval, recapitulated and advanced at a more mature level; the combination of outside visits linked with visitors to the school; and the way slide/tape presentations linked outside activities with work in the classroom. The rich interactions achieved in this project are illustrated in figure 7 (pp. 150–151).

The extract is an example of what may be achieved in curriculum when teachers make full use of resources beyond the school and organize them to make study relevant to the pupils, promote motivation and develop concepts that assist the pupils to place themselves in the scheme of things with growing awareness of the world they will enter.

Importance for special needs

The above example could be made to serve the needs of any group of pupils through alterations of specific content and adjustment of the level of objectives. That is because of the general agreement that the curriculum should be concerned with the community served by the school and the world that pupils will enter on leaving school – principles which are not changed by the fact that pupils have special educational needs. But there are features of special needs that give special importance to these aspects of curriculum. Here are some examples for which the special needs curriculum must compensate.

1. *Difficulties with self-concepts.* Part of each individual's self-concept involves the placing of the 'self' in terms of spatial location and time perspective. Pupils with disabilities that mark them off from the normality of their peers have additional difficulties to overcome. That part of the curriculum concerned with the management of disability plays the most important part in overcoming the difficulty, but studies such as those noted enable the individual to 'place' the self, relate to the natural and social environment, and enhance normalization.
2. *Difficulties with mobility and movement.* Pupils with special needs tend to be more restricted than their peers in movement around the local environment and make less use of travel. This

Theme: HOME & FAMILY

Topic: THE HOUSE

READING
1. books
2. newspapers
3. pamphlets
4. notices
5. own work

ART & CRAFT
1. making charts
2. mounting exhibits
3. making drawings & models
4. doing simple jobs at home

SCIENCE
1. investigating soil types & effect of damp
2. water supply
3. sanitation
4. lighting & power
5. weather & house design
6. heating & insulation

LANGUAGE ACTIVITIES
1. discussion & planning & reports
2. reading simple literature
3. collecting newspaper cuttings
4. collecting other printed material
5. discussion of family life
6. discussion of home entertainment
7. socio-drama of situations from family life

EXPLORATIONS
1. visit & discuss various types of houses
2. trace development: materials, techniques
3. survey houses in given area: types; relation to family size
4. visit homes under construction
5. visit builder's yard; architects' office; estate agent's office

VISITORS TO SCHOOL
1. master builder
2. building craftsmen
3. estate agent
4. building society officer
5. housing official
6. medical officer of health

THE HOUSE

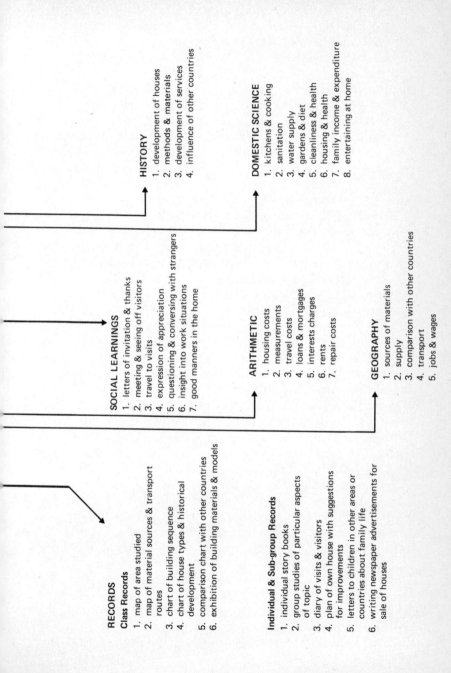

RECORDS

Class Records

1. map of area studied
2. map of material sources & transport routes
3. chart of building sequence
4. chart of house types & historical development
5. comparison chart with other countries
6. exhibition of building materials & models

Individual & Sub-group Records

1. individual story books
2. group studies of particular aspects of topic
3. diary of visits & visitors
4. plan of own house with suggestions for improvements
5. letters to children in other areas or countries about family life
6. writing newspaper advertisements for sale of houses

SOCIAL LEARNINGS

1. letters of invitation & thanks
2. meeting & seeing off visitors
3. travel to visits
4. expression of appreciation
5. questioning & conversing with strangers
6. insight into work situations
7. good manners in the home

ARITHMETIC

1. housing costs
2. measurements
3. travel costs
4. loans & mortgages
5. interests charges
6. rents
7. repair costs

GEOGRAPHY

1. sources of materials
2. supply
3. comparison with other countries
4. transport
5. jobs & wages

HISTORY

1. development of houses
2. methods & materials
3. development of services
4. influence of other countries

DOMESTIC SCIENCE

1. kitchens & cooking
2. sanitation
3. water supply
4. gardens & diet
5. cleanliness & health
6. housing & health
7. family income & expenditure
8. entertaining at home

Figure 7 Curriculum extract: senior slow learners

is not confined to those with sensory or physical obstacles to movement; pupils with learning difficulties and those with emotional disorders often lack the basic confidence required for free movement and exploration. The organized exploration of the curriculum not only broadens knowledge and outlook, it builds the knowledge and experience of movement that promote self-confidence in relation to journeying and exploration.

3. *Disability in a family often restricts family life.* The additional tasks facing families of handicapped children (especially where it is severe) often mean that families keep to themselves, there are fewer family outings, fewer visitors, and fewer visits are made. The outward looking curriculum compensates for all these restrictions through movement, places and people visited and visitors to the school. In later stages small-group or individual activities widen competence and confidence. There is also much social advantage in meeting people, receiving visitors in school and looking after their needs.

4. *Choice of career is often restricted.* Disability often limits the occupations and careers for which aspirations are realistic, and shaping the aspirations of individuals towards areas where satisfaction is possible is an important part of the education of pupils with special needs. The close study of local occupations and industry in the curriculum contributes to realistic insights into the demands that they make on individuals which may then be related to the self in the management aspects of curriculum. Without the reality of local visiting this curriculum task would be more difficult.

5. *Disability may restrict leisure outlets.* Developing satisfactory leisure activities often poses additional problems for pupils with disabilities. Choosing what is practicable, or working out means of overcoming limitation, is also an important curriculum matter. The experience of local facilities is necessary if suitable choices are to be made, and relating aspiration to personal resources is similar to that noted for occupations with almost identical curriculum consequences.

6. *Most handicapped people need outside support at some time.* Almost by definition, if support is not required the individual is hardly handicapped. Where support is needed it is important that its availability and location are known to those in need. The outgoing curriculum, by including official and voluntary agencies for handicapped people, builds the individual's knowledge, provides necessary experience, and ensures pupils will not be held back from seeking help by any fear of the unknown.

7. *Disabled people need to share experience with others similarly disabled.* There are experiences and insights concerned with disability that people without disability cannot share; hence the need of handicapped people to have some intimacy with their own kind. The outgoing curriculum can make these contacts for pupils before they leave school through association with other people and voluntary organizations. This aspect may become more important as small groups, or even individuals, are educated in ordinary schools, and the emphasis on integration increases the danger that this particular need of the handicapped may be overlooked.

8. *Disability often reduces the individual's contact with other people.* The more outgoing the curriculum and the wider the range of people contributing, the greater the possibility of broadening the social interaction of pupils with special educational needs.

9. *Pupils with special needs following normal curriculum may be subjected to additional academic pressure.* Because they are close to educational normality there may be a narrow focus upon what is required by public examinations as a consequence of which the personal and social aspects of curriculum may be overlooked. Those responsible for curriculum should guard against this. Examination curricula do not necessarily rule out personal and social objectives, but specific teaching arrangements may be necessary to make sure they are achieved. For some pupils their management curriculum may take up this point; for others counselling may achieve it; but in some cases it may require restriction of the pupil's participation in mainstream curriculum in order to secure the objectives implied above.

Throughout the discussion of resources it has been apparent that, apart from the specific management of disability, the resources required in curriculum for special needs are the same as those required in any curriculum. Differences that exist are twofold: the resources *must* be available, otherwise disadvantage is added to disability; and the resources must be utilized with exceptional efficiency if pupils with special needs are to be educated through the curriculum in a manner that will reduce the handicapping effect of their disability and allow them to live as closely as possible to normality. The use of resources beyond the school (and the quality of those aspects of curriculum) may be assessed through the answers to simple questions.

Assessing use of out-of-school resources

1. Has there been contact with public amenities and services?
2. Has there been contact with appropriate voluntary organizations?
3. Have employment prospects been fully explored in association with the specialist careers service?
4. Are pupils (where appropriate) competent in the use of public transport?
5. Have they explored the local environment—(i) town environs, (ii) countryside, (iii) links between the two?
6. Do they know how to observe, record and behave in town and country?
7. From the above experiences, have they identified leisure outlets of interest to them?
8. Are they in contact with groups or individuals who share their interests?
9. Can they use the equipment associated with their interests?
10. Are parents aware of the pupils' interests, aspirations and choice of leisure activities?
11. Has anything been done to ensure that parents are able to support the pupil in his activities?
12. Are parents and pupils aware of the desirability of further education and the opportunities for obtaining it?

The questions are not exhaustive, but where they can be answered in a positive manner they serve to indicate that the school is making use of outside resources. Positive answers also suggest that the school curriculum is reaching out into the world which the pupil will enter as a young adult.

Notes and references

1. Department of Education and Science (1959) 'Handicapped Pupils and Special Schools Regulations 1959', reg. 9; *Schools Regulations 1959*, reg. 20 (2), London, HMSO.
2. DES (1973) Circular 4/73, *Staffing of Special Schools and Classes*, Welsh Office 47/73, London, HMSO.
3. Ibid., para. 32.
4. Ibid., para. 25.
5. DES (1978) *Special Educational Needs* (Warnock Report), 8.41, London, HMSO.

6. Ibid., 7.22.
7. Ibid., 7.36.
8. Ibid., 12.24. The numbers show a slight fall from 1,239 in 1979 to 1,067 in 1980. Source: *Statistics of Education 1979* and *Statistics of Teachers in Service 1980*.
9. BRENNAN, W. K. (1979) *Curricular Needs of Slow Learners*, p. 16, London, Evans/Methuen Educational.
10. WILSON, M. and EVANS, M. (1980) *Education of Disturbed Pupils*, London, Methuen Educational.
11. DES (1978) op. cit., 12.4–15.
12. Ibid., 12.12.
13. Ibid., 12.35–64.
14. Ibid., 12.32.
15. DES (1981) Education Act 1981, 6a, 6b, London, HMSO. The responsible person may be the headteacher or a governor of a county or voluntary school or the headteacher of a nursery school. Duties: to make sure that the special needs of pupils are made known to all likely to teach them; to make sure that teachers are aware of the importance of identifying and providing for pupils with special educational needs (5b, 5c). As the duties involve the professional work of teachers, the headteacher would seem to be the better choice as responsible person, though he or she may delegate the duties to another suitable teacher in the school.
16. Ibid., 2 (5)–(7).
17. DES (1978) op. cit., 14.32.
18. Ibid., 14.34.
19. Ibid., Ch. 13. The chapter describes the proposed Advisory and Support Service for special Education. It discloses that, in a survey carried out for Warnock, 85 per cent of teachers who replied to a question on support had received no visits in the past year from an adviser in special education or from an advisory or peripatetic teacher.
20. Ibid., 12.75–81.
21. BRENNAN, W. K. (1979) op. cit., pp. 19–21.
22. For a more detailed discussion of accommodation for children with special needs in ordinary schools, see *Special Education in Mainstream Schools* from National Council for Special Education, 1 Wood Street, Stratford-upon-Avon, Warwickshire.
23. DES. (1981) op. cit., 2(3).
24. For a useful discussion of procedures with disturbed pupils, see WILSON, M. and EVANS, M. (1980) op. cit., Part 3.
25. *Special Education in Mainstream Schools*. op. cit.
26. BRENNAN, W. K. (1979) op. cit., pp. 23–8.
27. Centre for Educational Technology (June 1983) Information sheet 2, *Microelectronics and Children with Special Educational Needs*, Microelectronics Programme.
28.   (October 1983) Information sheet 4, Microelectronics Programme.

29. DES (21 November) *Microtechnology in Special Education*, presentation sponsored by DES, Bristol.
30. Dinsdale Park School, Durham LEA.
31. ILEA Resource Centre for motor and associated handicaps; Walsall LEA, Education Development Centre microelectronics development team.
32. Walsall LEA.
33. For a more extensive discussion in relation to special needs, see BRENNAN, W. K. (1979) op. cit., pp. 32–8.
34. See DES (1975) *Language for Life;* (1978b) *Mixed Ability Work in Comprehensive Schools*, London, HMSO.
35. DES (1978) op. cit., 3.39.
36. DES. (1978b) op. cit., also (1978c) *Primary Education in England*, London, HMSO.
37. McCALL, C. (1980) 'Ways of Providing for the Low Achiever in the Secondary School', in Raybould, *et al.*, eds. *Educational Review occasional publication No. 7*, Birmingham, Birmingham University.
38. See discussion in *Special Education in Mainstream Schools*, op. cit.
39. BRENNAN, W. K. (1979) op. cit., p. 18. See also DES (1978) op. cit., 7.36.
40. BRENNAN, W. K. (1982) *Changing Special Education*, Milton Keynes, Open University Press.
41. DES (1978) op. cit., Ch. 8.
42. HEGARTY, S. and POLKINGTON, K. (1981) *Educating Pupils with Special Needs in Ordinary Schools*, Windsor, NFER.
43. DES. (1978) op. cit., 3.34–45.
44. Ibid., 3.38.
45. Ibid., 13.30–31.

CHAPTER 6

Curriculum development and delivery

The development and the delivery of the curriculum are not separate; they are different aspects of a unitary process, and for that reason they are brought together in this chapter. Topics to be considered revolve upon basic curriculum problems. How are individual and common needs to be reconciled? It is possible to go some way to defeating the time pressures that have been shown to generate curriculum problems? Does the idea of mastery learning offer a way out? And is it related to the problem of individualizing curricula? Is efficient use being made of parents and community resources in the development of curricula? To many of these questions there are as yet no authoritative answers – and perhaps the nature of the curriculum will forever deny the possibility of such conclusions. But the discussion may assist in clarifying the problems facing those who educate pupils with special educational needs, identify interrelationships between topics, and suggest alternative approaches worthy of future investigation.

Curriculum and pupil development

Time, curriculum and development

The development of children and the working out of curriculum have in common that both are processes operating over time and both are concerned with learning and maturation. Yet there are qualitative differences. Though the development of pupils involves learning and leads towards maturity, it is an open-ended process, no absolute time limit is attached to it and there is no precise definition of ultimate, absolute maturity to mark the termination of the process. Moreover, in the process of development individuals will learn and mature at different rates, and those who learn slowly may, if allowed sufficient time, eventually achieve the level and standard reached sooner by their peers. Also, the life circumstances of individuals affect their experience and through it the pace and quality of their learning. This open-ended flexibility contrasts markedly with the circumstances of the curriculum. Though the curriculum is a process in time, the time element is limited by a precisely defined terminal age with no time allowed for individual differences in the pace of learning. Content is also selected, building up to a body to be established by the time defined as the end point of the curriculum process. In an attempt to ensure that most pupils will meet the curriculum demands, account is taken of the resources required for the purpose and the general standard of teaching available in the system. The end product tends to be a standardized concept of a curriculum, delivered by teachers with similar training mainly through a standard system of class teaching. When it is manifestly clear that individuals are incapable of meeting the demands of the standard curriculum, an attempt is made to introduce flexibility, first by some improvement of resources (e.g. smaller classes), but mainly by reducing what the individual is expected to learn by the end point of the curriculum. Put another way, it is the time element of curriculum that is regarded as fixed, and the content which is varied. The curriculum remains a closed process in contrast with the open nature of human development.

How, then, does the closed nature of the curriculum affect pupils with special educational needs? Take first the pupils who present for teaching but who are unable for various reasons to learn at the pace assumed by the curriculum norms. By this fact they are defined as 'educationally subnormal' or 'slow learners' or 'pupils with significant learning difficulties' according to the usage of the time, the common assumption being that the 'fault' lies with the pupils concerned rather than with the arbitrary nature of curriculum norms. Other pupils may be well able to learn at the required pace but are prevented from doing so by the demands of their disabilities. They may have the additional tasks of learning to manage their disability; there may be physical or sensory obstacles to learning; or medical or social intrusion may limit the time available for school work: circumstances not taken account of in fixing the norms of the main curriculum. Until 1972, when the statutory school leaving age was fifteen years, pupils with disabilities in special schools continued in school until sixteen years of age so that there was a recognized age allowance for their learning difficulties. However, when the statutory leaving age was raised to sixteen the additional special school year was allowed to disappear and there is now no legal recognition that pupils with special needs require additional time for learning.[1] All this takes the discussion back to the time-content pressures examined in Chapters 1 and 2 and to the conclusion that those pressures, when added to by the effect of disabilities, account for most of the curriculum problems connected with special educational needs.

Matching curriculum and development

Pupils with special educational needs face more than time-content pressures. Delayed in learning as they are by the effects of disabilities, they often find themselves forced into the pattern of curriculum developed to suit the majority of pupils who do not have special needs. The age-based class organization of schools, the assumptions about the content of the class syllabus, and the demands of internal and public examinations all presuppose expectations of normality for which the school provides. Not all pupils are expected to attain the norm. A small group will attain it easily, a larger group at a lower but acceptable level, while a further small group will fail to reach a satisfactory level. These are the expectations of a mass system with predetermined curriculum and standards, and into this framework the system forces many pupils with special educational needs. Even in special schools the pattern often remains, though with increased flexibility represented by rather wider age range in individual classes, itself often the result of the small number of pupils in the school.[2] In these circumstances it is not unusual for even a special school to measure its success on the basis of the upper and middle groups, overlooking those pupils who follow the curriculum but without successful learning. It could be said that such schools have developed 'norms' for their highly selected intake, in the process replicating the pattern of mainstream education. Both main and special schools with this type of curriculum stand in danger of regarding certain pupils as failing when in reality it is the school curriculum which is failing to meet their needs.

Among pupils most at risk from the above circumstances are those who deviate most from the normal expectations of mainstream schools, and the risks will be greater as more of them are placed in those schools for their education. Pupils with severe learning difficulties where the deviance may be intellectual, emotional and social are most at risk. Others, with moderate learning difficulties, may achieve an emotional and social match in the school that is complicated by severe deviance in intellectual potential, learning ability and scholastic achievement. Emotional immaturity or instability, on its own or with associated learning difficulty, is known to cause consternation in many ordinary schools through the problems generated. Any disability or combination of disabilities resulting in generally delayed learning or patterns of specific learning difficulty also introduce complications of curriculum, teaching and class placement. The common factor across all the disabilities is that the pupils do not 'fit' the main organization of the school, which may be perfectly appropriate and efficient for the majority of pupils.

There are many ways in which mainstream schools attempt to resolve the above problems. The widely practised banding or setting techniques represent a first approach; withdrawal or extraction from ordinary classes (however organized) is another method, specially useful where learning difficulties are specific; and the organization of special classes within the schools, with some controlled interaction, is another choice. The quality of balance between special classes (in particular those designated by the LEA) and mainstream classes may meet a wide range of needs – their organization was discussed in Chapter 5. Nurture groups in early primary and sanctuaries in secondary schools represent attempts to meet deviant emotional needs, while the so-called disruptive classes are intended to do the same for behaviour disorders.[3] Peripatetic teaching services meet a wide range of needs in primary schools and are increasingly adding to classroom flexibility by using their skills alongside the class-teacher without separation of the pupils; there are signs that teachers of special needs in secondary schools are beginning to use similar methods.[4] All these techniques help offset the inflexibility of the mass system but they have marked limitations. They do little to change the fundamental inflexibility; they mainly rely on separation; and they tend to be more concerned with organization, teaching methods and pupil learning than with the question of suitability of curriculum for those pupils for whom the mainstream curriculum is found wanting in content, objectives or phasing.

The case for extended curriculum

More serious in its effect on pupils with special educational needs is the limitation of curriculum imposed by the attempt to meet their needs within the common pattern of mainstream education. First, there is limitation in breadth arising from the restriction of subjects and experience made necessary by learning problems; second, the abrupt cut-off at sixteen years of age leaves the curriculum incomplete for many pupils.

At sixteen many pupils with special needs have not reached the level of personal and social maturity attained by most of their peers, and among these are some seriously backward in scholastic attainment. Other pupils, though normally mature and with adequate learning potential, are retarded in learning as a result of the many additional learning tasks they have faced because of their disabilities. Both groups require curriculum extension – in breadth, in continuation, or in both. The problems are not separate and both could be largely resolved by extending the curriculum in time so that pupils with special needs could more easily continue their education beyond sixteen and to the point necessary for the attainment of appropriate curriculum objectives. A time extension that applied with certainty wherever necessary would have a retrospective effect on curriculum by removing time pressures *from the beginning*. From the start there could be a realistic broader perspective in content planning, and the development of the curriculum could more closely match that of the pupils. On the social side it would no longer be necessary to attempt essential learning for which immature fifteen- to sixteen-year-olds were not ready simply because of the fear that if not attempted there would be no further opportunity.

The freedom arising from removal of time pressure would also affect the quality of education. Individualized learning and curriculum (always time consuming) would become more practical; reinforcement and generalization more liberal; knowledge and skill more closely related; and intellectual, emotional and social aspects of curriculum much better integrated in harmonious behaviour. Even greater benefit could be secured from time extension that was open ended. Children with severe or complex disabilities are continually subject to tensions and pressures, sometimes in repeated cycles of fluctuations, sometimes in a random and unpredictable manner, at other times as the result of planned medical intervention. An open-ended system would allow teachers to modify curriculum and teaching to accommodate changes with a minimum of stress for the pupils and in a way totally related to current and future needs.

Within the system as it currently operates schools do all they are able to secure curriculum extensions. Special schools link with secondary schools or colleges of further education in order to

broaden curriculum and similar techniques are used with children
with special needs in ordinary schools. In both types of school, 'life
skills' or school leavers' courses extend the curriculum base in the
final years, often including part-time 'bridging' or 'taster' courses
in the colleges. The transition from school to the wider world has
in recent years occupied a more important place in curricula for
special needs, combined in some LEAs with attendance at school
leavers' centres. Most of these measures go some way to broaden
curriculum for pupils with special needs, though there is evidence
that they are less successful where handicap is severe. However,
they contribute little to the resolution of the time-pressure
problem, as in general they operate within the statutory period of
education and to some extent displace other activities.[5] Also,
provision varies considerably between different LEAs and schools,
so there can be no certainty that the opportunities are available for
all pupils with special educational needs.

The importance attached to the transition from school to work
still falls below that accorded to it in the Warnock Report.[6] Two
major weaknesses have been identified. The first is that
insufficient attention is given to career guidance for pupils with
special needs, and this is reflected in the under-use of specialist
careers officers. Overall, most success appears to be associated
with physical disabilities, with least success associated with the
needs of pupils who are maladjusted or have moderate learning
difficulties.[7] The second weakness involves very immature pupils
with moderate learning difficulties and those whose learning
difficulties are severe. These pupils are often not included in the
work of specialist careers officers and there is an assumption in
their schools (which may be correct) that they are not employable;
unfortunately these circumstances are frequently associated with
school curricula that concentrate on basic subjects to the neglect of
attempts to establish positive leisure and associated activities.[8]

The situation appears to confirm the importance attached above
to the difficulties caused by a lack of 'match' between curriculum
phasing and the development of pupils with special needs.
Maladjusted pupils and those whose immaturity is associated with
learning difficulties are among those whose personal development
at the end of their school career may be inappropriate for many of
the activities associated with school leavers' courses or those
which anticipate the more mature behaviour of young adults. For
these pupils the answer may rest with extension in time to provide
guidance towards a level of maturity where the demands of such
courses may be appropriate and meaningful. The essential
requirement is extended school attendance or continuation in a
college of further education.

This conclusion replicates that of the Warnock Committee in 1978:

> We recognize that relatively few young people with disabilities or significant difficulties have achieved by the age of 16 either their full educational potential or an adequate degree of maturity to make a smooth transition to adult life . . . Educational provision must therefore be far more widely available to such young people beyond the age of 16.[9]

That conclusion was applied to all young people with special needs and was no doubt influenced by a research finding that the proportion of non-handicapped young people in continued education was five times higher than the proportion of those handicapped.[10] The report calls for strong encouragement for parents and young people to seek continued education; LEAs are reminded of their duty to provide continued education for all who want it between the ages of 16 and 19 and the need to ensure that there are adequate numbers of places for young people with special educational needs.[11] Progress towards the objectives of increased participation in continued education has been slow and uneven for a number of reasons. Many of the courses required involve curricula outside the experience of staff in continued education, for which planning and training are necessary; the increasing numbers of young unemployed also make additional demands in the same area; central government restrictions have curtailed available resources; and the absence of legislation on continued education in the Education Act 1981 appears to have concentrated initiatives arising from it mainly in the statutory years.

The adverse circumstances in no way weaken the case for extended education for pupils with special needs, in particular for those whose maturity or learning is delayed as a result of disability. There is evidence that much thought is being applied to the problem in further education, and this is discussed in the following section.

Further education and extended curriculum

The Warnock Report recognized that for many young people with special educational needs an establishment of further education would be a more appropriate setting than a school in which to continue their education. It saw a need for the development of a variety of courses in the colleges and for sensitive and skilful placement of students among the courses. Stress was put on courses for school leavers of low educational achievement and social competence, many of them deficient in basic skills, day- or block-release courses for young workers with special needs, and special vocational courses at operative level. Existing provision was regarded as having developed in a 'piecemeal and uncoordinated fashion', so in the necessary extensions a 'coherent pattern of provision should be developed'. In order to achieve efficiency the following critical developments were regarded as essential.[12]

Special education in further education – necessary critical development
1. Higher status for special needs work.
2. Awareness of special needs among all staff.
3. Appropriate training for teachers with special needs responsibility.
4. Development of suitable special needs curricula.
5. Necessary adaptations to premises.
6. Provision of appropriate special equipment.
7. Suitable and adequate input from supporting services.
8. Financial support for students with special needs where required.

The list accords with the view that provision for young people with special educational needs had received little attention, was relatively complex and largely uncharted.[13]

Though further education is subject to the obstacles to progress noted, recent surveys indicate some progress, albeit still lacking in cohesion, determined by chance factors, locally variable and falling short of systematic provision.[14] Important gaps in provision have been identified as lack of opportunity for young people with emotional problems or severe learning difficulty and those whose learning falls between the moderate and severe levels; absence of day places for able physically handicapped; and failure to provide for young people who are mentally capable but whose severe physical difficulties rule out placement in a sheltered workshop.[15] Other findings indicate that quality of provision is still variable, there is often insufficient attention to fundamental curricular elements, and where curriculum development exists it is usually carried out in isolation.[16]

On the positive side there is evidence that a good deal of planning of provision and thinking about curriculum is under way, though varying in quality and intensity between LEAs.[17] Some has reached the stage of formulated policy with officer responsibility; others respond to individual needs of students; but where services are substantially improved it is usually on the basis of well-established co-operation between special and further education advisers and the career services. More colleges, too, have formulated policies for special needs. Documentation is variable in quantity and quality, sometimes consisting mainly of a catalogue of difficulties together with future plans to overcome them, especially where the concern is mainly with physical disabilities. There is now a concern, however, stimulated by the Further Education Curriculum Review and Development Unit, that progress in the field shall be curriculum-led, with staff working together sharing materials and experience. A report sponsored by the FEC stressed the need for curriculum balance.[18]

> There is a balance to be found at two levels – ensuring special needs are met without further isolating students, and preparing them for the practicalities of work and adult living without unduly narrowing their educational experience and opportunities for personal development.

It also indicated that many new courses or adaptations would be needed, and pointed up the need for individualization:

> These courses need to be custom-built to an extent in order to take account of students' needs, their wishes and aspirations, and local conditions. At both school and FE levels there will be specific curricular concerns relating to older pupils such as the possible need for social skills training.

Note here the common concern for continuity between the curriculum the young person follows in school and that which he or she enters in the college. The more immature or scholastically retarded the pupil, the more important it is to secure continuity, for these are the pupils whose needs generate new curriculum requirements in the college. Note also the stress on local conditions. There is a regional or even national aspect of the curriculum of FE courses that contrasts markedly with the individual needs of pupils with disabilities, and with the acceptance of curriculum responsibility in individual schools which is the hallmark of special education and has been accorded first importance in earlier chapters. The local aspect may not be so immediately obvious as necessary to teachers who in their normal work are accustomed to work to FE syllabuses. Securing acceptance of this kind of continuity and responsibility may become an important part of the task of special needs tutors in further education.

A good example of curriculum thinking in FE is in the publication *Skills for Living*, subtitled 'A curriculum framework for young people in further education with moderate learning difficulties'.[19] The framework sets out to secure a balance between preparation for work, preparation for adult life including the development of coping skills, and preparation for a life in which there may be little employment but ample free time. A development strategy is worked out as 'defining the aims', 'defining the context', 'planning the content', and 'relating teaching and assessment strategies'. The *aims* selected were those considered appropriate from *A Basis for Choice*[20]. Nos. 1, 2, 4, 5 and 11, though these were re-defined as intermediate aims more appropriate for pupils with moderate learning difficulties with the following result. Young persons should be assisted to:

Aim 1.   1. Understand themselves and the society around them.
Aim 2.   2. Make good use of their time.
            3. Work.
Aim 4.   4. Get on with other people.
            5. Present themselves well.
Aim 5.   6. Be responsible.
Aim 11.   7. Stay solvent.
            8. Cope in most normal circumstances.

No order of priority was suggested by the list, which was left to local determination of the balance noted above. The probability is that most teachers of pupils with moderate learning difficulties would agree about the suitability of the aims for immature pupils who required a curriculum based upon living skills in further education.

Next came *defining the context*, a process which made the focus of attention local conditions: place of teaching and learning, family background, the community, proposed length of the course, time available, points of entry and exit (whether or not fixed), etc; from this the scope of the local course would be defined and decisions made about 'who would teach what', etc. In *planning the content* it was decided that instead of formulating precise objectives (which it will be recalled this study has regarded as a doubtful procedure at curriculum level) a 'brainstorming session' would be used to generate ideas for topics and areas from which a selection could be made. The selection resulted in a series of interconnecting 'webs' which might just as easily have been enumerated in checklist fashion. Connected with this was *assessment and teaching strategies*. Here the idea of a formal syllabus was rejected as inappropriate where students would be likely to have different starting points, learning needs, and rates of progress. The alternative chosen was a list of checkpoints of competencies which it was aimed to develop in the students, these being listed without sequence or priorities. Prerequisites for successful teaching were noted, though not elaborated, as pre-course assessment of students; sensitivity to their needs allied to continuous assessment and curriculum modification; general awareness by all teachers of the causes of learning difficulty; and precise identification of individual difficulties.

In the documentation the 11 aims are associated with 47 topics for which 21 activities are listed with over 100 suggestions for suitable resource material of reasonable availability. An example of the style of documentation follows.[21]

Aim 5 of ABC: to provide a basis on which the young person acquires a set of moral values applicable to issues in contemporary society.

Intermediate aim 6: to be responsible.

Items	Activities	Resources
Recognizing a problem.	Discussion on real or imagined situations, i.e. what would you do if . . . ?	Schools Council moral education project *Lifelines. Somebody's Daughter,* ILEA TV series.
	Taking responsibility in the family, and discussion of some associated emotion.	1. *Living in a City;* 2. *Learning in a City* – two packs from ILEA Learning Materials Service.
	Rejection/adoption/fostering.	
Consider other people.	Personal rights and responsibilities.	
	My rights, or your rights?	*Gamester's Handbook,* Hutchinson, 1978.
	The resolution of conflict.	*It's Your Future,* National Extension College, 1978.
	Games, e.g. Shipwrecked.	
	Balloon debates.	*Civil Liberty: The Guide to Your Rights,* National Council for Civil Liberties, 1978.
Safety and care of equipment.	Recognizing the value of equipment.	
	Careful use and packing away of equipment.	Cycling tests and traffic sense.
	Implications of breakage and loss of work for others.	Material from Royal Society for the Prevention of Accidents.
	Safety at home and on the roads.	Highway Code.
Time.	Telling the time.	
	Being punctual; planning time 'budgets' – how long it takes to do various things.	
	See also 'To cope' section.	

This curriculum document represents a commendable effort to generate thinking in an area of further education where the curriculum required by the students is likely to be new to the teachers and outside their experience. It also represents restraint in emphasizing local responsibility and refraining from setting a detailed syllabus in an area of education where teachers are accustomed to work to curriculum and syllabuses laid down by outside bodies. Nor does the document stand alone. It is part of an extensive effort to stimulate new thinking, as indicated in Appendix 4. This is just as well, for considerable skill and expertise will be required to translate the curriculum framework into relevant and successful classroom activities. The reality in the schools and colleges is that there is expertise in the area represented by the curriculum document; and it is to be found in the schools.

The pupils for whom the FE document is intended are those immature pupils who have been unable to benefit from similar curricula found to be the most successful in a Schools Council survey.[22] There also exists a body of experience and practice derived from relevant curricula which has been documented and reviewed.[23] With the extension of time and the added maturity of young people, the curricula developed in the schools should become appropriate, especially given the wider and more adult context of the FE college. The most direct way forward, locally, rests in co-operation between successful special schools for pupils with moderate learning difficulties and the local college; and the most immediate source of teachers with practical experience that is relevant is in the same schools. Unless the intention is to deliberately ignore existing experience, school–college co-operation offers the best hope for an early extension of the kind of curriculum envisaged in *Skills for Living*. Moreover, as already indicated, the existence of a college continuation course should allow schools to revise curricula for immature pupils and orientate it firmly to the establishment of readiness for the college course skills – a fact that might influence the college course. This indicates the need to see the college course as an extension of the school curriculum, not an appendage to it; there would be a powerful case for some interchange of teachers, another reason for which rests in the importance of a smooth transfer. It is as important as transfer at any point in educational progress and is essential if the development of curriculum is to match and keep in phase with the personal development of the pupils.

Mastery learning

The concept of mastery learning has been developed in the context of general education in complex modern societies.[24] It starts in a criticism of the assumption in mass education, and in many special schools, that not all pupils will succeed in learning curriculum material at a satisfactory, mastery level. Among those failing to reach this level in the ordinary curriculum, a different standard is applied – according to the concept – to the learning of personal survival skills, where all except the severely handicapped are expected to establish efficient mastery. Within modern society, mastery is necessary to ensure economic survival, to understand the complexities of citizenship and to assimilate essential values from the hidden curriculum of school and life. An educational system which assumes from the start that a sizeable group of children will fail to learn common aspects of curriculum effectively can no longer be regarded as appropriate for modern conditions.

Importance of the mastery concept

The basic assumption of mastery learning is that between 90 and 95 per cent of pupils are capable of effectively learning common curriculum material if provided with appropriate conditions for learning. The essential conditions involve time and educational needs. Each learner must be allowed the time required to master learning according to his or her aptitude for the subject matter. Techniques of teaching and learning must be developed that reduce to a minimum the time required to establish mastery by pupils with low levels of learning aptitude. To achieve these conditions requires changes in attitudes to teaching and learning.[25]

Aptitude for learning must be taken to represent the time needed to establish mastery and it may be modified by environmental circumstances in early life, by education or by learning about how to learn in later education, so that as far as possible the time element in learning is reduced to a minimum. Quality of instruction is to be assessed, not in current terms of effectiveness with groups, but by the flexibility with which instruction is modified to accommodate the learning needs of individuals. Variation in the ability of pupils to understand instruction must become a challenge to the teacher to devise techniques to overcome difficulties rather than regard them as deficiencies in the pupils. Likewise perseverance, the time the pupil is prepared to spend on learning, should be accepted as changeable – a question of securing and increasing motivation by appropriate means. Finally, there is the time available for learning. It is essential for mastery learning that the learner is allowed the time he or she needs for mastery, and that time will vary across curriculum areas according to the learner's aptitude for different subjects. The challenge to the teacher is that of reducing the time required by the pupil through strategies involving instructional methods, motivation, materials, and even school organization. The approach does not assume it is possible for every learner to achieve high aptitude, but it is assumed that the learning of almost all can be improved if instruction and the use of student time are made more effective. Bloom suggests that the ratio between fast and slow learners may be reduced from six-to-one to three-to-one.[26]

Nor does mastery learning assume that all students will acquire mastery in all areas of curriculum. It is most easily attained where pupils have a common minimum of prerequisite learning at the start of a course or where the subject itself demands little preknowledge; mastery is more difficult to attain where previous knowledge is important and exists at different levels among the pupils starting the course. On this basis early basic learning appears more favourable than later complicated sequential learning tasks. The importance of the curricular area also has influence. Where there is a requirement that all *must* learn a subject then it is logical to assume that its importance predisposes to mastery learning. Where later learning is dependent upon earlier stages then mastery in those stages is important if overall learning is to be effective. Curricular areas where knowledge is finite and stable with considerable agreement about the behaviours and ideas involved, or which emphasize convergent thinking processes towards generally accepted conclusions, offer clear opportunities for mastery learning. The time required to establish mastery in some areas may not be justified by the importance of the learning in the pupil's curriculum, especially if context learning will meet curricular needs. The interests, attitudes and aspirations of the individual pupils must affect the importance accorded to different curriculum areas when deciding where mastery is desirable.

This concept of mastery learning, then, reverses the current curriculum equation. Curriculum content and quality, formerly the variable, now becomes the fixed element – while time, formerly fixed, now becomes the variable. For most pupils the alteration is limited as their curriculum closes at sixteen years of age, and it could be argued that complete operation of the concept of mastery learning requires an-open-ended curriculum.

Applications of mastery learning

Within the closed curriculum as it exists, mastery learning must be applied through the selection of curriculum content priorities and the achievement of balance within them. Equally essential is the careful selection of the levels at which curriculum objectives are to be attained, so that sufficient time is available for even the slowest pupil to achieve mastery learning in areas essential to meet their curricular needs. This is exactly what the differential-learning approach and target priorities overlay – see Chapter 3 – were intended to achieve, at the same time ensuring that, in concentrating on essentials, breadth of curriculum was not neglected – see also figures 4 and 6. Mastery imperatives will appear in the *must* area of the 'function' level; that is *throughness* for Knowledge and *proficiency* for Skill in figure 4; and *direct* for Experience and *operational* for Attitudes in figure 6. How far these qualities are extended into the *should* or *could* areas of the 'function' level will depend on the aptitude of pupils, the quality of teaching, the degree of pupil understanding, the resolution of perseverence problems, and the efficient utilization of pupils' learning time that is, on the aspects of mastery learning discussed above.

Another approach to mastery learning was developed in the teaching of basic number in St Francis Residential Special School, Birmingham, during the 1960s. The content of the curriculum is set out in Tansley and Gulliford;[27] here the concern is with organization, which we may call 'curriculum setting'. First, the number curriculum from the readiness level up to the arithmetic and associated concepts required for social competence was separated into sections based upon sequences of curriculum *content* – what the pupils had to master in each section or 'set'. Then the timetable was arranged so that all pupils were engaged in number work at the same time, which made all teachers available to staff the sets. Pupils were placed in the sets on the basis of their learned achievement: what they had already learned to an acceptable mastery level. Once the scheme was in operation pupils joining the school (which they did at different ages) were placed in sets according to the level of their established mastery as indicated in individual achievement testing.

Each set had a closely defined content of number knowledge, computational skill, practical application and conceptual under-standing; allied to these were criterion-based assessment measures in continuous use by the teacher in classroom activities and checked independently before a pupil moved from the set; teachers knew exactly what learning the pupil had to establish in their set, what he knew on entry, and what learning followed. With this pattern of curriculum and teaching established, each pupil entered the curriculum at an appropriate set and moved through subsequent sets at a pace regulated by his own learning and mastery of content. As all teachers were available, the number of pupils in a set was small, around ten to twelve, all working on similar material though at different speeds, so that teaching within each set was highly individualized. Teachers also knew exactly what teaching materials were necessary for the limited objectives of their set; gradually a richness developed at each level that enhanced flexibility, the key to success. With pupils each progressing at their own rate, movement from set to set was dictated by progress and had therefore to be available as required. This meant that sometimes 'clusters' of pupils might develop at certain points and threaten to overwhelm a set. As the system matured this threat disappeared. Such clusters meant a reduction of the numbers of pupils in earlier sets; the availability of materials and adaptability of the teachers made it possible to organize additional sets at the point of the cluster.

The system at this Birmingham school had most of the features of mastery learning. There was a curriculum *must*, fixed for all except the most handicapped; there was individualization of materials and teaching methods; and there was time allowed for individuals to learn to mastery level at their own pace. There was even a group of pupils always in the school for whom the basic number curriculum proved inappropriate. Often emotionally disturbed, or with specific additional learning difficulties, they could not have completed the work by school-leaving age. The tight structure of the curriculum allowed these pupils to be identified as early as possible, though only after having opportunity to work in the curriculum. The alternative curriculum provided for them was based upon establishing awareness and the skills which would allow them to seek help when it was made necessary by their lack of number competence. This work, too, was organized in 'sets' so that it fitted the pattern common in the school.

Implications for curriculum

Of the implications of mastery learning for curriculum, first and foremost is that for full advantage for children with special educational needs the concept of mastery learning should operate in an open-ended curriculum. This may not require legal extension of statutory education but it does require the full implementation of the Warnock Report on continued education.[28] Second, mastery learning depends upon efficiency of teaching in order to minimize learning time for slower learners. Third, efficiency itself will rest on flexibility that enables teachers to individualize their work. And fourth, mastery learning may be pointless unless the priorities and balance of curriculum have been carefully derived from an informed study of the special needs of the pupils for whom it is intended. An added bonus would accrue from mastery learning in an open-ended curriculum in that it would make the ideal of a common curriculum easier to attain and enhance the contribution of education to social cohesion. There is far to go before these ideals are brought within reach.

Approaches to the common core

The School Curriculum,[29] as we saw in Chapter 2, extended the discussion of a common core curriculum to include special schools. Subjects in the common core were the concern of *A Framework for the School Curriculum*.[30] The DES document saw English, mathematics, religious education and physical education running through the whole of compulsory education, joined by science from the primary school onward, with, for most pupils, a modern language at the secondary stage. There was concern about the narrow curriculum usually on offer to less able pupils, as indicated by the comment that the curriculum should be judged by the range of subjects available for individual pupils rather than the total range in the school. A discussion of preparation for the post-school world indicated how a wider range of subjects might contribute at that level.

At about the same time a discussion from HMI made use of primary and secondary surveys to re-state the core in terms of understanding and experience to which all pupils should have access.[31] Summarized, the areas of experience are as follows: at primary level – language and literacy, mathematics, science, aesthetics (including physical education); secondary areas include – aesthetic and creative, ethical, linguistic, mathematical, scientific, physical, social and political and spiritual. These listings have much in common, the differences being those necessary to take account of the maturation of pupils as they progress through school. The document also commented on teacher expectations. The need for a school frame of reference within which subject teaching could operate; recognition that a subject could contribute in other areas or to many skills; awareness that individual pupils may need different programmes; curriculum continuity between stages of education and into further education: all these emphasized a common curriculum, not only within schools but between them. These two documents stimulated considerable discussion as well as fears that *A Framework for the School Curriculum* went too far, making the case for a common curriculum an argument for more central control. Professional opinion showed a strong preference for the HMI view and led to a revised statement from the DES, *The School Curriculum*, issued one year later.[32]

The School Curriculum represents a more acceptable case for a common curriculum. It is emphatic:

> It is the individual schools that shape the curriculum for each pupil. Neither the government nor the local authorities should specify in detail what the schools should teach. This is for the schools themselves to determine.[33]

At the same time the common curriculum was seen as going beyond individual schools. In each LEA there should be a framed policy for curriculum within which schools could work and for which local resources should be efficiently deployed. Within each school there should be co-operation between the governors and staff, with parents and the local community brought into discussion. Every school should set out its aims in writing and regularly assess how far they are being achieved, in the school and for individual pupils. The curriculum for each pupil should be broad and balanced, ensuring continuity within the school and between the stages of education, to which end records should be kept and passed between schools. The common curriculum should be challenging:

> All pupils should be encouraged throughout their school career to reach out to the limit of their capabilities. This is a formidable challenge to any school, since it means that the school's expectation of every pupil must relate to his individual gifts and talents. It is as necessary to meet this challenge for the ablest as for those who learn slowly and with difficulty or who have special educational needs, whether they are in ordinary or special schools: no group's needs should be subordinate.[34]

The subject areas from *A View of the Curriculum* were accepted with emphasis on the need to achieve curriculum unity and balance, the relationship to adult and working life, and the pupils' perception of the relevance of education outside the school. There was also acknowledgement of the importance of teaching methods, which were considered inseparable from what was being taught at every level of ability. In terms of the present discussion, the reference to special schools is of the first importance:

> But like all other schools special schools must try to offer a curriculum which fully meets the educational needs of each of their pupils in the way best suited to the pupil. They too need a written statement of their aims and, in the light of it, to appraise regularly the effectiveness of the programme offered to each pupil. Local authorities, therefore, will wish to engage special schools in local discussions on their policy for curriculum. This will also help to maintain continuity in the programmes of work of pupils who transfer between special and ordinary schools.[35]

If this is interpreted in terms of the rest of the pamphlet, then pupils with special needs (in ordinary or special schools) should be following a curriculum which includes English, mathematics, science, religious education and physical education; their humanities studies should be such that will give them 'lasting benefit' and they should have opportunities for practical and aesthetic activities. Where they can benefit from it, and where curriculum pressures allow, most pupils should study a modern language. The provision of this common curriculum would be through a combination of main and special curricula according to the needs of the pupil.

Common core and special schools

Mary Wilson[36] was concerned with curriculum in special schools, so she looked at common curriculum 'from the other side', including it in her discussion of the rationale of curriculum planning. She considers a core of subjects as 'extremely important for most if not all pupils.

These are: art, craft or home economics, English (language and literature), a foreign language, geography, history, mathematics, music, physical education and games, religious education and science.' These subjects are related to the areas of experience from *A View of the Curriculum*, which are accepted by Wilson, though she is aware of the extent to which that implies a reconsideration of curriculum. In her discussion, the interaction of subjects and experiences is highlighted and related to aesthetic and creative experience, wonder and mystery leading to the spiritual, and social and political morality leading to absolute ethical standards. More important, Wilson sees the need for curriculum unity and understands the reality that aesthetic, ethical and spiritual experience cannot be predicted but only made likely through the provision of curriculum – precisely the concern that led Eisner to formulate his expressive objectives.

Wilson is explicit about the attitudes which children with special needs should share: self-confidence, self-discipline, consideration for other, adaptability, perseverance and concentration, initiative, sensitivity and imagination are identified as common qualities planned for in special schools, and there can be no argument about their desirability for all pupils in all schools. The same applies to skills; many which are assimilated incidentally by most children must be taught to children with special educational needs and should form part of a common curriculum. On these Wilson is more forthright than HMI, and identifies:

> communication skills (listening, speaking, reading, spelling and handwriting), those related particularly to mathematics and science (computation, measurement, investigatory skills), and those relating to personal/social competence (dexterity, agility, self-care, social skills).[37]

Wilson's discussion makes clear how much there is in common between main and special curricula, and prompts the idea of a *curriculum shift*. This 'shift' refers to the fact that to some extent for special needs what is hidden in main curriculum becomes planned and what is planned becomes taught; and it refers to the associated difficulty of the increased pressure on the taught curriculum for special needs. Wilson relates her discussion to the broad based and core-and-periphery approaches described in Chapter 3, and she concludes her comments with the following insight:

> The core of an apple may be small, leaving a larger volume for tasting, but it is the core which contains the germ of future development.[38]

From that derives the quality of learning that was specified in Chapter 3 for the function level of differential learning.

Common core: an assessment

The common core of curriculum will be increasingly looked for and expected as a feature of education. It rests on concepts of equity and of common needs in children; it is made more manageable by the move to comprehensive secondary education and by more provision for special educational needs in ordinary schools; it reduces the problems associated with transfer between stages of education, or between schools where families move; and it offers the possibility of improving social cohesion in a time of social uncertainty. The advantages should not distract attention from weaknesses, however. The main curriculum itself requires improvement – in the teaching of science, the availability and standard of modern languages, observational and perceptual aspects of art and craft, and in relevance to the adult and working world.[39] Curricula for special needs also require improvement, in mainstream and special schools, with special attention to the humanities, social and aesthetic areas in a general raising of standards.[40] A common curriculum that is inadequate will do good to no one. Furthermore, the concept itself requires more thorough thinking through. Current statements concentrate overwhelmingly on the subject-content aspect of curriculum and on subject-based experiences. Skills are only implied, attitudes there as part of passing discussion, while objectives appear rarely and in an almost meaningless context. Statements tend to be in general with little attempt to define priorities or to establish minimum levels of competence to be achieved in the common areas. Wilson has moved the discussion in a more positive direction, and White[41] defined the core as consisting of subjects requiring participation for understanding, and the level as that which enabled the pupil to decide whether or not he wished to spend more time learning in the area. These are moves in the right direction, though there is still far to go to make common core curriculum an operational reality.

Individualization

Individualization is not a new concept. It has often been referred to as 'individualization of treatment', a form used by Descöeudres[42] in the 1920s and adopted by Tansley and Gulliford in the 1960s.[43] Wallin[44] made use of the concept in the USA as 'individualized instruction' and presented a wide survey of its use as a technique. In the following discussion a distinction is made between individualized teaching and individualized curriculum, for though these aspects are unified in practice the distinction contributes to clarity of understanding.

Individualized teaching
Individualized teaching does not mean one teacher to each pupil. It does mean that at any given time pupils will be in a teaching or learning situation most appropriate to individual learning needs, after those needs have been determined through comprehensive and continuing educational assessment. At one time a pupil may be

learning on his own; at another time in a group or class; teaching may now be individual, later in a small group, at another time in a class. Where necessary the pupil may be taught by a specialist teacher, in a situation outside the classroom if required. Pupils working towards the same objectives may use different materials, differently graded, with more or less teacher attention as required. When interacting with pupils, the teacher will vary his or her approach, language, questions, and the level at which answers are acceptable – the differences according with the learning aptitudes, the degree of understanding, the motivation and the curricular needs of individual pupils. Where there is a wide range of learning aptitude, or where pupils with special needs are in mainstream classes, it is important that the teacher communicates clearly through his or her manner that, though pupils are treated differently in terms of their learning, all are equally valued as persons. Where the teacher does this successfully it assists pupils to perceive the difference between the assessment of behaviour and the acceptance of a person, a valuable social and moral distinction, especially for pupils with learning difficulties or those who are emotionally disturbed. This, too, is a bonus from individualized teaching.

A more precise outline of individualized procedures comes from work in the USA.[45] Though derived from mainstream education, it points up approaches of value to teachers of pupils with special needs.

Principles of individualized teaching
1. Develop a general class programme within which sub-goals and topics are organized to allow individualization.
2. Ensure learning materials are sufficient for the range in the group.
3. When teaching, think of individuals and not of the class.
4. Individualize instructional tasks, rates of learning, amount of repetition, and grading of materials and tasks.
5. Allow each pupil to learn at his or her own pace.
6. Keep adequate individual records of learning.
7. Encourage self-directed learning by the pupils.
8. Establish standards and procedures that enable pupils to judge their own work.

In many respects the principles of individualized teaching are also those of efficient teaching. Individualized teaching means using the widest selection of available techniques –not just one-to-one situations – in a manner intimately related to the identified special educational needs of the pupils. There are three reasons for this emphasis. First, mainstream teachers are trained as class teachers, in normal circumstances teaching one curriculum through methods which focus on one level of the class distribution of learning ability. In future more pupils with special educational needs will join those classes for some part of their learning time, and if their needs are to be met some changes in methods will be essential. Second, some other teachers, particularly in special schools, base their teaching on a total *individual* approach in terms of both teaching methods and curriculum. This approach is rarely successful, because the available facilities (even in special schools) are not sufficiently adequate to support it, teachers have not been trained to operate it, and it demands a level of teaching skill found in only a small band of most excellent teachers. Third, education is concerned with social skills which for many pupils with special needs can be developed only in a situation of *social* interaction where teachers may exercise *individual* guidance. In the undifferentiated class situation the teacher is unable to offer guidance, while in the totally individual situation the pupil is denied social experiences. Individualized teaching avoids both dangers and contributes to the all-round development of the pupil.

Individualized curriculum

Individualized curriculum means that from all the curriculum resources of the school a selection is made of the objectives, curriculum content and learning experiences most calculated to meet the identified curricular needs of individual pupils. This does not require that each pupil will have a separate *individual* curriculum. A pupil may share some curriculum activities with all other pupils at the same stage of development, other activities may be shared with only some of the pupils, while some individual work may be provided for the pupil alone. At any given time each pupil in the school will be engaged in learning activities appropriate for himself or herself. In individualized curriculum that is the only criterion governing the selection of activities. The nature of the curriculum will permit many corporate activities shared by pupils as they work towards social objectives, but the criterion for their inclusion is that they meet the curricular needs of the individual pupils engaged in them. Some of these activities will form part of a common core and apply to all pupils, though there may be differences in the level to which they are taken by individuals. At its simplest level, where a pupil with special needs is following mainstream curriculum with special curriculum limited to the management of disability, individualized curriculum may require no more than an individual timetable to ensure the pupil is in the right place at the required time. The other extreme would be represented by a seriously handicapped pupil following a totally alternative curriculum but participating in social activities and corporate gatherings forming part of planned curriculum and contributing to hidden aspects.

Between the above extremes a wide variety of combinations will be necessary to contain the curricular demands generated by the range of special needs in pupils, spreading as they will across main and special curricula. Some of the combinations may be summarized as follows.

Individualization of curriculum combinations

1. Alterations in the pace by which the pupil moves through objectives of main or special curricula.
2. Refinement of curriculum objectives into smaller steps to assist pupils to overcome difficulties.
3. Changes in the curriculum content or learning experiences to overcome difficulty or maintain progress through improved motivation.
4. Changes in the level at which pupils are expected to attain objectives, e.g. function to context.
5. Any necessary combinations of 1 to 4.
6. Substitution of alternative curriculum for part of main or special curricula.
7. Full substitution in taught curriculum.

The concept of individualized curriculum rests on the important basic assumption that there exists in the school a carefully constructed general curriculum, effectively sequenced, and designed to meet most of the needs of most of the pupils in the school, though not expected to meet all needs without exception. This is the starting point for individualization: it gives point and purpose to the practical application of the concept by bringing it within the realm of practicality. It is equally important in ordinary or special schools.

Techniques for individualization

The most important technique for individualization of curriculum is the general or 'framework' curriculum noted above as a basic assumption. By effectively meeting the needs of as many pupils as possible, that curriculum reduces the demand for individualization with a real possibility that the demand will be kept within the range of resources and skills available in the school. Further, as indicated earlier, the sequence of intermediate objectives provides a framework that assists teachers in observing and recording the movement of pupils through the curriculum. Teachers are enabled to identify at the earliest possible point those pupils whose progress is not satisfactory so that their curricular needs may be carefully reassessed. And where there is need for modification of objectives, content, learning experiences or teaching methods the point of breakdown in the framework curriculum becomes the starting point for the planning of the necessary individualization.

Once the above point is reached, developing the individualized curriculum could mean the use of any combination of the approaches listed above for individualized teaching or curriculum. Other approaches might include the following.

Approaches to individualization
1. Use of materials and methods already organized in the school and classroom for alternative approaches to objectives.
2. Changes in the amount of individual work in the pupil's programme.
3. Alternative groupings of pupils.
4. Extended use of concrete or visual aids in teaching and learning.
5. The use of programmed texts or specially prepared programmed material.
6. Use of teaching machines or microelectronic aids.
7. Computer assisted learning.
8. Advice from supportive services: special education advisers, educational psychologist, subject advisers.
9. Input from peripatetic teaching service.
10. Discussion of pupils' difficulties with parents.

These are well-known techniques and the major variation between schools is likely to be in the efficiency of their use, but a breakthrough will be possible in the future. At present the use of computer assisted learning is just beginning, and it is likely to be a valuable and flexible addition to individualization techniques in the future. A most important application will be that of programming all the school curriculum resources into computer memory in a manner that allows them to be scanned and related to an input of pupils' curricular needs, in their entirety or at points of critical breakdown. Much more rapidly than is possible at present, teachers should be able to examine and assess all existing possibilities for meeting the needs. If computer control of teaching aids and material is also exploited, it should then be possible to secure a printout giving the structure of the chosen approach so that materials and teaching may be organized as quickly and efficiently as possible. Taking the technique a step further, computer aided control should make it possible for a teacher to supervise a larger number of individual learning programmes and modify them operationally as the pupils progress so that a new individual may be introduced into the 'net' without disruption for existing members.

Another possibility will come with the development of content-free programmes. These will allow a wide variety of basic learning structures into which teachers will be able to insert material of local content calculated to interest the pupil and motivate learning. The motivational value of computer assisted learning is already recognized and will have particular value for pupils with learning difficulty who are afraid of failure, or for those disturbed pupils who find sustaining relationships with others exhausting. Here the computer is the supreme accepter. It patiently repeats without sarcasm, adjusts to the pace of the learner, encourages endlessly, and asks for nothing other than a response.

These are short-term techniques and must not be allowed to dehumanize education. Keeping the teacher and relationships in the picture the computer may be useful in reducing the teacher's preparation time, minimizing routine work, and thus creating more opportunity for pupil–teacher interaction in other aspects of curriculum. In programmes intended for pupils with special educational needs, there is much to be said for writing the link with the teacher into the programme. The computer need not always reward, for it can direct the pupil to the teacher for that purpose. Similarly, and especially when work is complicated, the pupil may be directed to take work to the teacher for checking. This technique may have a special importance in freeing computer programmes from the behavioural-objectives limitation which seems to predominate at present. By writing the teacher into the programme it should be easier to secure generalization of learning from the computer to the environment, foster longer-term motivation, clarify relationship of learning with other learning and perhaps escape from undesirable complexity in the programme.

There is a place, too, for computer programmes that involve group learning. Programmes in which pupils may tackle problems together, each playing a part and communicating with each other as well as with the computer, in the process acquiring a feel for co-operation as well as experience of the techniques that make it possible, could make a significant contribution to social education. Writing the teacher into the programme may make these objectives easier to achieve.

Altogether, individualization of curriculum and teaching, and the benefits they may bring for children with special educational needs, should be enhanced by the advance of computer aided learning.

Individualization and integration

There are two aspects of integration to be considered, the integration involved in the unity of curriculum and the integration of pupils with special needs in ordinary schools; the former has implications for the latter, as will be shown. If earlier comments about the unity of curriculum are recalled, it should come as no surprise to find a pattern of relationships between individualization, differential learning, mastery learning and the concept of a common core curriculum. Individualized curriculum and learning are intended to make learning more efficient and in doing so they should reduce the time required for a pupil to achieve mastery in those areas considered essential. This should ease, if not remove, the time pressures that have been shown to be involved in many curriculum problems. The time released for learning may be used to extend mastery learning at the *function* level of the differential learning approach, or, where it is considered more essential for the pupil, to extend learning at the *context* level. So far as the common core is concerned, it is made more broadly applicable for pupils with special needs (especially those with learning difficulties or emotional disturbance) by the idea of differential learning and the associated concept of common objectives being attained at different levels by pupils with differences in aptitude. In this sense the thoroughness and proficiency at the function level of differential learning are relative to individual pupils: what may be adequate for one may be inadequate for another in terms of future needs. Once more this is individualization of curriculum.

Does this detract from the idea of a common core? Our contention is that it does not. A common curriculum is not an identical curriculum for all. As HMI put it:

> A common policy for the curriculum in this sense cannot be a prescription for uniformity. Enabling all pupils to achieve a comparable quality of education and potentially a common quality

of adult life is a more subtle and skilled task than taking them all
through identical syllabuses or teaching them all by the same
methods.[46]

Common curriculum is a matter of common experience which
links people across differences of time, place and intensity:

> It requires careful assessment of children's capabilities and
> continuing progress, and selection of those experiences and
> activities that will best enable them to acquire the skills and
> knowledge they need in common and to develop their own
> potential.[47]

Assessment should be continuous, made in the context of learning
by teachers in continuous interaction with the pupils, and it is in
that context that experiences should be selected. Individualization
of curriculum cannot be based upon any preconceived notions of a
pupil's aptitudes or abilities, for that would be inconsistent with
the principles of democratic curriculum aims discussed in Chapter
4.

Another aspect of individualization concerns the integration of
pupils with special educational needs in mainstream schools and
classes. In that it leads to efficient learning, individualization
should contribute to the extension of integration, the presence of
the pupils with special needs in the ordinary schools should
facilitate their participation in common core curriculum. On the
other hand, common curriculum does not imply identity of
content, place or time. Pupils with special needs who must be
educated in special schools for all or part of their school career are
not to be excluded from the experience of common curriculum. All
that has been written about differential learning, mastery
learning, individualization and common curriculum applies
equally to special schools, though minor modifications may be
required to accommodate the circumstances of some schools. In
developing their curriculum, special schools should take account
of common curriculum, in particular the arrangements that exist
in their LEA. This is necessary because, first, it is the right of every
pupil in the school to share as far as possible in aspects of
curriculum that should be common to all pupils; and second, the
common aspect of curriculum may be critical for those pupils who
at some stage of their school career might transfer from special
school to designated place in a mainstream school.

Contributors to curriculum

Chapter 1 discussed the influence on the school curriculum of central government through the Department of Education and Science, and of the local education authority. The tension between the centralist tendencies in the DES and the claims of the LEAs was shown, as well as the claims of the teaching profession that responsibility for curriculum should be within individual schools. That claim of the teachers appears to have been accepted – see the quotation from *The School Curriculum* on page 174. There appears to have been a rearrangement of a long-standing compromise about control of curriculum, which may be traced through official publications. The DES speaks out with increased emphasis and openness about the content and quality of curriculum.[48] It also increases emphasis on the responsibility of the LEA:

> The Education Acts lay on local education authorities the responsibility for securing efficient and sufficient primary and secondary education to meet the needs of their areas ... this implies a concern by authorities with the content and quality of education as well as with the facilities provided ... local authorities thus have a responsibility to formulate curricular policies and objectives which meet national policies and objectives, command local assent, and can be applied by each school to its own circumstances.[49]

The stress represented by 'command local assent' implies something wider than the LEA itself, possibly a concept of partnership, something spelled out at school level by HMI.

> There is a need for mutual confidence between school and the wider public in agreement about aims and in identification of the means to their realization. In practice that means that the broad definition of the purposes of school education is a shared responsibility, whereas the detailed means by which they may best be realized in individual schools and for individual children are a matter of professional judgement.[50]

The rearranged compromise appears to leave the position of the teachers unchanged while increasing central pressure and spelling out a role for the LEA which puts increased emphasis on the need for a stronger local structure within which schools will develop their curriculum. Properly handled, this may well improve democratic involvement in curriculum. But the relationships are spelled out largely within the context of mainstream education, and so far as education for special needs is concerned they fall short in one aspect. Both the Warnock Report and the Education Act 1981 stress the central role of parents in the assessment of their child's special educational needs and the arrangement made for special education. This is a right and proper role for parents of pupils with disabilities but the quality of parental knowledge is such that logic demands that it should have a special place in the shaping of curriculum.

The case for wider involvement

The case for wider involvement of contributing partners in the shaping of curriculum rests on a simple basis. However good the staff of the shool, and however wide their experience of life, it is a certainty that there is, somewhere in the community, relevant knowledge and experience that does not exist among the staff of the school. If that is so in general, how much more so where pupils have special needs that affect wide areas of their behaviour and outlook in a manner known best by people who have specialist knowledge of, or exceptional intimacy with them. At pre-school level, in out-of-school time, in the demands they will face in the post-school world, in the way disability affects their employment prospects, social perception, problems in sexual relationships or the demands made when they have their own families: in these aspects there is almost certain to be, somewhere in the community, knowledge, experience and insight beyond that which exists in the school. Some of the knowledge, because of the intimacy it implies, may be unduly subjective or influenced by emotion, but that is no reason for ignoring it. In any event, the role of the contributors is not to determine the curriculum; it is to contribute to the knowledge base from which professional teachers shape curriculum. The real problem is how to make use of contributions to curriculum in a manner that does not conflict with the professional role of the teaching staff of the school.

A framework for involvement

A framework for using contributing partners to curriculum may be developed according to some of the principles of curriculum advocated in this study, though it owes much to a detailed examination of the problem in relation to slow learners.[51] In developing the framework there are important assumptions, such as that the school has its own governing body; that the governors are widely representative of the local community; that there are governors who are parents of children in the school and others who are members of the teaching staff; and that in addition to subject or general advisers the LEA has special education advisers. There is also an assumption that the school has a commitment to curriculum development, that staff are involved in it and there is general agreement that wider involvement is desirable. This is the basis required for development, though it is helpful if a parent–teacher association exists which is not prevented from discussing curriculum and is accustomed to doing so. If the school, or that part of it concerned with special needs, has established some interaction with appropriate voluntary bodies, that is also a bonus.

The contributing partners to the curriculum consist of the headteacher and teaching staff of the school; the LEA through its advisory service; the governors of the school; and the parents of children in the school. Others may contribute from time to time, for example specialist professionals, representatives of voluntary bodies, local employers or trade union representatives, persons with disabilities or ex-pupils of the school. The permanent partners need the widest possible input of knowledge and experience relevant to the task of developing curriculum to meet the needs of the pupils with special needs.

For the purpose of this involvement the curriculum may be considered at three levels: first, the formulation of the curriculum aims that will guide work in the school; second, the definition of the general objectives that are to form the curriculum framework and their organization into sequences; and third, the definition of the specific objectives to operate in the classroom.

Curriculum aims

All curriculum partners are involved at this level. There is no hierarchy of knowledge here and the objective is to secure maximum inputs of knowledge and experience in order to provide the widest possible choices from which selection may be made. Brainstorming sessions as in the further education example may be useful – no suggestions or ideas should be ruled out at this stage. Gradually, as discussion develops, a selection will begin to take shape and a point arise where more precise formulations are required. Now is the time for the professional teachers to take the lead and prepare definitive statements for discussion with the governing body. Further refinement may be necessary to secure general assent and final versions will be for adoption by the governing body and the teaching staff. During this process it is likely that broad, tentative suggestions for objectives and content may emerge. These should not be ignored, but the record of them should be held for the guidance of staff in the next phase. Any presentation to governors at this stage would not be helpful.

At any point during the above discussions officers from the

advisory service, relevant professionals, or persons with special experience or knowledge may be invited to contribute to discussions. Contributions from parents and teaching staff, individually or collectively, should be encouraged, and all should be kept informed of the progress of the work.

It may be appropriate for procedures similar to the above to become part of the LEA framework for curriculum development, at least so far as pupils with special needs are concerned. In that event it would be appropriate for the adviser with responsibility for special needs, or the representative of the education officer on the governing body, to share the leadership role with the headteacher and have special responsibility where communications with outside persons were from the authority rather than the school. There probably should be some defined role for or relationship with the LEA at this stage, since the authority, as representative of the community, should have special reason for making sure that community and parental contributions to the process are neither overlooked nor undervalued.

General objectives; organization into sequences
A formulation of curriculum aims now exists with general agreement and there may also be tentative suggestions for content and general objectives. The process now becomes fully professional. There is no role here for parents or representatives of the community and governors should not be involved beyond receiving reports of progress. At the same time secrecy is something to be avoided and there is no reason why staff and parents should not know what is going on and feel free to comment. Such comment should be clearly understood for what it is, seriously received and seriously considered through a properly arranged procedure.

The staff of the school will be working on this part of curriculum development in the manner similar to that outlined in the section *Teachers' role in curriculum* in Chapter 5. Those directly involved will keep their colleagues informed, the headteacher will keep in contact to ensure continuity, and whenever requested by his colleagues he will arrange inputs from the subject and special needs advisers of the LEA. As work is completed it will be discussed at staff meetings, revised if thought necessary, and finally approved by the staff before being reported to the governors meeting.

Specific objectives for the classroom
This is also a fully professional procedure and resides with individual teachers in the classroom. They operate within the

framework previously established by work on general objectives and organization, and carry personal responsibility, for their own work. The responsibility cannot be 'shifted', though teachers should be discussing their work with colleagues and advisers. Parents should also be given insight into the teachers' work at this level as part of home–school relationships and any comments they make should be seriously considered.

The above framework, tentative though it is, is consistent with the principles of curriculum construction and development advocated in this study. It also offers the possibility of much closer involvement of parents and community in curriculum than has been usual. The parental and community inputs are at the level where they should have much of value to offer to the school, while the structure avoids their overlap with what is the area for trained professional teachers. Regarding the question of the evaluation of curriculum outcomes, here the contention is that, however sensitive the in-school evaluation, parents and people in the community see pupils with special needs in an entirely different context, from which could come valuable information relevant to evaluation. Whenever formal curriculum evaluation is in hand, the curriculum partners engaged as above at the first level should be brought into the evaluation process.

As ever when discussing curriculum, the discussion turns a dynamic situation into one that is static. What is described above is ongoing in practice. The whole of the curriculum is unlikely to be involved at any one time; different groups of people will be involved in different area of the curriculum; even in single areas only parts may be under revision at any one time; and modifications that involve individualization for individual pupils will not involve the range of people, though it is important that parents are intimately included in every phase and all discussions. Curricula for special needs are in a constant state of revision. At times, new knowledge and improved techniques force the change; at other times, changes in the school population bring about different combinations of need; or changes in staff skills call for different approaches. In these circumstances schools and teachers need all the assistance available. That is why it is foolish to rule out any source of knowledge relevant to curriculum.

The future

What schools teach, how they teach it, and their effectiveness in preparing the young for future adult roles will continue to be of concern in a democratic society. Democratic society is in a state of continuous change which affects individuals and is influenced by them. The pace of change and the pauses in the process are difficult to predict, making any attempt to forecast changes in education hazardous. Nevertheless, certain broad trends may be discerned.

Attitudes and resources

There is a direct connection between attitudes and resources, and major changes in education inevitably demand resources in a service prone to government economies and badly placed to resist them. The basic attitude change involves much wider acceptance of disabled people as people, the replacement of the very concept of disabled people by that of ordinary persons who have a disability. Thus their rights are those of all people, no more and no less, simply that society should meet their needs. Consequently their claim to an increased share of available resources does not rest on greater rights but on greater need. As people become more sensitive and responsible, exhibiting more care and concern for those who carry additional burdens through life, the claim of polititians in power that only by making society richer can the additional resources be made available will be seen for what it is, insensitive, lacking in understanding, and hollow. There will be a growing demand that the resources are made available by changes in the way existing riches are allocated. In other words, the resources required to improve the education of pupils with special needs could be made available *now* without increasing national expenditure, i.e. by spending less on other things.

Exactly the same is true about allocations within education where the plea that improvement must wait on increased resources is too often made the excuse for inactivity. But more important changes are required in the schools. Pupils with special needs (especially those with learning difficulties or emotional or behaviour disorders) must no longer be at the bottom of the list for school resources. Teachers must be given the resources and support to overcome their fears about their ability to teach pupils with special needs in ordinary schools; and those in special schools must learn to trust their colleagues in ordinary schools as being at least their equals in concern for the pupils.

Training and support

The implementation of the Education Act 1981, and of the broader more important Warnock Report recommendations, rests on improvements in the training of teachers – training not only in the colleges and universities, but in the schools, which is why support is here associated with training. A special-needs-awareness element in all courses of intial training is being implemented and will expand, though it is to be hoped that people with practical experience will be involved in the courses rather than otherwise redundant general lecturers. LEAs are reorganizing former 'remedial' services as support services for special needs with leaders broadly experienced in the field, and the services are providing courses on special needs for teachers in ordinary schools. Two things are required here. First, teachers working with pupils with special needs in ordinary schools must have almost immediate access to the advice and support of a suitably experienced colleague. Second, in-service courses must go beyond teaching methods and include work on the principles and practice of curricula for pupils with special educational needs. Here an associated development is required to which the training should contribute. In every large school there should be a member of staff with appropriate training and experience, responsible for all pupils with special needs in the school and acting as the link with the advisory and support service. Development of curricula for special needs starts within schools when the knowledge assimilated on courses is applied and refined. For that to happen informed leadership within the school is essential.

The special school

Special schools will continue to be required, but they must reassess their curricula as a result of the development of common core curriculum. The Warnock Report allocated to some of them the role of support to ordinary schools. In the initial stage of the movement of education for special needs into ordinary schools this role will exist. But as the movement proceeds the population of special schools will change in the direction of pupils with severe and mutliple disabilities. Problems hitherto concealed by success with less severely disabled pupils will begin to loom large, experimental curriculum and teaching become more important, and the deviance between special and ordinary schools become more marked. Yet association between the schools will continue to be necessary. Some suggestions for meeting this situation have been made. A new relationship must be evolved between pupils, staffs and, in particular, curriculum. This will be a totally new situation with no previous experience to guide those responsible for the development. Its successful resolution may be the supreme test of the new system and the people in it.

Notes and references

1. Good reasons were advanced for allowing the difference to disappear, in particular the desire to end the difference between ordinary and special education. See Warnock Report, 10.30. The situation is debatable.
2. Due to the small roll of most special schools the age range in classes often covers two or three years. This allows the formation of viable groups in relation to classroom accommodation.
3. BOXALL, M. (1973) *Multiple Deprivation: an Experiment in Nurture*, British Psychological Society occasional paper No.3; Department of Education and Science. (1978) *Behavioural Units: A Survey of Special Units for Pupils with Behaviour Problem*, London, HMSO; WILSON, M. D. and EVANS, M. (1979) 'Special Units for Disturbed and Disruptive Pupils', *Contact* 7(23), London, ILEA; see also WEBSTER, *et al.* (1977) 'Action for the Vulnerable Child', *Special Education*, V.4, pp. 26–8.
4. Recent research suggests that the trend for remedial teachers to work in ordinary classrooms has slowed down mainly due to tighter allocation of resources and falling school rolls. Only 3 per cent reported it in CLUNIES-ROSS, L. and WIMHURST, S. (1983) *Right Balance*, Windsor and Walton-on-Thames, NFER/Nelson.
5. HEGARTY, S. and POLKINGTON, K. (1981) *Educating Children with Special Needs in Ordinary Schools*, Windsor and Walton-on-Thames, NFER/Nelson; (1982) *Integration in Action*, Windsor and Walton-on-Thames, NFER/Nelson; HEGARTY, S. and BRADLEY, J. (1982) *Recent Curriculum Development in Special Schools*, Harlow and London, Longman for Schools Council; BRADLEY, J. and HEGARTY, S. (1982) *Stretching the System*, Further Education Curriculum Review and Development Unit.
6. DES (1978) *Special Educational Needs* (Warnock Report), Ch. 10, London, HMSO.
7. BRADLEY, J. and HEGARTY, S. (1982) op. cit.; WALKER, A. (1980) 'The Handicapped School Leaver and the Transition to Work', *British Journal of Guidance and Counselling*, V.8, pp. 212–23.
8. NESBITT, M. (1976) 'The Final Year in Special School' in Kedsey, R. and Whelan, E., eds, *The Education of Mentally Handicapped Young Adults*, Bolton College of Education (Tech).
9. DES. (1978) op cit., 10.27.
10. Ibid., 10.25. The difference was at age 18 years.
11. Ibid., 10.28. Places include those in school as well as in FE colleges.

Placement is for determination by the LEA.

12. Ibid., 10.33–46.
13. Ibid., 10.2.
14. PANKHURST, J. (1980) *Focus on Physical Handicap*, Windsor, NFER; FEU (1981) *Students with Special Needs in Further Education*, Further Education Curriculum Review and Development Unit; National Union of Teachers (1982) *Survey of Educational Provision for 16–19 Year Olds with Special Educational Needs*, London, NUT.
15. BRADLEY, J. and HEGARTY, S. (1982) op. cit; see also: NUT (1982) op. cit.
16. BRADLEY, J. and HEGARTY, S. (1982) op. cit; see also: NUT (1982) op. cit.
17. BRADLEY, J. and HEGARTY, S. (1982) op. cit.
18. FEU (1981) op. cit.
19. FEU (1982) *Skills for Living*, Further Education Curriculum Review and Development Unit.
20. FEU (1979) *A Basis for Choice*, Further Education Curriculum Review and Development Unit.
21. FEU (1982) op. cit.
22. BRENNAN, W. K. (1979) *The Curricular Needs of Slow Learners*, London, Evans/Methuen Educational.
23. Somerset LEA (1981) *Ways and Means: Children with Learning Difficulties*, pp. 158–67, 195–7, Basingstoke, Globe Education; HEGARTY, S. and BRADLEY, J. (1982) op. cit., pp. 11–26; *Preparing for Employment: A Model Programme for the Handicapped School Leaver*, Resource Centre, Salford LEA; HANSON, A. (1976) *Ready to Leave*, London, Collins; BRENNAN, W. K. (1979) op. cit., pp. 109–17; SPEAKE, B. and WHELAN, E. (1977) *Young Persons' Work Preparation Courses: A Systematic Evaluation*, London, Manpower Services Commission.
24. BLOOM, B. S. (1971) 'Mastery Learning and its Implications for Curriculum Development' in EISNER, E. W. ed. *Confronting Curriculum Reform*, Boston, Little, Brown; reprinted in Golby, M. *et al.*, eds. (1975) *Curriculum Design*, London, Croom Helm.
25. CARROLL, J. (1963) *A Model for School Learning*, Teachers' College Record; see also BLOOM, B. S. (1971) op. cit.
26. BLOOM, B. S. (1971) op. cit.
27. TANSLEY, A. E. and GULLIFORD, R. (1960) *The Education of Slow Learning Children*, Ch. 8, London, Routledge & Kegan Paul.
28. DES (1978) op. cit., 10.30–2, 37–40, 42–4.
29. DES. (1981) *The School Curriculum*, London, HMSO.
30. DES. (1980) *A Framework for the School Curriculum*, London, HMSO.
31. DES. (1980) *A View of the Curriculum*; (1978b) *Primary Education in England*, London, HMSO.
32. DES. (1981) op. cit.
33. Ibid., para. 10.
34. Ibid., para. 31.
35. Ibid., para. 29.
36. WILSON, M. D. (1981) *The Curriculum in Special Schools*, Harlow and

London, Longman, for Schools Council.

37. Ibid., p. 15.
38. Ibid., p.20.
39. DES. (1978b) op. cit.
40. DES. (1978) op. cit.
41. WHITE, J. P. (1973) *Towards a Compulsory Curriculum*, London, Routledge & Kegan Paul; see also LAWTON, D. (1975) *Social Change, Educational Theory and Curriculum Planning*, Dunston Green, Hodder & Stoughton, for discussion of five cores of knowledge, minimum levels of achievement and individualized timetables; WILLIAMS, R. (1961) *The Long Revolution*, Harmondsworth, Penguin; BRENNAN, W. K. (1979) op. cit., pp. 167–71.
42. DESCÖEUDRES, A. (1928) *The Education of Mentally Handicapped Children*, London, Harrap; reprint of 2nd French edition.
43. TANSLEY, A. E. and GULLIFORD, R. (1960) op. cit., pp. 90–91.
44. WALLIN, J. E. W. (1955) *The Education of Mentally Handicapped Children*, pp. 52–63, New York, Harper Bros.
45. BLOOM, B. S. (1971) op. cit.; see also GLASER, R. (1968) 'Adapting the Elementary School Curriculum to Individual Performance' in HOOPER, R., ed. *The Curriculum*, Edinburgh, Oliver & Boyd.
46. DES. (1980) op. cit.
47. Ibid.
48. DES. (1981) op. cit.
49. Ibid.
50. DES. (1980) op. cit.
51. BRENNAN, W. K. (1979) op. cit., pp. 155–67.

Further reading

General curriculum

BARNES, D. (1976) *From Communication to Curriculum*, Harmondsworth, Penguin. Emphasizes pupil responsibility, language and interaction.

JENKINS, D. and SHIPMAN, M. (1976) *Curriculum: An Introduction*, Shepton Mallet, Open Books. Straightforward expansion of sociological aspects.

Schools Council (1981) *The Practical Curriculum*, working paper No. 70, London, Evans/Methuen Educational.

SOCKETT, H. (1976) *Designing the Curriculum*, Shepton Mallet, Open Books. A direct, unpretentious exposition.

TAYLOR, P. H. and RICHARDS, C. (1979) *An Introduction to Curriculum Studies*, NFER. A review approach that extends most aspects of the general discussion.

WHEELER, D. K. (1967) *Curriculum Process*, London, University of London Press. An older book though still a valuable bringing together of philosophical and psychological aspects in a broad and interesting manner.

Readings

These books bring together a wide range of relevant papers on curriculum.

GOLBY, M. et al., eds. (1975) *Curriculum Design*, London, Croom Helm.
HOOPER, R., ed. (1971) *The Curriculum*, Edinburgh, Oliver & Boyd.
HORTON, T. and RAGGET, P., eds. (1982) *Challenge and Change in Curriculum*, Dunton Green, Hodder & Stoughton.
LEE, V. and ZELDIN, D., eds. (1982) *Planning the Curriculum*, Dunton Green, Hodder & Stoughton.

Official pamphlets

All Department of Education and Science publications from HMSO.

(1980) *A View of the Curriculum*, HMI, Matters for Discussion series.
(1981) *The School Curriculum*.
(1982) *Planning for Progress*, HMI Wales (occasional paper), Welsh Office.

Organization

BOLAM, R., ed. (1982) *School Focused In-service Training*, London, Heinemann Educational.
McGUINESS, J. B. (1982) *Planned Pastoral Care*, Maidenhead, McGraw Hill.
MARLAND, M. and HILL, S., eds. (1982) *Departmental Management*, London, Heinemann Educational.
WARWICK, D. (1982) *Effective Meetings*, Education for Industrial Society.   (1983) *Staff Appraisal*, Education for Industrial Society.

Special needs

AINSCOW, M. and TWEDDLE, D. A. (1979) *Preventing Classroom Failure: An Objective Approach*, Chichester, Wiley.
BRENNAN, W. K. (1979) *The Curricular Needs of Slow Learners*, London, Evans/Methuen Educational.

(1978) *Reading for Slow Learners: A Curriculum Guide*, London, Evans/Methuen Educational.

HINSON, M. and HUGHES, M., eds. (1982) *Planning Effective Progress*, Amersham, Hulton Educational.

LEEMING, K. *et al.* (1979) *Teaching Language and Communication to the Mentally Handicapped*, London, Evans/Methuen Educational.

MITTLER, P. and H. (1982) *Partnership with Parents*, National Council for Special Education.

Staff of Rectory Paddock School (1981) *In Search of a Curriculum*, Robin Wren Publications.

TANSLEY, A. E. and GULLIFORD, R. (1960) *The Education of Slow Learning Children*, London, Routledge & Kegan Paul.

WILSON, M. D. (1981) *The Curriculum in Special Schools*, Harlow and London, Longman for Schools Council.

and EVANS, M. (1980) *Education of Disturbed Pupils*, London, Methuen Educational.

Other reading

For microelectronics and special needs, see Appendix 2.
For further education and special needs, see Appendix 4.

Appendix 1

Schools Council projects: special needs

Visual Perception Training of Blind and Partially Sighted 5–11-
Year-Olds. Training in the use of residual vision. Publications:
*Look and Think Diagnostic Kit; Look and Think Teacher's File; Look and
Think Teacher's Handbook*, Schools Council and Royal National
Institute for the Blind, 1978.

Language Development for Hearing Impaired Children 4–12
years. Publications: *Level 1 Pre-reading Materials; Level 2 Step by Step
Reading Materials; Level 3 Theme Development Materials*, from: Globe
Education, Basingstoke, 1980.

Curricular Needs of Slow Learning Children. Publications:
Curricular Needs of Slow Learners, working paper No. 63, London,
Evans/Methuen Educational, 1979; *Reading for Slow Learners*,
curriculum bulletin No. 7, London, Evans/Methuen Educational, 1978, *Teaching the Slow Learners*, ten 30-minute video-
programmes, Schools Council and ILEA, available on sale or hire
from Central Film Library, 1976.

Education of Severely Educationally Subnormal Pupils 2–19
Years. Publications: *Teaching Language and Communication to the
Mentally Handicapped*, curriculum bulletin No. 8, London, Evans/
Methuen Educational, 1979. Three 30-minute video-pro-
grammes to go with the book from: Drake Educational
Associates, Cardiff.

Education of Disturbed Pupils 5–16 Years. Publications: *Education of
Disturbed Pupils*, working paper No. 65 (general principles),

London, Methuen Educational, 1980; *Special Provision for Disturbed Pupils* (statistical data), London, Methuen Educational, 1980.

Use of Project Materials by Teachers of Disadvantaged Children. 5–16 Years. A One-Year Project. Publication: *Teaching Materials for Disadvantaged Children*, curriculum bulletin No. 5, London, Evans/Methuen Educational, 1975.

Low Attainers in Mathematics. 5–16 Years. Publication: *Low Attainers in Mathematics: Policies and Practice*, working paper No. 72, London, Methuen Educational, 1982.

Kent Mathematics Project. 9–16 Years. Materials extended to a lower level in association with the Schools Council. Publications: *'L' Materials*, three kits, London, Ward Lock Educational, 1980.

Health Education 5–13 Years: Special Extension for Slow Learners. Publications: *Fit for Life*, Levels 1, 2 and 3, Basingstoke, Macmillan Educational, 1983.

Open Science, Science for the Less Able Child 14–16 Years. Publications: *Teacher's Guide* plus 13 *Pupil Units*, London, Hart-Davies Educational, 1980.

Communication Skills, 2–13 Years. Extended to cover pupils with moderate learning difficulties. Publications: *A Place for Talk: Teacher's Book*, London, Ward Lock Educational, 1981; workshop materials, Schools Council Publications, 1981; ten video-tapes, 1981. Workshop materials and video-tapes distributed by Drake Educational Associates, Cardiff.

Compensatory Education Research and Development Project (1967–72). 4–8 Years. Has wide application to special needs. Publications: *Deprivation and the Infant School*, Chazan, M. and Williams, P., 1978, Oxford, Blackwell; *Language Development and the Disadvantaged*, Downes, G., 1978, McDougall; *Swansea Test of Phonic Skills*, reissued by Schools Council, 1981; *Swansea Evaluation Profile*, handbooks and materials, 1978, Windsor/Walton-on-Thames, NFER/Nelson (researchers only).

Schools Council publications

Published by Longmans for the Schools Council: available from Longman Resources Unit, 33–35 Tanner Row, York Y01 1JP.

ADAMS, E. and BAYNES (1982) *Art and the Built Environment: Study Activities.*

ADAMS, E. and WARD, C. (1982) *Art and the Built Environment: A Teacher's Approach.*

BALOGH, J. (1982) *Profile Reports for School-leavers.*
EVANS, Mary (1981) *Disruptive Pupils.*
GREEN, F., HART, R., McCALL, C. and STAPLES, I. (1982) *Microcomputers in Special Education.*
HEGARY, S., POCKLINGTON, K. and BRADLEY, J. (1982) *Recent Curriculum Development in Special Education.*
KLEIN, G. (1982) *Resources for Multicultural Education: An Introduction.*
NUTTALL, D. (1981) *School Self-evaluation: Accountability with a Human Face.*
WILLEY, R. (1982) *Teaching in Multicultural Britain.*
WILSON, Mary D. (1981) *The Curriculum in Special Schools.*

Background projects

'Cross'd with Adversity': The Education of Socially Disadvantaged Children in Secondary Schools, London, Evans/Methuen Educational.
Geography for the Young School Leaver, three kits, Walton-on-Thames, Nelson.
Humanities Curriculum Project, introduction and eight themes, London, Heinemann Educational.
Lifeline (moral education project), York, Longman.
Nuffield Junior Science, teacher's guides and background, source books, London, Collins.

Appendix 2

Microelectronics Education Programme

Directorate: Cheviot House, Coach Lane Campus, Newcastle upon Tyne, NE7 7XA. Phone: 0632 664716. Fourteen regional centres.

The Special Education Microelectronic Resource Centres (SEMERCs)

These are resource centres for teachers and professionals who wish to use microelectronics in the education of children with special needs, whatever the disability. They are part of the MEP, set up by the DES in 1981 and due to finish in 1986. SEMERCS and the MEP regional centres work closely together. There are four SEMERCs:

Manchester SEMERC, Manchester Polytechnic, Hathersage Road, Manchester M13 0JA. Phone: 061 2259054. Manager: Bob Dyke.

Bristol SEMERC, Faculty of Education, Bristol Polytechnic, Redland Hill, Bristol B56 6U2. Phone: 0272 733141. Manager: Prue Greenwood.

Redbridge SEMERC, Dane Centre, C/O Teachers' Centre, Melbourne Road, Ilford, Essex IG1 4HT. Phone: 01 478 3706. Manager: Jean Tait.

Newcastle SEMERC, Newcastle Polytechnic, Coach Lane Campus, Newcastle upon Tyne NE7 7XA. Phone: 0632 665057. Manager: Colin Richards.

The National Co-ordinator for Special Education is: Mary Hope, Council for Educational Technology, 3 Devonshire Street, London W1N 2BA.

What do SEMERCs do?

INFORMATION. They are a wide information and advice source for teachers who wish to know about microelectronics. A wide range of hardware and software can be seen at the centres. They enable practitioners to exchange experience and so help to further knowledge in the field. By bringing together teachers and researchers, developers and manufacturers, they seek to forward the use of the new technology.

TEACHER TRAINING. They take part in and support courses, most away from the centres, as each covers a quarter of the country. Contact with and advice to individuals is also a most important part of teacher training.

CURRICULUM DEVELOPMENT. They stimulate discussion about efficient practice in the classroom and assist in the transfer of appropriate curriculum ideas into usable software programmes. There are funds available for these developments and SEMERCs are able to assist teachers in the formulation of curriculum development programmes. This is important as quality depends on the standard of software and the *curriculum* itself awaits development through microelectronic techniques.

A newsletter is available together with information sheets; demonstrations of equipment are possible; meetings with likeminded colleagues offer stimulation; copyright-free software may be available; and contact with SEMERCs keeps individuals abreast of developments.

Useful reading on microelectronics

CET/MEP information sheet (May 1982) *Microelectronics in Special Education*. Dated now but has some useful general information on applications for special needs. Lists activities on a regional basis.

GOLDERBURG, P. E. (1979) *Special Technology for Special Children*, Baltimore, University Press.

GREEN, F., HART, R. and STAPLES, I. (1982) *Microcomputers in Special Education*, York, Longmans Resources Unit.

HART, Bob and STAPLES, Ian (1980) 'Microcomputers in Special Schools', *Special Education*, V.7, No. 4, Dec. 1980.

HOGG, Bob (1984) Microcomputers and Special Educational Needs. A Guide to Good Practice. National Council for Special Education.

HOPE, Mary (1980) 'How Can Microcomputers Help?', *Special Education*, V.7, No. 4, Dec. 1980.

HOWE, Jim (1980) 'Computers: A Researcher's View', *Special Education*, V.7, No. 4, Dec. 1980.

PAPERT, S. (1980) *Mindstorms*, Brighton, Harvester Press.

SAGE, M. W. and SMITH, D. J. (1983) *Microcomputers in Education: A Framework for Research*, London, Social Science Research Council.

SCHOFIELD, J. M. (1982) *Microcomputer-based Aids for the Disabled*, Heyden for the British Computer Society.

(1982) *Learning to Cope – Computers in Special Education*, an Educational Computing Special.

Video

Micros for Special Needs, Salford Resources Centre for MEP, 40 minutes, free loan from SEMERCs.

Concept Keyboards – An Anthology, users in special education, Eclipse Videos for MEP, 35 minutes, free loan from SEMERCs.

IT and the Disabled, introduction to aids, Department of Industry, 25 minutes, free loan from Central Film Library.

Consultancy on communication aids in education

Two consultancy centres are concerned with schools for pupils with physical disabilities. Function is limited as they are on a part-time basis.

North of Birmingham: Phil Odor, Godfrey Thompson Unit, University of Edinburgh, 24 Buccleuch Place, Edinburgh EH8 9JT.

Birmingham and the South: Andrew Tollyfield and Patrick Poon, Electrical Engineering Department, Kings College, The Strand, London WC2R 2LS.

Acknowledgement

The author wishes to acknowledge the assistance of the following in the preparation of the microelectronic section and Appendix. Bob Hart and the staff of Walsall LEA microelectronics development team; Jean Taite of the Redbridge SEMERC; Centre for Educational Technology/MEP Information Service.

Appendix 3
Some examples
of microelectronics in
special education

MEP WEST MIDLANDS CENTRE. Working with local schools to exploit the microcomputer to increase children's understanding and use of language and problem solving.

CROWNBRIDGE SPECIAL SCHOOL, GWENT LEA. Using Big Track and Trilby in a class-based programme which modifies electronic toys for educational use by children with severe learning difficulty.

BRAYS SCHOOL, BIRMINGHAM LEA. MEP-funded project developing the use of concept keyboard as an alternative input for microcomputers – a flat A4 size touch-sensitive surface.

HUDDERSFIELD POLYTECHNIC. MEP project. A curriculum recording aid designed to assist teachers of children with severe learning difficulties who use individualized curriculum.

JAFFE CENTRE, BELFAST. Programmes to develop pupils' insight into housing needs and availability in association with the reality of the situation.

ILEA RESOURCE CENTRE FOR MOTOR AND COMMUNICATION HANDICAPS. The MACE-Apple writing/drawing/speech aid to offer severely physically handicapped children wider access to curriculum.

DINSDALE PARK RESIDENTIAL SCHOOL, DURHAM LEA. A wide variety of teaching aids using computer control. Staff able to make programmes without BASIC. Keyboard, adventure board or concept operation.

ELMFIELD SCHOOL, AVON LEA.   Working with profoundly deaf pupils. Visispeech displays voice patterns to encourage good quality voicing, lower pitch, flexibility and variation.

THE WESTGATE SCHOOL, HAMPSHIRE.   Programmes to promote advanced reading strategies and study skills.

BRIGHTON POLYTECHNIC.   Computer Aided Animated Arts Theatre to use micro-techniques to aid creative and communication abilities in disadvantaged children.

SHAWFOLD SCHOOL, STOCKPORT.   Use of LOGO computer language in schools: extending spatial, cognitive and social skills with children with moderate learning and behaviour difficulties.

ABBEY SCHOOL, ROTHERHAM LEA.   Creative story programme. Children create story using available text.

MICROELECTRONICS DEVELOPMENT TEAM, WALSALL LEA.   Catalogue of fifteen special needs programmes and thirty-two covering general language and number suitable for use with children with special needs.

Appendix 4
Further Education Curriculum Review and Development Unit: special needs publications

Students with Special Needs in Further Education. 1981. Review of research relating to young people with special educational needs in FE. Identifies provision requirements.

Stretching the System. 1982. Follow-up of a recommendation from *Students with Special Needs in FE.* Reviews provision: transitional courses in schools briefly, then various arrangements in colleges. Makes evaluations.

Making Progress. 1982. Reviews current literature and practice in assessment of students with special needs in FE. Emphasis on students with moderate learning difficulties. Case study examples. Guidelines for development procedures are related to curriculum.

Skills for Living. 1982. Suggests a curriculum framework for a course for young people with moderate learning difficulties. Sets out aims, activities and resources. Includes some case studies and records. Affords some insight into the method by which the curriculum was approached.

Route to Coping. In press. Will suggest guidelines for implementing coping aspects of *Skills for Living* guidelines.

A Basis for Choice. 1979. A more general document that has been made a starting point for some of the above curriculum publications. Is claimed to have proved useful to FE teachers working with students with moderate learning difficulties.

Index